ALSO BY DEB PERELMAN

The Smitten Kitchen Cookbook

smitten kitchen
EVERY DAY

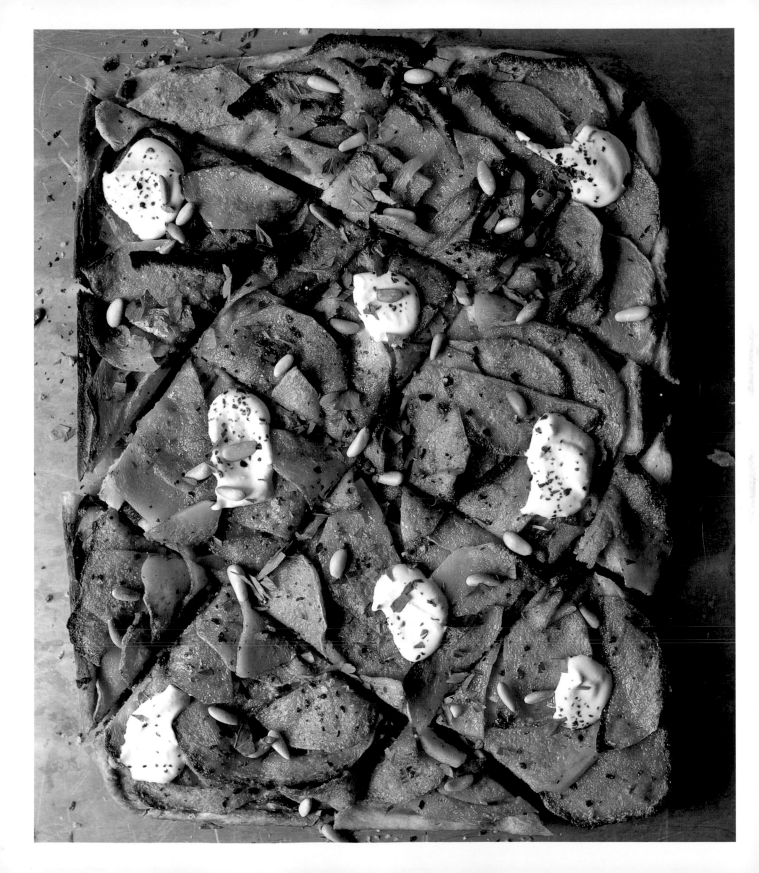

smitten kitchen
EVERY DAY

triumphant and unfussy new favorites

DEB PERELMAN

appetite
by RANDOM HOUSE

contents

against drudgery

(or, in praise of the unfussy but triumphant)

One of the delights of life is eating with friends; second to that is talking about eating. And, for an unsurpassed double whammy, there is talking about eating while you are eating with friends. People who like to cook like to talk about food. Plain old cooks (as opposed to geniuses in fancy restaurants) tend to be friendly. After all, without one cook giving another cook a tip or two, human life might have died out a long time ago.

—LAURIE COLWIN, *Home Cooking*

We home cooks have never gathered in force to speak out in defense of home cooking. So the image of cookery as drudgery lives on.

—MARION CUNNINGHAM, *Lost Recipes*

This isn't the cookbook I had expected to write. When *The Smitten Kitchen Cookbook* headed to the printer in 2012, we were a family of three. Our two-year-old was eating table food, but in a dabbling way. Mostly, I cooked the food that I was excited to eat, and little about having a kid changed how I went about it. In the years since, we've added another delicious little human to our family, and while most people will tell you that going from zero kids to one is the big adjustment, in the kitchen, the shift from one to two was more dramatic. All of a sudden, it wasn't just us plus an extra half-portion stripped of offending chile peppers or with some couscous on the side to bait a suspicious toddler to the table. Quickly, half our family (ahem, the noisier half) needed square meals at predictable times and I, well . . . I began to understand why not everyone jumps with joy when it's time to make dinner.

On any given night, most of us have countless really excellent reasons not to cook—be it picky kids, spouses, or roommates, or the extinction of a 9-to-5 workday that might actually get you home in time to assemble dinner for yourself, your friends, or your family. Even the people who are ostensibly

breakfast

deli rye english muffins

makes 12 miniature or 8 standard-sized muffins

M y favorite thing about this recipe is where it started, which, specifically, was in front of a library full of people in St. Louis while I was on a book tour. Someone asked me how I came up with recipes, and I'm sorry if it disappoints you to learn this, but I've never been good on my feet and was as fumbling and inarticulate as ever: "Uh, sometimes they just come to me? Or I'll just get an idea when I'm on the crosstown bus and . . ." It was pretty bad, but since there was no one to rescue me, I just blathered along. ". . . Like, this morning, I was thinking how cool it would be if you could make an English muffin that tasted like rye bread, because they're my two favorite kinds of toast to go with eggs," and someone said, "You should! Now you can start your second book!"

So, as fated—eh, 4.5 years and one kid later—I began here. I learned a few things along the way. English-muffin recipes are divided into two camps: those that require pastry rings to hold the batter in shape, and those that use a thicker dough but allow you to free-form them. The first category make for great nooks and crannies, but are unquestionably a pest to maneuver. The second category have some nooks and a few crannies but don't require any specialty-store purchases. To get the results of the peskier method without the hassle, I found you had to use a softer dough.

And then, once you've made English muffins that taste like a good deli rye bread, what do you do with them? They're excellent with a heap of scrambled eggs or a crispy fried one, maybe with a little hash underneath. They're good for any kind of sandwich you'd normally put on rye. But toasting them with sweet butter is always my first choice.

2¼ teaspoons (from a 7-gram or ¼-ounce packet) active dry yeast

¼ cup (60 ml) lukewarm water

¾ cup (175 ml) milk or buttermilk

2 tablespoons (30 grams) unsalted butter, plus more for the bowl

1 tablespoon (15 grams) granulated sugar

⅔ cup (80 grams) dark rye flour

1⅓ cups (175 grams) all-purpose or bread flour, plus more for your work surface

1½ teaspoons coarse or kosher salt

2 teaspoons (5 grams) whole or 1 teaspoon ground caraway seeds

Oil, for greasing bowl and coating skillet

Cornmeal, for sprinkling

Combine the yeast and water in the bowl of a stand mixer fitted with a dough hook. Let rest 5 minutes; the yeast should dissolve and look slightly foamy. Gently warm the buttermilk, butter, and sugar to lukewarm (not hot), and add it to the yeast mixture, followed by the flours, salt, and caraway. Use the dough hook to combine until a shaggy, uneven dough forms; knead it on the lowest speed for 5 minutes, until the dough is stretchy and cohesive. Butter or oil a large bowl (or do as I do and remove the dough long enough to oil the mixing bowl, then return the dough to it), and let the dough proof at room temperature, covered with a dishcloth or plastic, for 1 hour. (Until it has risen by at least one-third.)

to the parchment-lined baking sheet, and lay flat in a single layer. Bake for another 20 minutes, until toasted and crisp. (If you like, you can flip them halfway for more even browning, but you will have good color on them either way.)

Cool the biscotti on the baking sheet, or transfer to a rack.

note This recipe should prove very tweakable; you could use cinnamon, or almond extract, add citrus zest, vary the fruits and sweeteners. You could swap half the flour for whole wheat or even oat flour. Or you could add some chocolate chips. Who could blame you?

do ahead Biscotti keep in an airtight container at room temperature for up to 2 weeks, and longer if well wrapped in the freezer.

jam-bellied bran scones

makes 10 scones

In the Muffin Olympics, my favorite—bran muffins—would never even make the team. I get that gritty brown masses hardly have the appeal of blueberry-buttermilk, sweet-cornmeal, banana-walnut, and pumpkin-spice, but I've always enjoyed their quiet, nutty complexity—plus, it's kind of adorable, the way I convince myself that they're healthier, right? So I decided that they needed a makeover, and I reformatted them as scones, and pretty ones at that. Preloading the scones with jam makes them self-contained packets of breakfast luxury. Yes, like a jelly doughnut but still craggy and wholesome enough that we get to enjoy them way more often.

1½ cups (195 grams) all-purpose flour, plus more for your work surface

1¼ cups (75 grams) wheat bran

1 tablespoon (15 grams) baking powder

½ teaspoon fine sea or table salt

½ cup (95 grams) dark-brown sugar

6 tablespoons (85 grams) unsalted butter, chilled, cut into small pieces

½ cup (120 grams) sour cream

½ cup (120 ml) heavy cream

1 large egg, lightly beaten with 1 teaspoon water

¼ cup (80 grams) jam or marmalade of your choice, or more if yours is on the thick side

1 tablespoon (10 grams) coarse or raw (turbinado) sugar, to finish

Heat the oven to 375 degrees, and line a baking tray with parchment paper.

Combine the flour, bran, baking powder, salt, and brown sugar in a large bowl. Add the butter and, using your fin-gertips or a pastry blender, work it into the flour mixture until the largest bits are the size of small peas. Add the sour and heavy creams, and stir until the mixture forms big clumps. Knead once or twice, just by sticking your hands into the bowl, until it comes together in one mass.

On a very well-floured surface, roll out the dough to about ½-inch thickness. Cut into 2½-inch rounds and then gently reroll scraps as needed. Use your thumb to make an impression in the "belly" (center) of half of them. Dollop ½ to 1 teaspoon jam in the center, brush the edges with egg wash, and use one of the plain, nonindented rounds as a lid. Press gently together at edges, sealing in the jam. Repeat with the remaining rounds.

Transfer the scones to the prepared baking sheet, and brush the tops with egg wash. Sprinkle each scone with about ¼ teaspoon coarse sugar, and bake for 16 to 19 minutes. Let the scones cool on the tray for 5 or so minutes before carefully lifting and transferring them to cooling racks.

baked oatmeal with caramelized pears and vanilla cream

makes 6 portions

T his is my deep-into-winter escape from hot-cereal drudgery, a casserole-formatted, lightly lux-urious baked oatmeal that I make at the start of a week and heat up one portion at a time. I really love fruit with my oatmeal, but it usually ends up falling to the convenience of dried fruit stirred in. This is better. You begin by roasting lemony pears in a bit (just a bit!) of butter, sugar, and vanilla bean seeds until the juices begin to release and *self-caramelize* in the pan. From here, you build a somewhat standard baked oatmeal on top, something we should thank the Amish for including in old cookbooks—but I'm actually going to thank Heidi Swanson of 101 Cookbooks for introducing this to the wider web audience. Eggs and a little bit of baking soda give the oats some cohesion and lift; the pear caramel makes it otherworldly. So does one other thing: the tiniest trickle of a sweetened vanilla cream on top. You could use milk, I suppose—but I don't, because once I tried this at a restaurant there was no going back. It is, in one pour, a coolant, a sweetener, and something to loosen the whole bit up. If this sounds like work, keep in mind that you're going to get six amazing breakfasts from it, a better return on investment than I get from most from scratch soups, dinners, or cakes, and—ahem, I'm just saying—none of them self-caramelize.

vanilla sugar
½ cup plus 2 tablespoons (125 grams)
granulated sugar
½ vanilla bean

pears
2 tablespoons (30 grams) unsalted butter
3 pears (preferably D'Anjou, Forelle, or firm Bartletts)
1 lemon

oatmeal
1 cup (235 ml) milk
1 cup (235 ml) water
2 tablespoons (30 grams) unsalted butter

2 large eggs
1½ teaspoons coarse or kosher salt
2 teaspoons baking powder
3 cups (240 grams) rolled oats

to finish
1 cup (235 ml) heavy cream or half-and-half

make the vanilla sugar Place the sugar in a small bowl. Split the vanilla bean, scrape the seeds into the sugar, and use your fingertips to distribute the seeds throughout; the abrasion helps release more flavor. Save the pod: there's tons more flavor to be had, and we're going to use it.

is tender, 1 to 2 minutes more. Drain in a colander, and cool under cold running water. Gently squeeze handfuls of spinach to remove as much liquid as possible, then coarsely chop it. You will have about ½ cup fairly tightly packed cooked spinach.

Wipe the skillet dry, turn the heat to medium-high, then add olive oil to the skillet. Once the oil is hot, add the sausage (if using) and cook until browned breaking it up with a spatula, for about 5 minutes. Remove with a slotted spoon, and discard all but 1 tablespoon of drippings. Stir the onion and garlic into skillet. Cook over medium-low heat until the onion is tender, about 5 minutes. Add the mushrooms, increase heat to medium-high, and cook, stirring, until the mushrooms have softened and exuded liquid, and that liquid has cooked off, about 5 minutes. Stir in the cream, salt, pepper, nutmeg (if using), chopped spinach, and reserved sausage (if using) and bring to a simmer. Remove the skillet from heat and let cool slightly.

bake the frittata In a large bowl, whisk together the eggs, salt, and pepper. Stir in the vegetable mixture, scallions, and goat cheese. Pour into the prepared dish, and bake until golden and set, about 30 minutes.

to serve Cool on a rack for 5 minutes before serving in squares.

everything drop biscuits with cream cheese

makes 12 biscuits

They're going to throw me out of New York City for saying this, but there are times when a bagel can feel like too much, too heavy to go with a simple breakfast. I'll head toward the Holland Tunnel now; I know I've shamed my adopted home. But if I go far enough south, nobody is going to question my occasional preference for a biscuit—quick, tender, with crisp edges, and just the right size to scoop up some scrambled eggs without sending me back to bed for a nap. Don't trust New Yorkers around biscuits, though—they're liable to do things like this to them. An everything biscuit may seem a poor replacement for a well-made bagel, but we find it to be an enjoyable riff on a standard biscuit. It's also fun to make: you fling a simple cream-cheese-enriched biscuit dough from a big spoon into a seed pit of flavor, give it a tumble, and bake it in the oven. Once the biscuit is broken open and slathered with butter, you get the best of both worlds. If you halve it and add more cream cheese, lox, and capers, you've created a brunch that people can neatly eat with their hands. As the holster for a fried-egg sandwich, it trumps a bagel any day. [Ducks.]

seed mix

2 tablespoons (15 grams) sesame seeds

2 tablespoons (15 grams) poppy seeds

1 tablespoon (7 grams) dried minced onion

2 teaspoons (6 grams) dried minced garlic

1 teaspoon coarse salt

biscuits

2½ cups (325 grams) all-purpose flour

2½ teaspoons baking powder

1 teaspoon coarse salt

4 tablespoons (55 grams) cold unsalted butter, cut into cubes

4 ounces (115 grams) plain cream cheese (half an 8-ounce foil brick), cold, cut into cubes

1 cup (235 ml) buttermilk

Heat the oven to 450 degrees. Line a large baking sheet with parchment paper. Combine the seeds with the dried onion, garlic, and coarse salt in a small bowl. In a larger bowl, combine the flour, baking powder, and 1 teaspoon salt. Scatter the butter and cream cheese over the dry mixture, and use your fingertips or a pastry blender to work them in until the mixture resembles rubbly sand. Add the milk or buttermilk, and stir until just combined, with the dough clumping together.

Drop the dough in about twelve equal mounds (it's okay if you get more or less), one at a time, into the everything-seed mixture. Use your fingertips to give them a little half-roll through the seeds, and space them evenly on the baking sheet. Repeat with remaining dough. (You'll have some extra seeds. I love these as a garnish.) Bake until golden and your home smells like a bagelry, about 12 minutes.

note The biscuits are best on the first day. You can freeze the unbaked dough in mounds. Let warm slightly from freezer, then roll in the seeds before baking.

to make the hazelnut cream in a food processor Combine ¾ cup of the hazelnuts—reserve remainder for garnish—the salt, and the sugar in a food processor, and grind as finely as possible. Add butter, and blend until combined, scraping down the sides if needed. Add the egg and extract or flavoring; blend until combined. Transfer to a bowl, and chill until firm but spreadable.

to make the cream without a food processor Mince ¾ cup hazelnuts to a fine powder and mix with sugar and salt. Whisk butter with the hazelnut-sugar mixture, egg, and flavoring until combined. Chill until firm but spreadable.

make the syrup Combine the water, sugar, and orange peels in a small saucepan, and bring to a simmer. Stirring frequently, simmer until sugar has dissolved. Remove from heat and let cool slightly, then fish out and discard the peels and add any liqueur or flavoring.

Heat the oven to 375 degrees. Place an oven-safe cooling rack on a baking sheet and arrange the brioche slices in one layer.

Generously brush each slice with the syrup. Divide the raspberries among slices of brioche and mash them roughly, unevenly, into the syrup-soaked bread. Dollop each slice with equal amounts of hazelnut cream, and use a small offset spatula or butter knife to spread it evenly over each surface. Don't worry if it makes a mess of the raspberries already mashed on—that's the point! Coarsely chop the remaining hazelnuts, and sprinkle some over each slice.

Bake the brioche for 10 to 15 minutes, until puffed and golden all over. Remove from the oven, and dust with powdered sugar. Eat warm or at room temperature.

note Brioche is traditional here, but you can use any enriched bread instead (such as challah).

polenta-baked eggs with corn, tomato, and fontina

makes 2 hearty or 4 petite breakfasts

These might be the coziest baked eggs I know how to make. Polenta (or grits) is cooked until soft and studded with sweet corn kernels, a couple dollops of sour cream, melty fontina, parsley, chives, and a swirl of tomatoes; then eggs are nested on top and baked. Because of dishes like this, the overlapping seasons of tomato and corn are one of my favorite points in the summer—which seems like a good time to tell you I also made this in January.

Gasp! It's true. Don't get me wrong: nothing makes me happier than getting in-season, exquisite fresh produce from a farm stand. It's just that this only happens for a couple months of the year in the Northeast. The rest of the time, what's left is what the grocery store carries. It's never as good, but I've found that it's a great baseline in recipes—as in, if I can make the saddest-looking corn taste incredible in the dead of winter, just imagine how great this will be when the good stuff arrives.

Thus, do know that this will work with cheap cornmeal, frozen kernels, and jarred sauce; it's exceptional, even. We licked our plates clean. But should you find yourself with access to Anson Mills grits, Early Girl tomatoes, and the kind of corn that New Jersey excels at in August—oh man, you're in for a treat. Trust us. We were lucky enough to have it both ways.

2 cups (475 ml) water

½ cup (70 grams) fine polenta or yellow cornmeal

½ cup (60 grams) fresh corn kernels,
from 1 small cob (or use frozen, defrosted)

½ cup (55 grams) coarsely grated fontina,
plus 3 tablespoons for sprinkling

Salt and freshly ground black pepper

2 tablespoons (30 grams) sour cream or crème fraîche

¼ cup (60 grams) prepared tomato sauce
or tomato purée

4 large eggs

Fresh flat-leaf parsley or chives, for garnish

Heat the oven to 400 degrees.

Bring the water to a simmer in a medium-sized saucepan over medium-high heat. Slowly whisk in the polenta, trying to avoid lumps then lower the heat to medium-low and simmer the mixture, stirring almost constantly, for 15 minutes. Stir in the corn kernels, and cook for 5 minutes more, continuing to stir regularly. Add ½ cup cheese, and stir until melted; then season well with salt and pepper. Add the sour cream, and stir until partially combined. (I like to leave a few creamy bits throughout.)

Coat a 1-quart baking dish or an 8-to-8½-inch oven-safe skillet with butter or nonstick cooking spray. Transfer the polenta to the dish, then dollop with spoonfuls of tomato; swirl them unevenly into the polenta, so that there are pockets of tomato throughout.

Smooth the top of the polenta and use a spoon to make four deep wells, and crack an egg into each hole. Sprinkle the whole dish with salt and pepper, then sprinkle with the 3 tablespoons cheese. Bake in the heated oven until the whites are firm and the yolks are runny; you can check progress by inserting a toothpick into the whites to see if they've firmed up. If you plan to serve this dish more than a few minutes after taking it out of the oven, remove the eggs from the polenta before they are done, because otherwise they will continue to cook in the hot polenta. If you'd like it to be a little brown on top, run the pan under your broiler when the eggs are only halfway as cooked as you like.

Sprinkle with parsley or chives, and serve with a spoon.

note This scales up well for a crowd.

magical two-ingredient oat brittle

makes a heaped ½ cup brittle

You'd think that as someone who boasts craftsmanship of three granola recipes—or as much as one can over a dish that she hardly invented—I would always have a jar of it around. I don't. I mean, we're happier when we do, but the reality is that the overlap in the Venn diagram of All Granola Ingredients Are in Stock, and Desire to Make Homemade Granola and Not, Say, Binge on *Orange Is the New Black* is, for the sake of honesty, pathetically slim.

Enter: Magical Two-Ingredient Oat Brittle, in which the title is almost longer than the ingredient list. After making a maple-oat topping for a fruit crumble a few years ago, I wondered how it would stand up on its own and was delighted to find that it did. It's a cinch to make and, once cool, can be lifted from parchment paper in large sheets with about 10 percent of the usual number of ingredients considered essential to do so. It keeps forever, which you can correctly read as me saying I happily ate from a jar of it that was at least a year old and I've lived to tell about it. It may not have the complexity of a twelve-ingredient granola recipe, but it has an intense crunch, a light sweetness, and as many clusters as your heart desires.

½ cup (50 grams) old-fashioned rolled oats
2 tablespoons (30 ml) maple syrup
A couple pinches of sea salt

Heat the oven to 350 degrees.

In a small dish, stir the oats, syrup, and salt together until the oats are coated with liquid. Spread the sticky mixture out on a small parchment-lined baking sheet in a thin layer; the oats should be touching each other but not in any piles. Bake for 10 minutes and take a look. You want it to be toasted light golden at the edges—this usually takes 3 more minutes, but it's always safer to check. Remove from the oven, and let the brittle cool completely on the baking sheet, then lift it off in one pleasing sheet and break into chunks.

flipped crispy egg taco with singed greens

makes 2 tacos

I have never met an intersection of eggs and tortillas I could walk away from without ordering it. My obsession was always bad—scrambled-egg burritos, enchiladas, baked eggs in black beans— but it went into overdrive when, a few weeks before I finished this book, my husband surprised me with a birthday weekend away in Mexico City. I would have needed a month to get through all the glorious ways to eat eggs, from *huevos revueltos al gusto* (scrambled with additions), *rancheros mexicanos* (fried with tomato, onion, and chiles), *divorciados* (two fried eggs, one with red salsa, one with green), *motuleños* (black beans, cheese, and then some), and *al albañil* (scrambled with hot salsa and fresh cheese) to *ahogados* (poached in salsa), all usually served with refried beans, avocado, and corn tortillas, not to mention *chilaquiles. Hold me.*

I came back with an aching desire to find the breakfast taco I could eat any day of the week that might even offset the effects of all the *pan dulce* (sweet breads and pastries) we also couldn't resist. I found everything I needed right in the fridge, where a container of washed curly kale for salads, a bag of corn tortillas, eggs, and plain yogurt are almost always in stock. The greens are singed in a smoking-hot skillet for about 30 seconds, until they just start to crisp and collapse; the egg is fried until bubbling and crisp, and then flipped for just enough seconds so it's still loose but will mostly stay within the confines of the taco; the tortillas are charred a little over the gas flame; and the whole mess is finished with a dollop of yogurt and as much hot sauce as makes your heart happy. Use avocado if you don't want yogurt; use some diced tomato if you don't like hot sauce; but, please, do not skimp on those greens and eggs.

Olive oil

1 ounce (30 grams) curly kale leaves, washed, torn into largish chunks

Salt and freshly ground black pepper

2 small corn tortillas

2 eggs

2 dollops of plain yogurt

Hot sauce

Heat a small heavy skillet over the highest heat for a full minute. Coat the bottom of the pan with a glug of olive oil, and heat the oil until it is almost smoking, about another 30 seconds. Add the greens, and be careful, because they're going to hiss and splatter. Use tongs to press them against the bottom of the pan so they singe on one side; then flip the greens and do it again. They should begin to wilt. Transfer them to a plate, and season with salt and pepper.

Again using tongs, hold the tortillas over a gas flame until they're warmed and slightly charred. Add them to the plate with the greens.

Return the heavy skillet to a very high flame, heating it for another full minute. Add a good glug of olive oil (don't skimp; most will stay in the pan, but a stuck egg is a sad one), and heat this for another full minute. Drop your egg in, and jump back—it's going to pop and splatter insanely. This is not for the faint of heart. If you have the nerve to get closer, you can spoon a little of the cooking oil over the egg white to help it bubble. Season well with salt and pepper, and cook until the underside is a deep-golden color and crisp, about 2 minutes. Use a thin spatula to loosen the egg carefully from the pan and flip it; cook it for another 20 seconds or so. Transfer to a plate with the other ingredients. Repeat with the remaining egg.

Assemble the tacos by piling each tortilla with singed greens, placing an egg on top, then a dollop of yogurt, and a few shakes of hot sauce. Eat immediately, folding the taco as you pick it up, breaking the yolk.

alex's bloody mary shrimp cocktail

makes 4 drinks

Nobody knows who really invented the Bloody Mary, although there have been many claims—one Fernand Petiot in 1921 at what later became Harry's New York Bar in Paris, the Hemingway Bar at the Ritz Paris, and also New York's "21" Club. None of the above, however, can answer the question an alien might ask if dropped into a boozy weekend brunch in the year 2017 to find people drinking tall glasses of tomato juice and vodka enhanced with anchovyish steak sauce, hot sauce, horseradish root, olives, celery, lemon, and salt and pepper by choice, which is, forgive me, "Really?" But don't listen to the skeptics; the drink has legions of fans including my husband and his family, which means I've had countless opportunities over the years to tweak my own version to their tastes: heavy on the horseradish, heat, and pickled things. It was only a matter of time before I mashed it up with my husband's other classic restaurant favorite, shrimp cocktail, a more natural fit than it sounds when you consider that traditional shrimp cocktail sauce uses tomatoes enhanced with horseradish, spice, and lemon. We prefer quick-grilled shrimp to poached, and grilling on skewers allows you to use those skewers to prop the shrimp over the drinks. A salt, celery, and pepper rim makes it fancy. A rib of celery makes it traditional. And making it at home means you get all the shrimp, refills, and fixings you want without having to flag down a waiter.

cocktail

1½ cups (12 ounces or 355 ml) tomato juice

¾ cup (6 ounces or 175 ml) vodka

2 teaspoons (10 ml) Worcestershire sauce

3 tablespoons (45 grams) prepared horseradish

8 dashes of hot sauce, plus more to taste

4 pinches of celery salt

A couple shakes of sweet smoked paprika, hot smoked paprika, or chipotle powder

4 pinches of fine salt

¼ teaspoon ground black pepper

Juice of ½ lemon

shrimp

1 pound (455 grams) large shrimp, unpeeled

2 tablespoons (30 ml) olive brine, from jar

Salt and freshly ground black pepper

6 to 8 skewers

1 tablespoon (15 ml) olive oil

Juice of ½ lemon

Cocktail onions (optional)

Olives (optional)

assembly

A pinch or two of celery salt

1 tablespoon kosher salt

¼ teaspoon ground black pepper

4 cups (680 grams) ice cubes

4 celery stalks, ideally with leaves still attached

make the cocktail Combine all the drink ingredients in a pitcher, saving the empty lemon half. Refrigerate until needed.

prepare the shrimp Toss the shrimp with the olive brine and salt and pepper to taste. Thread 3 onto the top half of each skewer, leaving an inch clear above the top shrimp. Brush the shrimp on the skewers with olive oil. Heat the grill as hot as you can. Once it's fully hot, place the shrimp skewers on the grill. Grill for 4 to 5 minutes, flipping once or more as needed for even browning. Remove the skewers from the grill to a platter and squeeze the lemon juice over them.

You can serve the shrimp in one of two ways: leaving them on the skewers (you may wish to add an olive or cocktail onion to the empty inch on top) or removing them from skewers and hanging them off the edge of the glasses, classic shrimp cocktail style.

assemble the cocktails Mix the celery salt, kosher salt, and pepper on a very small plate. Use the empty lemon half from the cocktail-mixing step to wipe the top rim of four 11-to-12-ounce tumblers. Dip the rims in the salt mixture. Carefully drop 1 cup ice into each glass. Give the cocktail mixture in the pitcher a stir and divide it among the four glasses. Garnish with a celery stalk and a shrimp skewer or loose shrimp. Toast and feast!

note We triple this for a crowd.

perfect blueberry muffins

makes 9 muffins

When early summer blueberries first show up at the market, it feels like sacrilege to bake with them—ditto with raspberries, blackberries, and strawberries. Mother Nature made them perfectly! Why drown them in batter, wilt them with heat, and then leave them out to dry? What brutes we'd be! But there's a day in late August when something shifts. The high for the day is in the 60s and you wish for a cardigan. I live for cardigan weather. Suddenly the prospect of a berry baked into something warm and cozy, something that you might eat with your first hot coffee of the season, seems absolutely right.

I want these to be the last blueberry muffins you ever make because I culled everything I had ever eaten, read, or loved about muffins and squashed them into 9 overfilled cups. From *Cook's Illustrated*, I learned that a muffin with a thick batter suspends blueberries, no coating in flour necessary. From Blythe Danner, I realized you could put an inordinate amount of berries in each muffin and still have a very good muffin. From Stella Parks at Serious Eats, I came to agree that a full teaspoon of coarse sugar on top of each muffin sounds crazy but actually makes for a delightfully crunchy lid. If the muffin underneath it isn't too sweet, the extra sugar doesn't put it over the top at all—it's just right. From my own muffin recipes over the years, I knew I could one-bowl this (yes, it's a verb, at least around here), and while I was at it, I could ditch the creaming of the butter and the sifting (sifting! To make muffins! NO). And FTLOG, who—in practice, not just in ambitious recipe writing—measures zest in half-teaspoons?

Finally, it had always bothered me that my recipe made 10 to 11 muffins only. A muffin recipe should make an even dozen! Did I make it happen? Nope. I went the other way and found this makes 9 much prettier towering muffins with perfectly bronzed domes; double it for a dozen and a half.

---

5 tablespoons (70 grams) unsalted butter (cold is fine)

½ cup (100 grams) granulated sugar

Finely grated zest from ½ lemon

¾ cup (175 grams) plain unsweetened yogurt or sour cream

1 large egg

1½ teaspoons baking powder

¼ teaspoon baking soda

¼ teaspoon fine sea or table salt

1½ cups (195 grams) all-purpose flour

1¼ to 1½ cups (215 to 255 grams) blueberries, fresh or frozen (do not defrost)

3 tablespoons (35 grams) raw (turbinado) sugar

Heat the oven to 375 degrees. Line a muffin tin with 9 paper liners or spray each cup with a nonstick spray. Melt the butter and pour into the bottom of a large bowl, and whisk in the granulated sugar, lemon zest, yogurt, and egg until smooth. Whisk in the baking powder, baking soda, and salt until fully combined, then lightly fold in the flour and berries. The batter will be very thick, like a cookie dough. Divide between the prepared muffin cups and sprinkle each muffin with 1 teaspoon turbinado sugar. Bake for 25 to 30 minutes, until the tops of the muffins are golden and a tester inserted into the center comes out clean (you know, except for blueberry goo). Let the muffins cool in the pan for 10 minutes, then the rest of the way on a rack.

These, like most muffins, are best on the first day. But we've found—through extensive "research"—that if you heat them split open under a broiler on day two with a pat of salted butter, they are so good that you're going to forever hope for more blueberry-muffin leftovers.

notes

The smaller amount (1¼ cups) of blueberries listed in the ingredients will make a well-berried muffin. The larger amount (1½ cups) is for people—me! me!—who like just a little bit of muffin with their blueberries.

salads

cauliflower wedge

makes 4 servings

My great salad love, the iceberg wedge, is a study in impracticality. Have you ever tried to sprinkle bits of things over the steep sides of a wedge? If you ever see a photo of a wedge salad with everything caught mid-slope, do know that you're witnessing some food-styling voodoo. In real life, or at least mine, all the wonderful, nubby, crunchy bits that make a bland old wedge magical end up in a puddle on the plate. I addressed this (ahem) Great Problem of Our Time in my first book by making my "wedge" instead with thick slices of iceberg that could be stacked, and nothing was lost. But I realized I was missing out on one of the best parts of eating a wedge—scooping up all the bits on your plate with each forkful.

This wedge—big char-roasted, Parmesan-crusted cauliflower quarters—embraces its topography. Closest to you are those *Brassica oleracea* ridges, but as you slice into them, your fork scoops up an explosion of flavors from the plate: bits of fricoed Parmesan, vinegar-plumped currants, thinly sliced green onions, and one of my favorite "fixings" ever, capers that have been dropped in oil and cooked until their layers expand and crisp like the world's tiniest blooming onion. The cauliflower remains firm enough for the fork-and-knife treatment, as any good wedge should, but the flavors are as complementary to cauliflower as blue cheese and bacon are to iceberg.

2 small, compact-looking heads cauliflower (1¼ to 1½ pounds or 569 to 683 grams each)

3 tablespoons (45 ml) olive oil, plus more for frying capers

Coarse or kosher salt and freshly ground black pepper

⅓ cup (35 grams) finely grated Parmesan

Juice of ½ lemon

1½ tablespoons (25 ml) white wine vinegar

2 tablespoons (20 grams) currants

2 tablespoons (25 grams) capers, brined variety

1 scallion, thinly sliced

1 tablespoon chopped fresh flat-leaf parsley

prepare the cauliflower Heat the oven to 450 degrees. Trim the outer leaves from the cauliflower, then slice the heads in quarters through the stem. Coat a large foil-lined baking sheet with 1 to 2 tablespoons olive oil. Arrange the cauliflower wedges with the cut side down. Drizzle another tablespoon of olive oil over the top of the cauliflower. Season it generously with salt and pepper. Roast on one cut side until nicely browned underneath (15 to 20 minutes), then flip each piece onto its other cut side, sprinkle with more salt and pepper and half of the Parmesan (don't worry if some lands on the tray), and return to the oven to roast for another 10 minutes, until browned. Sprinkle with the remaining Parmesan, and return the baking tray to the oven for another 3 to 5 minutes, until the top layer of cheese is fricoed.

make the currants While the cauliflower is roasting, place the lemon juice, vinegar, and ¼ teaspoon salt in a small bowl. Add the currants; set aside and let them soak while you prepare the other ingredients.

make the capers Drain the capers, and spread them on paper towels until most of their moisture has wicked out, about 5 minutes. Pour ½ inch of olive oil, or another oil that you prefer to fry in, in your tiniest skillet or saucepan. Heat it over medium-high heat. When it's hot enough so a droplet of water makes the oil hiss, carefully add the capers and take a step back! They're going to sputter a bit for the first 10 seconds. Once it's safe to get closer, give

them a stir. Depending on how dry the capers were at the start, it can take 1 to 2 minutes for them to get first lightly golden at the edges, and then crispy. Remove the capers from the oil with a slotted spoon. Drain them on paper towels, and set aside.

to serve Arrange the cauliflower wedges, any loose cauliflower rubble, and any fricoed bits of Parmesan from the roasting pan on a platter. Sprinkle with the scallions, then the currants with their lemon-vinegar mixture, then the capers and parsley. Eat with a fork and knife while standing at the kitchen counter, and order takeout for your family; I won't tell if you don't.

mango apple ceviche with sunflower seeds

makes 2 generous servings or 4 sides

I f a salad could have a month of the year, this one would unequivocally be March. March in the Northeast, in a good year, gives you glimpses of spring but far more reminders of winter that make you grumpy. December snow flurries as you walk down Fifth Avenue checking out the department-store windows, gazing at the trees, are charming. Snowstorms in January are delicious days off. Snow in March is unloved and unwelcome. Meanwhile, your friends in California—but are they really your friends if they taunt you so?—are welcoming their first strawberries.

This salad is here to help. Inspired by coastal Latin America, where I imagine few are averting ankle-deep slush puddles while crossing the street, I give mango a treatment usually reserved for fresh seafood—that is, I souse it in lime juice, salt, red onion, and chiles. After that, I drag it back to New York (kicking and screaming, just like I would be) with one of the few stalwarts of the winter grocery aisles, green apples, before topping it off with something that would make ceviche traditionalists shudder but makes your narrator extremely happy: roasted salted sunflower seeds. Please, trust me, here they're meant to be. I tried more than once to skip them, and it just wasn't as good.

2 large ripe mangoes, peeled, pitted, and sliced ¼ inch thick

½ small red onion, very thinly sliced

½ or 1 fresh red chile pepper, such as limo (traditional for ceviche) or serrano (but go easy on it!), seeded and finely chopped, added to taste

¼ cup (60 ml) lime juice, or to taste

¼ teaspoon coarse or kosher salt

3 tablespoons (45 ml) olive oil

1 unpeeled green apple, cut into matchsticks

⅓ cup (10 grams) roughly chopped fresh cilantro or flat-leaf parsley leaves

3 tablespoons (25 grams) roasted salted sunflower seeds, shelled

Place the mangoes, onion, and chile in a nonreactive (i.e., not metal) bowl, and toss with the lime juice and salt. Let marinate in the fridge for 15 minutes to 1 hour, if you can spare the time, tossing occasionally. Remove from the fridge, then stir in the olive oil and the apple. Adjust the seasonings to taste. Right before serving—seriously, right before—stir in the cilantro, and sprinkle the salad with sunflower seeds.

note Don't get good mangoes where you are? Try this in the summer with firm-ripe peaches, nectarines, or even apricots.

potatoes and asparagus *gribiche*

makes 6 servings

The very best thing about *sauce gribiche* isn't that it contains five things I enjoy and want together as often as possible (shallots, capers, cornichons, mustard, and hard-boiled eggs). Or that they form something of a piquant mayo, where nothing is blended or smooth.

The very best thing about *sauce gribiche* is definitely not that it's traditionally used on top of cold boiled *tête de veau*. Or, I mean, I'm sure there are many people out there for whom calf's head is the best thing, people who get excited about it the way I might about, like, brownies. But ever the American, when I hear mayo, pickles, and hard-boiled eggs, I think of potato salad—or, at minimum, a top-notch dressing for cold potatoes. Adding parcooked vegetables makes it an even less traditional potato salad and more a really great salad *with* potatoes. This also means you can eat it more often, which definitely sounds like it should be the best thing about the sauce. But still it's not.

My actual favorite thing about *gribiche* is that if you dig around you'll find references to its being a word for "a mean old woman who scares children," and this delights me; it sounds straight out of Hans Christian Andersen before Disney cleaned him up. The origins are a little vague—the Dutch word *kribbich* means "grouchy" or "petulant," and it might have sifted out from there—but around here, it's forever stuck.

gribiche dressing

2 large hard-boiled eggs, yolks separated, whites chopped

2 tablespoons (30 grams) Dijon mustard

2 tablespoons (30 ml) white wine vinegar

6 tablespoons (90 ml) olive oil

1 tablespoon (12 grams) capers, brined variety

2 tablespoons (20 grams) finely chopped cornichons (from about 4)

1 small shallot, minced

½ teaspoon kosher salt

Freshly ground black pepper

assembly

2 pounds (about 1 kilogram) small new or fingerling potatoes

1 pound (455 grams) asparagus, trimmed

1 tablespoon chopped fresh parsley, tarragon, or chervil

make the sauce/dressing Mash the yolks with the mustard in the bottom of a bowl. Whisk in vinegar and oil. Stir in capers, cornichons, chopped egg whites, shallot, salt, and pepper to taste. Adjust the seasonings.

make the salad Place the potatoes in a medium saucepan and cover with 2 inches of salted water. Bring to a boil, and cook for about 13 minutes, or until the tip of a knife pierces through a potato with a little resistance. Add the asparagus to the pot, and cook them together for 2 minutes. Drain and rinse under cold water. Let the potatoes and asparagus cool completely.

Cut the potatoes in halves or quarters, depending on their size, and place them in a large bowl. Cut the asparagus into ½-to-¾-inch segments, and add to the bowl. Toss with *gribiche* sauce, and season well with salt and pepper. Garnish with the herbs.

winter slaw with farro

makes 6 to 8 servings

Two of my biggest ongoing salad fixations are non-mayo-sogged slaws, and grain salads where the grain is the minority ingredient, not just a foundation that vegetables are dotted across as an afterthought. Thus, it was only a matter of time before they collided.

Much ink has been spilled on the glories of heirloom tomatoes, shucked corn so sweet it feels wrong to cook it at all, and baby field greens freshly picked from an actual field . . . but for most of us living in places where the ground is dormant for more months of the year than it is productive, great winter salads are an elusive concept. Slaws, untethered from creamy picnic dressings, deserve a place on our January plates. Whole and well-wrapped halved heads of cabbage seem to hold up indefinitely in the fridge, and even once shredded into a salad, far longer than your average leafy green; they deserve equally dependable (or at least easy to ransack your cabinets for) complements. Here, inspired by what became our favorite West Village restaurant all of five minutes after it opened, Via Carota, hearty bits of farro are scattered throughout the vegetable salad like nubby crouton accents, where they're joined by diced dried apricots soaked in vinegar long enough to give them a little pop, roasted almonds, and flakes of Parmesan. Together they make a subtle, crunchy winter salad, and an ideal take-with-you weekday lunch that keeps all week in the fridge.

½ cup (100 grams) finely diced dried apricots

¼ cup (60 ml) white wine vinegar, plus more to taste

1 small-medium (2 pounds or a bit less than 1 kilogram) head green cabbage

1⅓ cups (145 grams) cooked farro, cooled (from about ¾ cup uncooked)

⅓ cup (45 grams) roughly chopped roasted almonds

2 ounces (55 grams) Parmesan, thinly shaved on a grater or with a vegetable peeler

3 tablespoons (45 ml) olive oil, plus more to taste

½ teaspoon kosher salt, plus more to taste

Freshly ground black pepper

Place the apricots in a small bowl with the vinegar, and set aside while preparing other ingredients.

Cut the cabbage in half, and remove the core; then cut the halves again so that you have quarters. With a mandoline or a knife, slice the cabbage into very thin ribbons. You'll have about 12 cups total, which will seem ridiculous, but it will wilt down with dressing on it. Pile it in your largest bowl.

Add to the bowl the apricots and their vinegar, the farro, almonds, and most of the Parmesan, plus the olive oil, salt, and a good helping of freshly ground black pepper. Toss to combine, and try to give it 15 minutes, if you can stand it, to let the ingredients settle a little before making seasoning adjustments; then add more vinegar, Parmesan, oil, salt, and pepper to taste. Heap on plates in piles, and top with remaining Parmesan.

do ahead The slaw keeps for up to 1 week in the fridge.

smashed cucumber salad with salted peanuts and wasabi peas

makes 4 servings

ook, if a food writer ever compares his or her moment with a dish to Proust and his madeleines, I think you should be like that gif that flips a table over and storms out. I promise, I would never do that to you. This is not that kind of story. All I want to say is that when I moved to New York City, almost two decades ago, we used to go out very often to this place that was definitely a symbol of the gentrifying that was already well under way in Williamsburg, and I used to find myself sitting at the bar alone very often, because my friends were always late. My favorite thing to order there was cold sake, because they brought it to you with a cucumber spear in it, along with a dish of a mix of salted roasted peanuts and wasabi peas as a bar snack, and I went through this procession of flavors—cold, faintly sweet, crisp, refreshing, with sinus-clearing pop and salty crunch—with delight. And I've been wanting to get it back into my life without, you know, spending, er, *as many* evenings on a barstool.

I finally found my version in a Chinese smashed-cucumber salad, one of the best things to make a habit of when it gets warm. Cucumbers are smashed or smacked with the side of a knife or mallet, then torn apart—all of which is just as much messy fun as it sounds—briefly salted, drained, and returned to you crisp, skins beaming, completely ready to absorb any dressing you throw at them, far better than a freshly sliced cucumber ever does. I dress mine in a splash of sake, rice vinegar, and toasted sesame oil, but the real magic comes at the end, when you coat it with a fiery, salty, crunchy mix of crushed wasabi peas and peanuts—bizarre if you've never had it, forever habit-forming once you have.

2 large seedless cucumbers (a little shy of 2 pounds or 1 kilogram)

1 teaspoon kosher salt, plus more to taste

2 tablespoons (30 ml) plus 1 teaspoon (5 ml) sake

1 tablespoon (15 ml) rice vinegar

2 teaspoons (10 ml) toasted sesame oil

Hot pepper flakes, to taste

2 tablespoons (20 grams) salted peanuts, crushed or coarsely chopped

2 tablespoons (15 grams) wasabi peas, crushed or coarsely chopped

Cut the cucumbers in half crosswise, then split lengthwise. Put on an apron (you'll thank me) and, on a solid work surface, lay the cucumbers cut side down and whack them firmly with the flat side of a meat pounder or the bottom of a cast-iron skillet until the skin has torn and the seeds largely separate. Use your hands to swipe out any loose or lingering seeds, then tear or chop the cucumbers into rough 1-to-2-inch pieces. Toss in a bowl with 1 teaspoon salt and 2 tablespoons sake, then let sit in a colander set over a bowl for 10 to 15 minutes at room temperature, or up to a few hours in the fridge.

Discard the liquid in the bowl, wipe it out, and drop the cucumbers back into it. Pour in the rice vinegar, sesame oil, last teaspoon of sake, and salt and hot pepper flakes to taste. Scatter generously with crushed peanuts and wasabi peas, and eat immediately.

note I promise, this isn't nearly as boozy at is sounds—most of the first glugs of sake drain off with the salt, leaving just a kiss of flavor behind. It's only that last spoonful that goes right onto your plate. But if you want to omit it, simply add a couple of pinches of sugar to the initial liquid.

do ahead (or don't) The cucumbers get slippery pretty quickly, so it's better not to dress or garnish them until you're ready to eat.

sushi takeout cobb

makes 6 servings

A few years ago, I shared a recipe for the carrot-ginger dressing you get with salad at a lot of sushi restaurants, but I kind of thought nobody would be excited about it. It seemed so obscure, too specific; for all I knew, it was just a New York thing. From the responses I got, I began to wonder if we are all wading through unagi, toro, and tomago just to score a few wan leaves of iceberg draped with this sauce. People are bonkers for it in a way that would seem impossible for something made by grinding a raw carrot with miso, ginger, raw shallot, rice vinegar, and toasted sesame oil, but if you've tried it, you probably know that they form something so special it could probably make an old shoe taste good. (Please note, this is not actually a tested theory.)

Thus, the only logical thing was to find a way to have more of it in my life. With more salad, you get to make more dressing, and so I've taken to creating an assembly of the ingredients you might find in a sushi takeout salad, plus edamame, tofu, and avocado, which is to say that this is full of protein and even vegan, but in the best way: accidentally. I've never been big on "detox" foods or mostly raw meals, but if my week's menu looked like this plate, I might reconsider.

dressing

2 medium carrots (115 grams),
peeled and roughly chopped

2 medium shallots or ½ small white onion,
finely chopped

2 tablespoons (25 grams) minced or
very finely chopped fresh ginger

¼ cup (60 ml) unseasoned rice vinegar,
plus 1 teaspoon for avocado

¼ cup (70 grams) white miso

¼ cup (60 ml) toasted sesame oil

6 tablespoons (90 ml) neutral oil

salad

1 large avocado, diced

3 to 4 cups thinly sliced napa cabbage
(½ medium, 2-pound or roughly 1-kilogram head)

⅔ cup (110 grams) shelled edamame,
cooked and cooled

1 cup diced silken tofu
(half of a 12-ounce or 340-gram container)

1 cup (170 grams) diced tomatoes

1 cup (70 grams) diced cucumber
(from about ½ large seedless cucumber)

1 cup (115 grams) daikon, cut into matchsticks

garnish

2 tablespoons minced fresh chives

make the dressing In a food processor or blender, blend the carrots, shallots or onion, ginger, and vinegar together until very finely ground. Add the miso, sesame oil, and neutral oil, and blend until as smooth as possible. Taste, and adjust the seasonings if desired.

make the salad Toss the avocado with 1 teaspoon rice vinegar to prevent it from browning. Scatter the cabbage on a large platter, then arrange the remaining ingredients—avocado, edamame, tofu, tomatoes, cucumber, and daikon—in rows. Garnish with chives. Serve with dressing on the side.

notes

I adore toasted sesame oil, but I've heard from others that they don't always like the full 2 tablespoons in this recipe (though we do, very much). If you're nervous that it will be too strong a flavor, use just 1 tablespoon and hold off on the rest until the end. If you have enough sesame flavor, add 1 tablespoon more of a neutral oil instead; if you can never have enough, use the remaining sesame oil.

The dressing makes 2 cups, which is way more than you'll need. You could even halve it. But this is a real pour-it-on dressing; I don't think you'll mind the extra.

If you're nervous that your cranky old blender won't handle raw carrot well, you can grate or chop it smaller first.

tip Juliennes always look really complicated to cut but are anything but. I even (weirdo alert) find it fun. Take any long vegetable and cut it into thin slices on the diagonal. Stack the slices, and cut them into thin matchsticks.

kale caesar with broken eggs and crushed croutons

makes 2 hearty or 4 smaller salads

The terrain of kale salads, dishes with runny eggs on top, and variations on caesar salads has been so thoroughly trodden, trampled, and squeezed for life that about the only excuse left for creating variations on it is, to be completely honest, about the only good reason to cook anything ever: it's so good you basically cannot shut up about it.

And so it happened that we fell in love with a caesar salad riff we make at home, in which the usual romaine hearts are replaced by kale, runny eggs run amok throughout, and the croutons are crushed to fragrant olive-oil/toasted-Parmesan crumbs that cling to the eggs and dressing—dressing that has about as much to do with authentic caesar salad as I have to do with being tall.

We call it my Hopelessly Inauthentic Caesar Dressing, and I began making it over a decade ago out of convenience, but the thing is, everyone likes it now more than the real deal. Instead of raw egg yolks, there's mayo, which—wait, come back—is technically raw yolks and oil, right? Instead of minced anchovies, there's Worcestershire, which, in fact, has anchovies in it, so it makes more sense than it sounds. The rest is olive oil, lemon juice, Dijon, and some minced garlic, and no fancy blender work is required to emulsify it. It's fantastic. We wouldn't change a thing about it. We've tried, but we always come back to it.

I have monthlong benders throughout the year when I don't understand why I have to eat anything else. Even if it wasn't a balanced composition of raw greens and inexpensive protein, the salty, tangy, crunchy indulgence of it all would make it impossible not to put this on repeat. My best advice? Make extra dressing (it keeps in a jar for weeks), wash extra greens, cook extra eggs, and assemble them as needed—because you're going to want this again.

salad

2 large eggs

5 ounces (about 5 cups or 140 grams) baby or regular kale leaves, the latter sliced into thin ribbons

¼ cup (30 grams) grated Parmesan

breadcrumbs

1 tablespoon (15 ml) olive oil

1 small garlic clove, minced

A few fine gratings of lemon zest

⅓ cup (20 grams) panko breadcrumbs

dressing

2 tablespoons (25 grams) mayonnaise

1 small garlic clove, minced

1 teaspoon (5 ml) Worcestershire sauce

1 teaspoon (5 grams) smooth Dijon mustard

1 to 2 tablespoons (15 to 30 ml) lemon juice

¼ cup (60 ml) olive oil

Salt and freshly ground black pepper

prepare the eggs Bring a medium-sized pot of water to a boil. Carefully lower in the eggs and lower heat to a simmer. Cook for 7 minutes, drain, and run under cold water.

make the breadcrumbs In a small skillet, heat the olive oil over medium heat. Add the garlic, and cook, stirring, until barely golden about 30 seconds. Add the lemon zest and breadcrumbs, and sauté them until golden, 2 to 3 minutes. Set the breadcrumbs aside until needed.

make the dressing Whisk all ingredients together, and season to taste with salt and black pepper.

assemble the salad Carefully peel the cooked eggs—running them under cold water if it helps—and rinse them of any clinging shells. Toss the kale with half the dressing. Pile a third of the dressed kale in a large serving bowl. Sprinkle with a third of the crumbs and a third of the Parmesan, and then, right over the salad, chop the first egg into rough quarters (I do this right over the salad so I don't have any spillage) and scatter a few of the pieces over it. Repeat twice. Serve with remaining dressing on the side.

charred corn succotash with lime and crispy shallots

makes 4 servings

I can tell you from experience that a recipe is a great place to sublimate wanderlust. There's been this period of time—let's call it adulthood, or, more specifically, parenthood—in which we've again and again found it harder to travel the way we used to, and always imagined that we would. What with all of the warm, glowy stories of babies on planes and young children eagerly embracing cuisines unfamiliar to them in places unfamiliar to them in time zones unfamiliar to their sleep routines, I cannot imagine why we have run into this problem. I'm sure it's just us. In the interim, we spend a lot of time gazing enviously at the vacations of others on social media, and, more relevantly here, thumbing through cookbooks that can take us where cheap airfare during peak travel weeks has not.

It was over the course of digesting a few Thai cookbooks that I became fixated on giving succotash—an American summer casserole classic—the treatment of a green papaya salad: that is, slivers of chiles and garlic, a lime-and-fish-sauce vinaigrette, and crispy shallots, my other favorite garnish, on top. And the idea wouldn't let up until I made it happen. This salad is a tiny little bit fussy. There are crispy shallots; you could skip them, but I think you shouldn't. There's charred corn; charring gives even the blandest off-season corn a smoky depth without requiring a grill. There are green beans that need to be parboiled, in place of the traditional shell beans. But when I put it together, we couldn't get over it, and by "we couldn't get over it," I mean we ate it standing up in the kitchen and it never made it to the table that night. (Which is too bad; it would be excellent with a simple skirt steak rubbed with sugar, salt, and pepper, or with grilled shrimp.) I could never pick a favorite salad, but I can assure you that this will forever be near the top.

crispy shallots

Vegetable oil, for frying

2 large shallots, thinly sliced

dressing

Juice of 2 limes

2 teaspoons (10 grams) dark-brown sugar

2 tablespoons (30 ml) fish sauce

salad

1 cup (115 grams) green beans, sliced on the diagonal into 1-inch segments

4 medium ears corn, shucked

1 tablespoon (15 ml) neutral oil

2 shallots, thinly sliced

2 garlic cloves, thinly sliced

1 fresh Thai or other green or red chile (more or less, to taste), thinly sliced

Fine salt, to season

1 cup (155 grams) cherry tomatoes, halved

1 tablespoon thinly slivered Thai or other basil leaves

make the crispy shallots In your smallest skillet, heat ½ inch of oil over medium heat. (I use 8 to 10 tablespoons in my 6-inch skillet.) Add the shallots to the skillet, breaking the rings up a little as you drop them in. Cook, stirring, until the shallots are a good golden brown, then transfer them with a slotted spoon to a plate lined with several paper towels and sprinkle them with salt. The shallots will keep cooking a little after they leave the skillet, so removing them just a bit early is recommended.

make the dressing Whisk together the dressing ingredients.

for the salad Cook the green beans in a pot of salted water until crisp and just barely tender, about 3 minutes. Drain, and plunge them into ice water to stop them from cooking and to cool. If you've got better things to do than draw a bath of ice water, you could remove the beans at 2 minutes; they'll continue cooking as they cool. Drain and pat dry.

Remove any small children from the kitchen. Over a hot grill or an open gas-stove flame, char the ears of corn until most of the kernels are blackened, turning with tongs to get at all sides. The corn has a tendency to crackle and splatter, so wear oven mitts and be cautious. When the corn is cool enough to handle, shave off the kernels with a large knife, and reserve.

In a large skillet, heat the neutral oil over medium heat. Add the shallots, garlic, and chile, and cook for 1 minute, until just softened. Add the corn, season with salt, and cook for 2 to 3 minutes, just to soften the corn. Turn off the heat, quickly stir in the green beans and tomatoes, and pour half the dressing over the top. Pile on a plate, and garnish with basil and crispy shallots. Serve with the remaining dressing on the side.

whitefish and pickled cucumber salad

makes 6 rectangular toasts or 3 to 4 cups salad

When Ina Garten says she's going to make a dish for her husband, Jeffrey, you kind of know it's going to be awesome—a towering chocolate cake, the most comforting roast chicken, unseemly large chocolate-chip cookies that, let's be honest, are the only kind we want to eat anyway. I think my husband has similarly positive effects on my cooking. Alex's great loves (that, um, are not me—sorry, that was horribly twee) are chocolate, peanut butter, bourbon, pretzels, radishes, pickles, and smoked fish. If I say peppers, he suggests *peperoncini*. If I suggest deli meat, he suggests prosciutto or a spicy salami. And whenever the weather gets warm and I start talking about American-style potato salad with the minced sweet pickles and the chopped hard-boiled eggs, mustard, and mayo, he reminds me that it's been *x* number of days since I last made his favorite potato salad. Basically, for every North American whim I have, he counters with an Eastern European/Slavic/Mediterranean one.

This dish, of course, is not potato salad, but it includes Alex's favorite parts from his favorite version, which makes overnight dilled pickles of two giant cucumbers, then tosses them with sliced onion, radishes, dill, and mayo. Then, instead of using potatoes, here we combine the pickles with smoked whitefish, to make a salad that would be as much at home on a bagel as it is on a thin slice of grainy bread.

pickles

6 tablespoons (90 ml) distilled white vinegar

1 tablespoon Diamond kosher salt
(use ½ tablespoon of other brands)

Two 1-pound (455-gram) English hothouse cucumbers, very thinly sliced

A few sprigs of fresh dill (no need to chop)

dressing

2 tablespoons (25 grams) mayonnaise

2 tablespoons (30 grams) sour cream

2 teaspoons (10 ml) pickle brine (from above)

1 tablespoon chopped fresh dill, plus more to taste

Salt and freshly ground black pepper

assembly

12 to 14 ounces (340 to 390 grams) flaked smoked whitefish (see note)

½ recipe pickled cucumbers

½ small white onion, very thinly sliced

2 or 3 radishes, very thinly sliced

2 tablespoons (25 grams) capers plus 1 teaspoon (5 ml) of their brine

4 thin slices pumpernickel or another dense bread, such as A Dense, Grainy Daily Bread (page 112), toasted and cooled

make the pickles Place the vinegar and salt in the bottom of a gallon freezer bag, and swish it around. Add the cucumbers and dill, and seal the bag. Toss to combine well. Refrigerate overnight, turning the bag occasionally. The next morning, pour the cucumber mixture into a large sieve set over a bowl. Fish out and discard the dill. Drain well, and reserve a little of the brine.

make the dressing Whisk the mayo, sour cream, pickle brine, and all but 1 teaspoon of the dill in a small bowl, and season to taste with salt and pepper.

assemble the salad In a larger bowl, combine the flaked fish, half of the pickles, the onion, radishes, and all but 1 teaspoon of the capers. Add half of the dressing to start, and stir gently to combine.

Dollop on the toasts and garnish with the remaining dill and capers. Serve extra dressing on the side.

note You'll want about 1½ pounds whole (bone-in, skin-on) smoked whitefish to get 1 pound skinned and flaked. Most whole smoked whitefish clock in at 2½ to 3 pounds, so you'll need about half of one here.

fennel, pear, celery, and hazelnut salad

makes 2 hearty or 4 small servings

W e jokingly call this the Haters' Salad. Well, mostly jokingly. If there's anything I've picked up in a decade of sharing recipes, it's that people have strong feelings about fennel, and they're generally not positive. Ditto about celery and, at least from my at-home peanut gallery, pears. ("Why can't they taste like apples?" is a question I have been asked by a member of my own family, in case you want to know what I'm up against.) But I love all of these things enough for me and you and everyone else, and together they make an enviable winter salad that feels about as light as anything can in months that require sleeping bags for coats. Crisp, tangy in some parts, lightly bitter in others, the ingredients wind around each other with nutty punctuations from the hazelnuts, and you'd be surprised how many fennel disavowers have been well converted. That is, when I'm nice enough to share.

1 small-medium (1-pound or 455-gram) fennel bulb, very thinly sliced, some fronds reserved for garnish

2 or more celery stalks from the center, plus leaves

¾ medium pear (I use a red D'Anjou), halved, cored, and thinly sliced

Juice of 1 lemon

2 tablespoons (30 ml) olive oil

Coarse salt and freshly ground black pepper or red pepper flakes

½ cup (69 grams) hazelnuts, toasted, skinned, and cooled

One ½-ounce (15-gram) chunk Parmesan, shaved or peeled

Toss the fennel, celery, and pear together in a big bowl, and dress with the lemon juice, olive oil, and an unfrugal amount of salt and pepper. Taste, and add more of any seasoning if needed. Scatter the hazelnuts and Parmesan on top, lightly toss one more time, then dig in. The salad keeps in the fridge for 2 days, but the pear will eventually soften a little, long before the salad goes "bad."

note I also adore this salad with blood orange segments in place of the pear and celery, with Parmesan optional.

fall-toush salad with delicata squash and brussels sprouts

makes 2 large or 4 small servings

This probably makes no sense. The classic Levantine fattoush salad that I've mercilessly punned upon is the epitome of summer: tomatoes, cucumbers, scallions, mint, parsley, garlic, and lemon with pita chips that both do and do not soak up the dressing, in the best of both ways. It's bright, crunchy, and the absolutely ideal thing to eat on a hot day. But what about when the tomatoes wane? A *fall*-toush salad is like your summer fattoush put on a thick sweater over a plaid shirt and went on a hayride, drinking hot apple cider. A fall-toush salad keeps the brighter parts of the summer version—the lemon, scallions, parsley, mint, garlic, and pita chips—but stirs them over warm roasted squash and brussels sprouts. A fall-toush salad accepts that when it's going to be cold out for the foreseeable future, your salads must adjust accordingly.

I'd originally made this as a side salad to simple roast chicken, but was delighted to find that it's really meal-level hearty, almost an all-in-one-bowl dinner with a killer dressing. But my favorite part of this salad is that it's squarely a fall dish that, with the lemony, crunchy ingredients, holds on to a glimmer of summer.

salad

3 tablespoons (45 ml) olive oil

1¼ pounds (565 grams) delicata squash (about 1 medium squash)

Kosher salt and freshly ground black pepper or Aleppo-pepper flakes to taste

½ pound (225 grams) brussels sprouts

1 large pita bread

2 scallions, thinly sliced

About 1 tablespoon finely chopped mint leaves

About 1 tablespoon finely chopped flat-leaf parsley or cilantro leaves

Ground sumac or paprika, to finish

dressing

2 teaspoons (10 grams) ground sumac or paprika

2 teaspoons (10 ml) warm water

1 to 2 tablespoons (15 to 30 ml) lemon juice

1 small garlic clove, minced

1 teaspoon (5 ml) white wine vinegar

¼ cup (60 ml) olive oil

Salt and freshly ground black pepper or Aleppo pepper flakes

prepare the vegetables Heat the oven to 400 degrees. Coat two baking sheets with a tablespoon or so of olive oil each.

Cut the ends from the delicata squash, and scrape out the seeds with a spoon. (Did you know you can toast these like pumpkin seeds for a crispy garnish? You can!) Slice the squash into ½-inch-thick rings, then cut each ring into 1-to-2-inch chunks. Spread them on the first baking sheet in one layer; sprinkle with salt and pepper. Roast for 20 to 25 minutes, until bronzed underneath; then flip and roast for another 8 to 10 minutes, until browned at the edges and tender in the center. Set aside to cool slightly.

Meanwhile, trim the ends and any discolored leaves from the brussels sprouts, and halve them lengthwise. Spread, cut side down, on the second baking sheet; sprinkle with salt and pepper. Roast for 15 minutes, then flip the sprouts and roast them for another 5 to 10 minutes, until toasty and crisp. Set aside to cool slightly.

prepare the pita chips Split the pita into two layers, and cut or tear into large bite-sized chunks. Toss in a bowl with the remaining olive oil and a couple pinches of salt. Spread on a baking sheet, and toast in oven with vegetables for 5 to 8 minutes, until golden and crisp.

make the dressing Soak the sumac in water for 5 minutes, then whisk in the remaining dressing ingredients. Adjust the seasonings to taste; you may find you need more lemon juice or vinegar.

assemble the salad In a medium-large bowl, combine the warm roasted vegetables and scallions. Toss with half to two-thirds of the dressing, or to taste. Stir in the chopped herbs, then the pita chips; add more dressing, and adjust the salt and pepper levels if needed. Sprinkle with sumac to finish, and serve.

do ahead Keep the roasted vegetables separate from the pita chips until ready to serve, so the chips don't get soggy.

carrot salad with tahini, crisped chickpeas, and salted pistachios

makes 2 large or 4 small servings

One of my favorite carrot salads is the classic French *carottes râpées,* exquisite in its simplicity of lemon juice, olive oil, a pinch of sugar, some salt, pepper, and roughly chopped parsley, all applied in that old-fashioned taste-as-you-go method that basically guarantees it will be perfectly seasoned when you're done. (You do this with everything you cook, right? Yeah, I forget, too.) And yet this isn't that; this is what happened one time when I decided to mess with the classic and ended up creating the kind of carrot salad that doesn't hang quietly off to the side and let other dishes shine.

Zinging with lemon, nutty with tahini, flecked with parsley, topped with almost smoky roasted chickpeas and then some chopped salted pistachios—I don't think I've ever had a bowl of grated carrots with so much complexity, so much to consider. On a weeknight, you could pile it atop some leafy greens for a more meal-like salad, or serve it with sesame-spiced turkey meatballs (from my first book—no pressure or anything, but they're pretty awesome). For a work lunch salad, keep the chickpeas separate and sprinkle them on as croutons just before you eat. This salad would be welcome at a cookout, maybe with some lamb skewers and grilled pita wedges. Just put the lamb/meatballs/other dishes on notice that they're the sides now, that this carrot salad is the centerpiece, and also a bit of a diva. When you try it, you'll see why.

chickpeas

1¾ cups cooked chickpeas,
or one 15.5-ounce/440-gram can, drained
and patted dry on paper towels

1 tablespoon (15 ml) olive oil

½ teaspoon coarse sea salt

¼ teaspoon ground cumin

dressing

1 medium garlic clove, minced

¼ cup (60 ml) lemon juice

3 tablespoons (25 grams) well-stirred tahini

2 tablespoons (30 ml) water, plus more if needed

2 tablespoons (30 ml) olive oil

Salt and red pepper flakes to taste

salad

1 pound (455 grams) carrots, peeled and coarsely grated

¼ cup (10 grams) coarsely chopped fresh parsley

¼ cup (30 grams) shelled salted pistachios, coarsely chopped

roast the chickpeas Heat the oven to 425 degrees. Toss the chickpeas with the olive oil, salt, and cumin until they're all coated. Spread the chickpeas on a baking sheet or pan, and roast them in the oven until they're browned and crisp. This can take anywhere from 15 to 20 minutes, depending on the size and firmness of your chickpeas. Toss them occasionally, to make sure they're toasting evenly. Set aside until needed.

make the dressing Whisk all the ingredients together until smooth, adding more water if needed to thin the dressing slightly. Taste and adjust the seasoning; don't worry if the lemon juice makes it taste a little sharp; it will marry perfectly with the sweet grated carrots.

assemble the salad Place the grated carrots in a large bowl, and toss them with the parsley. Mix in two-thirds of the dressing, adding more if desired. Add more salt and pepper if needed. Sprinkle with a large handful of chickpeas (you'll have extra, and if you're like us, you won't regret it) and the pistachios.

do ahead The salad keeps well in the fridge for 2 days; however, I'd add the chickpeas and pistachios right before serving, so they don't get soft.

soups and stews

red lentil soup, dal style

makes 4 servings

once read an article by a food writer in which she said that for years it seemed that everyone she knew had a special lentil soup that sustained them and kept them warm all winter, but she didn't, although she wished she did. I was riveted. I had never considered this before. Was this yet another of those things that other grown-ups—the kind who had their acts together—all knew about, and I—being me—did not? What else was on this list? How was I ever going to catch up? At least, I decided, I could teach myself to make a mean red-lentil soup.

I am not convinced that I have my act together any more now than I did a decade ago, but I knew exactly what "my" lentil soup would be. It would look humble and be a cinch to put together, but would fly off the spoon with Indian spices. I dreamed not as much of a lentil soup but a loose dal. It took me another few years, however, to learn of the manna that is *chaunk* (sometimes called "tadka" or tempering): an oil sizzling with spice seeds that's added to soups and curries as a finish. Mustard seeds are common, and for good reason—I think the oil smells like popcorn as it cooks. This toasted nuttiness is a delicious finish and adds a bit of richness without adding heaviness. Whatever you do, wherever your hunt for your togetherness-as-evidenced-by-a-signature-red-lentil-soup takes you, please don't miss this.

soup

3 tablespoons (45 ml) neutral oil

1 large onion, minced

1½ tablespoons (40 grams) minced ginger

2 garlic cloves, minced

1 fresh hot green chile pepper, minced, or ½ teaspoon ground cayenne pepper

¼ teaspoon turmeric

1½ teaspoons ground cumin

1 teaspoon ground coriander

2 teaspoons kosher salt, or more to taste

½ cup (125 grams) chopped fresh or canned tomatoes

1 large carrot, diced (just shy of 1 cup)

6 cups (1.4 liters) water

1 cup (210 grams) red lentils

to finish

3 tablespoons (45 ml) canola oil or ghee

1½ teaspoons (5 grams) mustard seeds

Handful of chopped fresh cilantro

A squeeze of fresh lemon juice per bowl

In a large pot, heat the neutral oil over medium-high heat until hot and shimmering, then add the onion, ginger, garlic, and any fresh chile you are using, and cook, stirring, until browned, about 5 minutes. Turn the heat to medium-low, and add the turmeric, cumin, coriander, cayenne (if you're not using fresh chile), and salt. Cook the onion mixture for a minute or two, then add the tomatoes, and scrape up any bits that have stuck to the pan. Add the carrot, cook for 1 minute more, then add the water and lentils. Bring back to a simmer, partially cover, and cook for 25 to 30 minutes, until the lentils and carrot are soft. Taste, and adjust the seasonings as needed. If desired, blend for a second or two with an immersion blender to create a mixed smooth-rough texture.

Heat the canola oil in a small skillet over high heat. When the oil begins to smoke, add the mustard seeds and cover the pan with a lid or splatter screen. When the seeds stop popping, immediately pour the oil over the soup. Add a squeeze of lemon juice and garnish with cilantro.

note I make an all-mustard-seed *chaunk,* but you can also replace half with cumin seeds for a more varied flavor, or add a chopped garlic clove and red pepper flakes at the end for more punch.

pea tortellini in parmesan broth

makes 8 servings

once read that if someone makes you homemade-from-scratch tortellini they must be absolutely in love with you, because it takes a hellacious amount of work. I thought this was a bit melodramatic until the day I decided to tackle it—i.e., cranking out 2-inch squares of paper-thin pasta dough and then filling, folding, and pinching them into a "napkin" shape and repeating this process upward of two hundred more times, because it's too much work not to make a lot to stash in the freezer, all for something most people will eat in a single bite and forget. Oh, and don't try to make them larger to get it done faster, or you might end up a spinster. Legend has it that Italian brides have been judged by how many of their tortellini fit on a spoon.

Needless to say: Nope, nope, nope. Or, at least, not unless you all come over to help.

This puts me in a position, because tortellini *in brodo* could rival any matzo-ball or chicken-noodle soup for my ideal bowl of comfort. Sure, you can make it with frozen pasta and boxed stock, but if you've had it made fresh, you're already ruined. This is the way I compromise—not on the *brodo,* which we are going to make with Parmesan rinds, onion, and garlic, and it's going to be life-changing and completely worth it, or it was for me—but with packaged wonton wrappers.

The benefits are manifold: Most are already impossibly thin, far more so than the ones I usually pull off with homemade dough. Because I'm making my own filling, I can make the filling I really want—in this case, peas with lemon, Parmesan, and ricotta—and, well, because I'm already married (I mean, *phew,* right?), I can make them big enough that one fills a spoon, and I don't have to share them with anyone for whom that isn't good enough.

broth

12 ounces (340 grams) Parmesan rinds

12 cups (2¾ liters) water

1 large onion, quartered or roughly chopped

4 unpeeled garlic cloves, lightly smashed

2 teaspoons peppercorns

Large handful of fresh flat-leaf parsley

½ teaspoon kosher salt, plus more to taste

tortellini

1 cup (150 grams) cooked peas, cooled

½ cup (125 grams) ricotta

½ cup (65 grams) grated Parmesan

½ teaspoon kosher salt

Several grinds of black pepper

A few fine gratings of lemon zest

2 teaspoons (10 ml) lemon juice

Two 48-count packages of wonton skins or wrappers

to serve

Handful of pea shoots, for garnish (optional)

Olive oil and Parmesan, for serving

to finish

1 large carrot, julienned

1 large parsnip, julienned

1 tablespoon minced fresh dill, parsley, or chives

make your stock Heat the oil in the bottom of a stockpot (6 to 7 quarts is ideal) over medium-high heat. Add the leeks, onions, carrots, parsnip, celery, and mushrooms, and cook, stirring occasionally, until they're browned in spots and a little soft, 10 to 15 minutes. Add the rutabaga, potato, garlic, parsley, dill, peppercorns, cayenne, salt, and bay leaf, then the water and bring to a simmer. Cook, covered, for 45 minutes to 1 hour, then taste and adjust the seasonings as desired. Strain the stock, and set aside.

meanwhile, make the matzo balls Mix all the matzo-ball ingredients in a bowl. Cover, and chill in the refrigerator for 30 minutes. Bring well-salted water to a brisk boil in a large, wide pot such as a sauté pan, then reduce the heat to a simmer. Run your hands under water so they are thoroughly wet. Form matzo balls by dropping teaspoonfuls (as in, 1 teaspoon measurement or the equivalent tiny scoop) into the palm of your wet hands and rolling them loosely into balls. Drop them into the simmering salt water one at a time. Cover the pot, and cook them for 20 minutes.

assemble the soup Meanwhile bring the stock back to a simmer. About 5 minutes before the matzo balls are ready, add the julienned carrots and parsnips, and let them simmer until tender, about 5 minutes. Add the matzo balls to the pot. Ladle into bowls, and garnish with herbs.

notes

A julienne peeler was used to make the spaghetti-like vegetable strands you see here. A spiralizer would make fun, curly vegetables.

Why seltzer? It makes matzo balls extra light, insist both my mother and mother-in-law.

roasted tomato soup with broiled cheddar

makes 4 mugs of soup

Thisis, depending on your perspective, either the greatest intersection of grilled cheese sandwiches and tomato soup that could exist, or the kind of terrible thing that happens when you let an American get her hands on French onion soup. You don't have to choose. I published a version of this on the website more than 6 years ago and have opened the page again and again, because I still make it the same way. Or, at least, I did. The peskiest thing about it was that it started with fresh tomatoes, which are great if you desire a piping-hot cup of heavy soup in the dead of summer or are lucky enough to have tomatoes that last until it cools off in late September. But why should you be tomato-cheddar bereft in January, just when you need this soup the most? An update was in order.

This new version allows you to enlist the canned tomatoes that are better than fresh ones the vast majority of the year, and more budget-friendly, too. But I don't let you off the hook that easily. In a trick I picked up from an old *Cook's Illustrated* recipe, we're going to roast them first. This adds a concentration of tomatoey flavor that isn't reliably present in canned tomatoes. It also allows you to throw in some roasted garlic cloves, making the soup even more complex. And when we ladle this into mugs (you're not going to want a larger portion) and broil an open-faced grilled cheese sandwich on top, it's going to be booming with flavor and complexity, but also messy and charred. Okay, I changed my mind. You do have to choose sides, and you'll know where to find me.

soup

Two 28-ounce (794-gram) cans whole tomatoes

2 tablespoons (30 ml) olive oil,
plus a drizzle more

2 large or 4 small garlic cloves, unpeeled

Salt and freshly ground black pepper

A few fresh thyme sprigs, or ¼ teaspoon dried

1 tablespoon salted or unsalted butter

2 large shallots, minced, or about ⅓ cup minced white onion

2 cups (475 ml) vegetable or chicken stock

A few pinches of red pepper flakes

grilled cheese lid

Four 1-inch slices firm sourdough or country bread, lightly toasted

¼ cup (30 grams) coarsely grated cheddar per slice

make the soup Heat the oven to 450 degrees. Pour the tomatoes into a strainer set over a bowl, and use your fingers or a fork or spoon to break them open so that they release their juices. Reserve the juices, and set aside. Put 1 tablespoon of olive oil in the bottom of a roasting pan, and spread the tomatoes out in the pan. Wrap the garlic cloves tightly in a foil packet with a few drops of olive oil inside, and place the packet in the roasting pan as well.

Finish the tomatoes with a drizzle of oil, salt and pepper to taste, and thyme. Roast the tomatoes and garlic together for 30 to 35 minutes, until most of the liquid has evaporated, the tomatoes begin to color, and the garlic is tender. Discard any wiry thyme stems.

Heat a large pot with the butter and 1 tablespoon olive oil over medium heat. Sauté the shallots until translucent and sweet-smelling, for 3 to 5 minutes then add the roasted tomatoes, 3 cups of the reserved tomato juices, stock, garlic squeezed from its skin, and red pepper flakes, and bring it all to a simmer. Cook with the lid slightly ajar for 20 to 25 minutes. Use an immersion blender (or transfer to a blender or food processor) to blend the soup to your desired texture.

make the grilled cheese lid Heat the broiler. Arrange four ovenproof mugs on a foil-lined baking sheet. Divide the soup between mugs. Float a slice of bread on each, then top with grated cheddar. Cook under the broiler until melty and browned in spots, usually for just 1 to 2 minutes. Serve immediately.

note Deb, can I skip the roasting step? Yes, you can, but there is a lot of extra flavor to be had, I promise. I am far too lazy myself to do it otherwise.

do ahead The soup can be prepared 1 day ahead, and kept covered in the fridge. Rewarm before serving, or before finishing with the cheddar crouton.

cucumber yogurt gazpacho with mint, almonds, and grapes

makes 4 servings

Any older sibling can tell you that the arrival of a younger one ruins your life (also messes with your toys and follows you from room to room, totally unlike the puppy you'd rather have). So, when the noise (and pea-throwing antics) at dinnertime approached a fever pitch in the spring after his little sister arrived, we started picking one night a week to take my son out for dinner and have some quality time and uninterrupted conversation. For a few weeks, we let him choose, and it was (shockingly) all pizza, all the time, but then we decided to nudge him to new places, which is how we found ourselves at a restaurant one night with the menu written fancily on the wall, and I was asked to explain what a Baked Alaska was. Don't try to mention ice cream, cake, and setting a dessert on fire to a kid and then not order it, not unless you are some kind of monster.

What a cruel tease it is now for me to talk about cold soup, huh? Before it was understandably upstaged by the Baked Alaska, I, too, had a life-altering experience, of a less revolutionary variety: I ordered a cold soup and I loved it. I had never found cold soups particularly enjoyable (although, because I am a generous person, I'd long held that if anyone wanted to put me on a plane to the gazpacho motherland of Andalusia, Spain, and I had it locally and authentically, I'd see the light). But this one—gazpacho, really, in name only, and, ingredient-wise, closer to a Turkish *cacik*—was something else: cucumber, yogurt, and mint with toasted Marcona almonds, thin slices of green grapes, flecks of green pepper, and a kiss of chile oil on top. I would have drunk it from a straw. I went, in one spoonful, from being a person who felt nothing about gazpacho, to being a person who wasn't sure she'd be able to survive the summer without a bowl of it each day. This is the simplified result, the culmination of everything I remembered and loved: coolness, crunch, tang, a bit of sweetness, and a kiss of bracing heat.

soup

2 large seedless cucumbers (a little shy of 2 pounds or 1 kilogram), halved and seeded (no need to peel), chopped into chunks

1 cup (230 grams) plain Greek yogurt

½ cup (120 ml) buttermilk, well shaken, or ½ cup (115 grams) additional plain yogurt

2 tablespoons (30 ml) white wine vinegar

1 shallot, chopped

¼ cup (60 ml) olive oil, plus more for drizzling

¼ cup (10 grams) loosely packed fresh mint leaves

½ teaspoon fine sea salt, plus more to taste

Cayenne, to taste

to finish

¼ cup (20 grams) almond slices, well toasted

6 green grapes, thinly sliced

A few slivers of a fresh green chile
A few droplets of olive oil
A few fresh mint leaves, julienned

In a blender, combine the cucumbers, yogurt, buttermilk, vinegar, shallot, ¼ cup olive oil, and mint leaves, plus the salt and a pinch or two of cayenne. Blend until smooth, and taste to adjust the seasoning. Chill overnight if you can bear it; the flavor will be much more developed in the morning.

When you're ready to serve it, if you desire a silky-smooth texture, strain the soup through a fine-mesh sieve; otherwise, you can skip this step. Ladle into bowls, and garnish the servings with almonds, grapes, chile slivers, oil, and mint leaves.

note For a less green color, peel the cucumbers first.

spiced carrot and pepper soup with a couscous swirl

makes 4 to 6 servings

T his is that rare, magical soup that looks pretty and has enough going on to keep an adult with, ahem, *relatively* developed tastes engaged but is also loved by kids, or at least the two I was assigned. What I mean is, if I were being smart, I'd just quit now—these things don't happen twice. It probably didn't hurt that I was inspired by two different soups I've loved—one, a simple summery red-pepper soup; another, a carrot soup with spices—and also by couscous, which was pretty much a staple for us when I was growing up but has fallen out of rotation around here thanks to the tempting whole grains available these days. I've missed it. It's really quick to make, and it also has a lightness and delicacy that go well with vegetable dishes. Plus, I have a theory that just about every seemingly lightweight blended vegetable soup is exactly 2 tablespoons of cooked grains dolloped into the center away from being passed off as a meal to the soup-suspicious, even without the usual assists of dumplings, meat, or glugs of cream. Swirling the couscous in right before we eat it keeps it fluffy.

---

soup

2 tablespoons (30 ml) olive oil

4 garlic cloves

1 large yellow onion, roughly chopped or sliced

6 large red bell peppers, cut into 1-inch pieces

1 pound (455 grams) carrots, thinly sliced

1 teaspoon ground cumin

1 teaspoon sweet paprika

⅛ teaspoon ground cinnamon

¼ teaspoon ground ginger

A few saffron threads, crumbled (optional)

3 cups (710 ml) vegetable or chicken broth

1 teaspoon kosher salt, plus more to taste

1 tablespoon prepared harissa, plus more to taste

to serve

½ cup (120 ml) broth or water

A pinch or two of salt (if using water)

½ cup uncooked dried fine couscous

Handful of chopped fresh flat-leaf parsley or cilantro

Lemon wedges

make the soup base Heat a large heavy pot over medium-high heat. Add the olive oil, and once it is very hot, add the garlic and onion. Cook until lightly browned, 5 to 10 minutes, then add the peppers. Cook until they begin to soften, about 10 minutes, then add the carrots and cook for 5 minutes together. Add the cumin, paprika, and other spices, and cook for 1 minute more. Pour in the broth and salt, and bring to a simmer. Cover, and simmer over gentle heat until the carrots and peppers are tender, 25 to 30 minutes. Use an immersion blender (or transfer to an upright blender) to purée the mixture until smooth. Add the harissa a dollop at a time, to taste.

meanwhile, make the couscous Bring the broth or water and salt to a simmer. Stir in the couscous. Cover the pot, and remove from the heat. Let stand for 5 to 10 minutes. Right before serving, stir to fluff the couscous.

to serve Ladle the soup into bowls, and spoon a couple tablespoons of cooked couscous into the center of each, swirling it in slightly. Scatter the herbs over, and serve with lemon wedges.

grandma-style chicken noodle soup

makes 8 hearty servings

A t some point, and with the best of intentions, chicken noodle soup has gotten more complicated, intimidating, and expensive than it needs to be, and I'm guilty as any cook as charged. Almost every first-page search result for chicken noodle soup implores you to start with canned chicken stock and then add chicken (sometimes already cooked) with the understandable goal of speed, but at the expense of efficiency. On the other end of the spectrum, some of the more popular recipes out there—with a chef-level "best" and "ultimate" in mind—require a couple birds just to make the broth and then have you discard them when you're done, using additional fresh chicken to finish, as if there is nothing else a boiled chicken is good for.

I don't say this to tut-tut someone else's soup happy place or warble about the good old days; I throw no shade at boxed broths, bouillons, and shredded rotisserie chickens and don't think my way is the only way. I just think it's a bummer that somewhere along the way, a really useful piece of kitchen knowledge has been lost: how to boil a chicken. How to buy a chicken, a couple onions, a bag of carrots, and celery, and some egg noodles at a store and turn it into eight substantial bowls of dinner. How to stretch $20 of ingredients into a series of meals you cannot buy anywhere else for that price. How to wake up on a day that's too cold or too dark or knowing that a flu is closing in on you . . . and know exactly how to make it better.

And I think if we knew how to do those things, we would, because this recipe is hard not to feel victorious about once you know how to make it. For years I too bounced between overly hasty methods that left me short on flavor, and overly complicated methods that meant homemade chicken noodle soup became a rarity. So when we made it this way one cold Sunday afternoon, simmering away and leaving us free to be lazy (you'll need between 2 and 3½ hours, which allows for at least one Harry Potter movie), it was a revelation, and this has become a frequent Sunday tradition ever since. It's a satisfying result to coax out of a few ingredients and a triumphant feeling to start the week with Monday's dinner already made.

broth

1 tablespoon (15 ml) oil of your choice or butter

2 large onions, unpeeled, quartered

2 medium carrots, cut into 1-to-2-inch segments

2 celery stalks, cut into 1-to-2-inch segments

2 garlic cloves, unpeeled and lightly smashed

A handful of parsley stems (save the leaves for garnish)

2 teaspoons peppercorns

1 bay leaf

One 3¼-to-4-pound (about 1¾-kilogram) chicken, either whole or cut into halves so it fits better in your pot

3½ quarts (14 cups or 3⅓ liters) water

to finish

8 ounces (225 grams) dried egg noodles

5 celery stalks, in ½- to-1-inch chunks

5 medium carrots, in ½- to-1-inch chunks

Kosher salt and freshly ground black pepper, to taste

Chopped fresh parsley leaves, to finish

make the broth Heat the oil or butter in the bottom of your largest pot (8 quarts is ideal here; see note) over medium heat, and add the onions, carrots, and celery. Cook, stirring occasionally, until they're browned in spots and a little soft, 10 to 15 minutes. Add the garlic, parsley stems, peppercorns, bay leaf, and chicken, then the water, and bring to a boil. Reduce the heat to a simmer and cook, mostly covered, for 25 minutes, then use tongs to remove the chicken from the broth, leaving the broth covered on the lowest heat. As soon as the chicken is cool enough to handle, discard the skin and pick the meat from the bones, covering it and setting it aside until needed. Return the bones to the stock and bring it back to a simmer. Cook, mostly covered, for 1 to 2 hours; less time will make a fine

pot of soup; a longer amount of time will make an even more developed flavor.

Pour the soup through a fine-mesh strainer, wipe out your stockpot, and return the broth to it. (You should have about 3 quarts of stock.)

cook the noodles Bring a separate pot of well-salted water to a boil and cook the noodles according to package directions; drain when finished.

finish the soup Meanwhile, bring the soup broth back to a simmer and add salt and pepper to taste—I usually need at least 1 tablespoon kosher salt and ½ to 1 teaspoon of pepper adds a nice warmth—then add the additional celery and cook for 5 minutes; then the additional carrots, and cook everything together for 7 to 10 minutes more, or until the vegetables are tender. Add the reserved chicken and noodles, taste again for seasoning and adjust as needed, and heat just to warm through. Ladle into bowls and finish with fresh herbs.

notes

I often swap one onion in the soup base for 2 leeks, halved, cleaned, and cut into 2-inch segments, and 1 carrot for a parsnip. I'll sometimes add another leek, sliced in ½-inch rings, to the final soup vegetables. And I insist on finishing my soup with fresh dill as well, but these are of course personal preferences.

You can put the whole chicken directly in your pot, but I do find if I split or quarter it (kitchen shears make easy work of this and your soup won't know whether you've "properly" butchered the bird), it's a little easier to get the meat off later.

Once I strain the broth, I discard the vegetables; to me, they have imparted all the flavor they can, and I resume with fresh ones for additional flavor and a prettier finish. I have heard from many people over the years that this feels wrong to them in every way. If you are in this camp, return the original vegetables to the final soup and skip the addition of new ones.

Why boil the noodles in a separate pot? Because I have experienced the heartbreak of spending hours making a glorious soup broth only to have the noodles drink all my hard work up and don't want this to happen to anyone else. Some people add a bouillon cube to the boiling water, which will impart a more soupy flavor to the noodles, but I find that they pick up plenty enough when you return them to the soup.

I haven't always had an 8-quart pot, but I had a little trick I used instead. I put in all the ingredients and as much water as I could in my pot, often having a quart that didn't fit.

Because liquid will evaporate as you simmer the base, I'd keep adding the water throughout, keeping the pot as full as possible until all the extra water was used. You can also divide this recipe between two smaller pots. It's really just for the first part (with the whole chicken) that you'll need the biggest pot. Once you return the chicken carcass, you can get away with a 5- or 6-quart pot.

do ahead You can easily make the soup base one day and finish it with the noodles, reserved chicken, and additional vegetables the next. Assembled, this keeps in the fridge for up to 5 days and for up to 2 months in the freezer. (To store the soup in the freezer, I transfer it to freezer bags and try to remove as much air as possible.)

manhattan-style clams with fregola

makes 4 servings

I f you'd ever like a human being to make a beeline for something, be sure to tell them that it's terrible and they wouldn't enjoy it at all, which is exactly what happened to me when I learned that the great paterfamilias of American cookery, James Beard, once called Manhattan clam chowder "horrendous." How could I not want to try it? Manhattan clam chowder is best understood as everything the New England clam chowder is not—cream-free and loud with garlic, pepper flakes, tomatoes, green peppers, carrots, and celery, flavors influenced by Italian immigrants to the Brooklyn and Jersey shores.

I like it even more as a springboard to a brothy riff on linguine and clams. Steaming the clams open right in the soup is less work (no shelling required), and tiny confetti-like pearls of toasted pasta called fregola, unlike heavier linguine, nestle inside the open shells and fit neatly on your spoon. For a little extra luxury, sizzle a minced garlic clove, pinch of salt, and red pepper flakes in olive oil and drizzle right over the finished dish. Grilled bread—garlic or other—on the side is always welcome.

4 ounces (115 grams) thick-cut or slab bacon, diced

½ large (yellow or Spanish) onion, diced

½ large green bell pepper, diced

2 medium celery stalks, diced

2 garlic cloves, minced

½ teaspoon dried oregano

One 28-ounce/794-gram can whole peeled tomatoes in juice

1 cup (235 ml) chicken or seafood stock

Salt

Red pepper flakes, to taste

½ cup (90 grams) dried fregola

24 (about 2 pounds or 1 kilogram) littleneck clams, rinsed

Freshly ground black pepper, to taste

¼ cup roughly chopped fresh flat-leaf parsley

Scatter the bacon in the bottom of a medium-sized Dutch oven or a deep 4-quart sauté pan, and set over medium heat. Let the bacon warm and sizzle in place; then, when it begins to brown, stir it around, continuing until it is browned and the fat has rendered out, about 5 minutes. If there is extra, discard all but 1 tablespoon of the bacon drippings and add the onion, bell pepper, and celery. Cook, stirring, until softened, about 5 minutes. Add the garlic, and cook for 1 more minute; then stir in the oregano, tomatoes (with juices), and broth, scraping up any stuck bits, and bring to a simmer. Season with salt and red pepper flakes.

Stir in the fregola, and simmer, covered, for 10 minutes. Stop here if you are prepping the soup ahead of time. If serving immediately, stir in the clams and simmer, covered, stirring occasionally, until the clams open wide, 8 to 10 minutes. (Discard any clams that have not opened after 10 minutes.) Season with salt and black pepper, and add the parsley. Want garlic bread? See page 144.

sandwiches, tarts, and flatbreads

broccoli melts

makes 8 small-medium toasts

M ost of my understanding of the diner sandwiches we know as "melts" comes from the hyper-local archive of culinary amusements I know as Foods My Husband Will Order for Himself When Left to His Own Devices. I can't give away all of his secrets—well, I can, but for a fee—but I have been given permission to tell you that the list is topped with Regrettable Chinese Takeout with a Life-Threatening Amount of Sichuan Peppercorns (to be repeated the next time, no lessons learned), and, somewhat farther down the list, only if the day has been long and terrible enough, is a tuna melt—as in jarred mayo meets canned fish meets something square and flat that only passes for cheese in America. Did it not always come with a side of steak fries, which I want to steal because you should know by now that fries don't count when I say I'm not hungry for dinner, I'd probably be breaking our house "don't yuck my yum" rule even more often than my offspring.

So, when I read that melts were having a moment again, I wondered if we were in for more dark times for Deb, such as when the entire universe decided that beets were delicious and it was 24 months before I could safely order a salad again. Instead, I decided to take matters into my own hands and rewrite the melt script in a way that I could enjoy, endlessly. Because I like bread. I like cheese. And though tuna salad may not be my thing, I hope you will soon agree that the mess I call "broccoli rubble" is ever as much deserving to be a star.

1 pound (455 grams) broccolini or regular broccoli

Coarse salt, to taste

2 tablespoons (30 ml) olive oil

3 garlic cloves, minced

A few pinches of red pepper flakes

Finely grated zest and juice of ½ lemon

½ cup (65 grams) finely grated aged Pecorino Romano

8 slices bread of your choice
(I use a seeded white country loaf)

8 thin slices totally unfancy deli provolone

prep the broccoli rubble If you're using broccolini, cut it into 2-inch segments. If you're using regular broccoli, peel the stems with a vegetable peeler first, so that they cook evenly, and cut the rest into large chunks.

Pour about a 1-inch puddle of salted water into a large sauté pan and bring to a boil. Add the broccoli, cover with a lid, and steam for 2 minutes. Drain the broccoli well, and pat it dry on paper towels, wringing out as much extra liquid as possible. Chop it into small (roughly ½-inch) bits.

Wipe the sauté pan dry, and place over medium heat. Add the olive oil, and heat it for a full minute. Add the garlic and the pepper flakes, and cook for 1 minute, or until the garlic is just beginning to turn golden. Add the broccoli, and cook for 1 to 2 minutes more; season with salt. Transfer the mixture to a bowl, and add the lemon zest and juice, Pecorino, and more salt and pepper flakes to taste.

make the toasts Heat the broiler. Arrange the slices of bread on a tray, and lightly toast on both sides, about 1 minute each. Scoop the broccoli mixture onto each slice of bread, lay a slice of provolone over it, and run it under the broiler until the cheese has melted and begun to blister, anywhere from 1 to 4 minutes, depending on the robustness of your oven. Eat. Repeat. Don't forget to share, or at least hide the evidence if you decide not to do so.

note I usually make this with broccolini, which I prefer because it much less noticeably discolors when hit with lemon juice. Outside of aesthetics, both broccolini and regular broccoli work about the same here, and are equally delicious. If you're the sort of person who enjoys anchovies, they meld well here with the garlic and pepper flakes.

artichoke and parmesan galette

makes 6 to 8 servings for a light meal

My mother, eager to have another artichoke lover in the family—i.e., an excuse to bring them home more often—taught me when I was young how to pull off the leaves from artichokes we'd boiled forever, dip them into a mixture of mayo, lemon juice, salt, and pepper, and rake off the meaty bits with our teeth. Teenaged Deb thought this was all there was to know about artichokes—I mean, what more could an artichoke lover ever want or need? But adult-aged Deb is whispering "Rome" right now, *"carciofi alla romana, alla giudia . . ."*—which is why I had my mind blown in college when someone brought a baked artichoke dip to a party and I'd never had anything so good. My friend couldn't believe I'd never heard of this hack of canned artichoke, mayo, and Parmesan, but it quickly became my favorite thing.

I probably haven't had it in the better part of two decades, mostly because the narrow window of time in my life when I knew about this dip and could get away with eating it freely has long since passed. I had great fun, however, figuring out a way to get the flavors I love in that catastrophically unhealthy dish into a vegetable tart we could eat on a weekday night by pairing it with salad. Nobody can accuse me of not having admirable goals.

crust

1¼ cups (165 grams) all-purpose flour, plus more for your work surface

¼ teaspoon fine sea or table salt

¼ cup (35 grams) finely grated Parmesan

½ cup (4 ounces or 115 grams) unsalted butter, cut into pieces

2 tablespoons (30 grams) sour cream

2 teaspoons (10 ml) fresh lemon juice (from about ¼ of a juicy lemon)

¼ cup (60 ml) very cold water

Nonstick cooking spray or spray oil for coating pan

filling

Two 14-ounce (400-gram) cans artichoke hearts, drained very well, then patted out on towels (2⅓ cups drained)

2 large eggs

¼ cup (50 grams) mayonnaise

¼ cup (60 grams) sour cream

½ cup (120 ml) milk

Finely grated zest and juice of ½ lemon

1 garlic clove, minced

½ teaspoon kosher salt

Freshly ground black pepper

½ cup (65 grams) plus 2 tablespoons (15 grams) finely grated Parmesan

2 tablespoons chopped fresh flat-leaf parsley

optional glaze

1 large egg yolk and a few drops of water

make the dough Stir the flour and salt together in a large bowl. Sprinkle the Parmesan and butter over this and, using a pastry blender or your fingertips, work it into the flour until the mixture resembles coarse meal, with the biggest pieces of butter the size of tiny peas. In a small bowl, stir together the sour cream, lemon juice, and water, and add this to the butter-flour mixture. With your fingertips or a wooden spoon, mix in the liquid until large clumps form. Pat the clumps into a ball. Wrap with plastic, and refrigerate for 1 hour, or up to 2 days.

Heat the oven to 350 degrees. Coat a 9-inch cake pan, a standard pie dish, or a 9-inch pastry ring with nonstick spray, and place on a baking sheet.

make the filling Roll out the crust, on a floured counter, into a roughly 12-inch round. Transfer it to the prepared baking dish, and let the extra dough drape over the sides.

Drain the artichokes well, pressing out any extra liquid you can before spreading them out on a couple layers of paper towels for a few minutes, to remove as much moisture as possible. Cut them into thin slices, and place them in the bottom of the crust. Whisk together the eggs, mayo, sour cream, milk, lemon zest and juice, garlic, salt, pepper, and ½ cup of the grated Parmesan. Stir in the parsley. Pour the custard over the artichokes. Sprinkle with the remaining 2 tablespoons Parmesan. Gently lift the sides of the dough up over the custard filling, and pinch them together—you're going to want to do this in the air, hovering over the filling, not by pressing down on it, of course, because the filling is primarily liquid. Let the creased dough edges gently, loosely rest on the surface of the tart. Repeat all around.

finish and bake If desired, because it will add a deeper color and shine to the crust, whisk the yolk and water together, and gently brush over the surface of the crust. Bake for 35 to 40 minutes, until the eggs are set. If the top is not quite brown enough, run under broiler for 1 minute.

Let the galette cool on a rack. Eat warm or at room temperature.

note I also attempted here to mash up a quiche—everyone loves to eat them but hates the fussiness of a rolled and parbaked crust—and a galette, which is far more rustic and forgiving. Galettes do not excel at holding in liquid, however, because they're baked on a flat pan. I solve this problem by dropping the galette dough into any round baking dish with sides—a cake pan, pie pan, or tart ring—which gives the sides enough structure to hold in liquid but keeps it as easy to make as a rustic galette. Just a heads-up: the bottom of the crust doesn't get fully crisp.

leek, feta, and greens spiral pie

makes a dozen 4-inch pies

blame growing up far outside the Phyllo Belt that stretches from Bosnia through Greece and Turkey and around to Egypt for that fact that until recently I considered this papery, flaky pastry that cracks if you even look at it askance my mortal enemy. I mean, sure, I love those massive squares of spanakopita cut from a sheet tray at Greek restaurants and cafés, but I was perfectly happy to leave the crafting of it to the pros. It took not a trip to the Aegean to break my phyllo impasse but a gelato-and-coffee shop down the street from me, which, in a nod to its Greek owners, brought in the most wonderful spiral-shaped spinach pies from a lady in Astoria every morning. They were my lunch at least once a week for a year before they disappeared, and the only thing left for me to do was to conquer my phyllo-phobia and try them at home.

Traditional spanakopita has a surprisingly—well, if you, like me, always thought it was just spinach and feta—long ingredient list. There is usually an onion, a few scallions, a leek, garlic, plus dill, parsley, and sometimes mint, a little nutmeg, pine nuts, and not just feta but graviera or kasseri cheeses, too, as well as eggs, to hold it together. It's really nuanced when you make it properly. But I felt like every time I went to buy the ingredients at the store, I came back with fewer than last time—since the leeks were in packs of three, why not use them instead of the onion, scallions, and a single leek? And it's sometimes hard to find good-quality spinach—spinach, of all things—in these kale-obsessed times, so I began making it with any mix of greens that looked better (yes, kale, but also chard or any mix with spinach). I left out the garlic one day, and we didn't even notice. My store sells feta by the ½ pound, and I ended up throwing it all in instead of just the cup I'd intended. The result? Well, I won't call it spanakopita anymore, but we liked it just as much. All from fewer ingredients, which yielded fewer leftovers.

filling

2 tablespoons (30 ml) olive oil

1 pound (455 grams) spinach, or other leafy greens, stems removed

3 large leeks, very thinly sliced

Salt and freshly ground black pepper

2 garlic cloves, minced

2 tablespoons finely chopped fresh dill

1 tablespoon chopped fresh mint (optional)

A pinch or two of freshly grated nutmeg

2 large eggs, lightly beaten

¼ cup (35 grams) pine nuts, toasted

8 ounces (225 grams) feta, crumbled

assembly

12 large sheets phyllo

½ cup or more butter, melted for brushing

1 tablespoon (10 grams) sesame seeds, toasted (optional)

make the filling Add 1 tablespoon of the olive oil to a large pan, and heat over medium heat; then add the damp spinach and cook until wilted, 2 to 3 minutes. Transfer to a colander and, once cool enough to handle, wring it out; coarsely chop it on a cutting board, and set aside.

Wipe out the pan and add the second tablespoon of olive oil. Heat over medium heat, add the leeks, and season with salt. Sauté for 1 minute. Reduce the heat to the lowest flame, add 1 tablespoon water, cover with a lid, and let the leeks cook for 10 minutes, stirring once or twice throughout. Remove the lid, increase the heat back to medium, and cook for 5 minutes longer, until the leeks are sweet and only just beginning to brown. Add the garlic, and cook for 2 minutes more. Add the wilted spinach, the dill, and the mint, if desired, and cook just until warmed through. Add more salt and pepper to taste. Stir in the nutmeg. Let cool to lukewarm, then stir in the eggs, pine nuts, and cheese.

assemble the pies Heat the oven to 375 degrees. Line two baking sheets with parchment paper. Place one phyllo sheet on your counter, with the wider side closer to you. Cover the remaining sheets with a damp towel so they don't dry out, which they otherwise will do quickly. Brush the phyllo sheet lightly with butter all over. Make a small (about 1-inch) fold across the side closest to you, to reinforce it a bit. Add about 5 tablespoons of the greens mixture, and spread it out in a thin log. Begin to roll carefully from the reinforced side; it should be moderately tight, with no sagging spaces, but not so rigid that you'll have trouble snaking it. Dab both ends of the log with additional butter, and carefully roll it into a spiral. Seal the final end onto the snail body as best as you can.

bake the pies Transfer the pie to a prepared baking tray, and brush it with additional butter; then sprinkle the top with sesame seeds, if desired. Repeat until you've used up all of the dough. Bake the pies for about 35 to 40 minutes, until they are golden brown. Eat warm or at room temperature. Leftover pies reheat fantastically.

note You can also use this recipe and technique to create a larger spiral pie that's a total centerpiece. In a butter-brushed standard pie pan, with an 8½-to-9-inch diameter, I made one using six ropes of spanakopita, sealing the ends together as I wrapped them around.

grilled yogurt flatbreads

makes 4 large flatbreads

Depending on what your food orientation is, you might call this anything from a pita to naan, but in my mutt of a cooking outlook, it's just a flatbread—and a good one at that. This recipe was missing from my cooking repertoire for way too long, a dead-simple yeasted bread that you can grill and use with anything and everything: as a pockletless pita or naan, yes, but also a grand thing to cut into strips and serve with soup, or dice and toast again as croutons. The dough is impossibly forgiving; mix it now and use it in an hour, or mix it now and keep it in the fridge for a few days, until you need it. Maybe you pull off some tonight and more in 2 days. It freezes well once cooked; I tend to grill it a little on the lighter side if I'm planning to freeze it, so I have a chance to recrisp it later without burning it. The yogurt provides moisture and depth; the simple foundation can be used to build flavors in almost unlimited ways.

¾ cup (175 ml) warm water

Heaped 1 teaspoon (about ½ of one ¼-ounce or 7-gram packet) active dry yeast

2 tablespoons (30 ml) olive oil, plus more for bowl and brushing

½ cup (115 grams) Greek or other thick plain yogurt

2½ cups plus 2 tablespoons (340 grams) flour, all-purpose (or blended; see note), plus more for your work surface

1½ teaspoons coarse or kosher salt

flavoring ideas: 1 tablespoon finely chopped fresh herbs (such as parsley, thyme, basil, mint, oregano, or dill); zest of ½ lemon, 1 minced garlic clove; Indian or Middle Eastern spices, such as za'atar, and/or a little crumbled cheese.

Place the warm water in the bottom of a medium bowl. Sprinkle the yeast over the top, and let it dissolve for 10 minutes. Stir in the olive oil and yogurt, then 2 cups flour and all the salt plus flavorings of choice (except za'atar, which is best at the end). Combine with a wooden spoon until everything is incorporated. Add ½ cup flour, and stir it in—the dough will be getting stiff, so flex those guns—and then the remaining 2 tablespoons. Bash it around in the bowl, then scrape it onto the counter while you roll 1 tablespoon olive oil around in the bowl. Return the dough immediately to the bowl, cover it with plastic wrap, and set it aside until it has about doubled in size, 60 to 70 minutes.

Flip the dough out onto a floured counter, and divide it into quarters (or more pieces, for smaller breads). Flour a baking tray. Roughly stretch each dough piece flat on the tray with your equally floured fingers. Repeat with the remaining pieces. Brush the bread tops with olive oil.

Heat your outdoor grill or a stove top grill pan to medium-high. Once it's hot, place the dough, oiled side down, on it and grill until dark grill marks appear underneath, about 5 minutes. Brush the tops of flatbreads with more oil, then flip the breads over and cook until the second side is dark, too.

note You can replace any portion of the flour with whole wheat or another flour you like, although on your first round I might limit the substitution to a third of the total.

corn, bacon, and arugula pizza

makes one 12-inch thin round pizza, serving 2 to 4

The inspiration for this pizza is, illogically enough, the worst meal we had on a vacation. (I really know how to entice, eh?) They say you can't have a bad meal in Rome, and we almost proved the theory, but near the end we chose a place that was no doubt awesome when the person who recommended it to us spent many evenings there but had likely changed hands a few times before the night when we were served a series of flabby pastas with ketchuplike sauces and mealy antipasti. Yet we hardly suffered, because we ate one dish that redeemed the evening—the dish we were the most skeptical about will forever cement that mediocre meal in our minds as "totally worth it." Bacon—yes, American-style bacon in Rome; not exactly the pork product I most associate with the city, but who am I to question these things—was grilled to a perfect lightly charred crisp, then topped with peppery wild arugula and drizzled, so very lightly, with an aged balsamic and a few diced tomatoes. Together this mixture was magical; it achieved immediate cult status when we came home and made "bacon salad" (definitely the healthiest salad ever) for all of our friends.

For this pizza, I returned to the salad as dinner and added some sweet corn and sharp cheese to the broiled, crispy, salty foundation before piling a lightly dressed baby-arugula salad on top. Do you like egg pizzas? Because adding one here is amazing, too. The tomatoes are sprinkled on top. I ended up eighty-sixing the balsamic, because it felt like excess—a hilarious concept for a pizza involving bacon, cheese, and a runny egg, I know—but, trust me, this is not something you make only once.

Olive oil

Cornmeal, for sprinkling your baking surface

½-pound (225-gram) unbaked, fully risen pizza dough (½ of the recipe on page 108)

¼ pound (115 grams) thickly cut bacon, very cold (so it's easier to handle)

Fresh corn kernels from 1 ear of corn (about ¾ cup or 100 grams)

Salt and freshly ground black pepper

⅓ cup tomato purée (from a can or jar, or blended from fresh)

1 cup (130 grams) finely grated aged Pecorino Romano or Parmesan

1 large egg (or more if desired)

1 cup (15 grams) baby arugula leaves

Heat the oven to 500 degrees. Brush a large round pizza tray lightly with olive oil, then sprinkle with cornmeal. Roll the dough on a floured counter into a roundish shape, then transfer it to the tray and use oiled fingertips to press it thinner, if desired.

Cut the bacon crosswise into ¼-inch-wide strips. In a large frying pan, cook the bacon over moderate heat until the pieces are crisp. With a slotted spoon, transfer the bacon to paper towels, and drain off all but 1 tablespoon of the fat in the pan. Add the corn to the frying pan, season it with salt and pepper, and cook for just 2 to 3 minutes, until crisp but tender.

Spread the tomato purée over the dough, leaving a 1-inch margin at the edge. Season with salt and pepper. Sprinkle with ¾ cup cheese, then add bacon and corn. Clear a small area of the filling in the center (if using 1 egg; clear more space for each egg) and break the egg into it.

Season with more salt and pepper and sprinkle with the remaining cheese. Bake for 10 minutes or until the cheese is melted and the egg white is set. Sprinkle with arugula, drizzle lightly with olive oil, and cut through the center egg into eight wedges.

roasted tomato picnic sandwich

makes 8 large or 16 smaller portions

Okay, let's for the duration of this page pretend we live in a world where we have picnics, like, all the time. A place where we all have those colossally expensive English picnic hampers with the linens, porcelain plate settings for four, hand-blown wineglasses, wine duffels, and full coffee services.

Do know that I can picture this idyll (did I mention that our hair looks amazing that day?) and still inwardly fret, just a little, about what to put in that picnic basket. I mean, it's not that I don't know what we *would* do—we're New Yorkers, we'd just go to a deli—but what if we wanted to do better, something that we'd actually be really excited to eat, because it was exceptional in every way, flexible enough to feed different-sized crowds and not involving in any way the assembly-line-style toasting, schmearing, and stacking of individual slices of bread? I always wanted to do this, but I finally understood how to make it happen when I had a square of Genovese *foccacia ripiena* (literally, refilled or stuffed focaccia) that was, at the same time, two excellent layers of home-baked bread with a meat-and-cheese filling. Think of this as a stuffed pizza, but served in squares and so much more flexible.

You can fill yours with anything you wish—combinations of cured meats and cheese are popular, but so are sautéed greens, and roasted eggplant. Here, I use one of my favorite mixtures: slow-baked tomatoes, all chewy, tart, and intense, tossed with crumbly, salty ricotta salata, well-chopped cured black olives, and a happy amount of garlic and oregano. This is a meat-free sandwich that isn't genteel and doesn't play second fiddle to anything.

This recipe makes a 9-by-13-inch "slab" sandwich. You can easily double it, in two pans or in a half sheet pan. It makes great packed lunches; you could make one at the start of the week and take portions with you; it reheats well.

tomatoes

4 cups (21 ounces or 600 grams) cherry or grape tomatoes

2 tablespoons (30 ml) olive oil

½ teaspoon flaky sea salt, or to taste

4 medium garlic cloves, unpeeled

assembly

1 tablespoon (15 ml) olive oil, plus more for the pan and your fingertips

1-pound (455-gram) unbaked, fully risen pizza dough (see page 108)

4 ounces (110 grams) coarsely grated mozzarella

¼ cup (35 grams) pitted olives of your choice, finely chopped (my favorite here is oil-cured Gaeta)

2 teaspoons dried oregano, crumbled

3 ounces (85 grams) crumbled salty cheese, such as ricotta salata

Kosher salt and freshly ground black pepper

assemble flatbread Heat the oven to 450 degrees. Brush either one 13-by-18-inch rimmed half sheet pan or two 9-by-13-inch quarter sheet pans with olive oil. (Divide the dough in half, if using two pans.) With oiled fingertips, press, nudge, and stretch dough to fit the shape of the pan(s). Thin, imperfect dough is just fine here. If holes form, patch them together.

In a large bowl, combine 4 tablespoons olive oil, cumin, coriander, Aleppo pepper, and several grinds of black pepper. Add the squash and toss to evenly coat. Spread the mixture over the dough(s), going all the way to the edges so that there are no uncovered spots. The edges brown more quickly, so you can make the squash slices a little thicker there.

bake the flatbread(s) Bake for 25 to 30 minutes, until the squash is golden at the edges but tender and baked through. Remove from the oven and cool slightly.

meanwhile, to serve Stir together the yogurt and hummus, and add lemon juice and salt and pepper to taste. When the flatbread has cooled a bit, dollop the yogurt-hummus mixture all over, and sprinkle with za'atar, pine nuts, and herbs. Cut into desired shape.

a dense, grainy daily bread

makes one 2-pound loaf

I've long been an enthusiast of those dense, hearty, grainy sourdoughish thin-sliced breads you might see as part of an hors d'oeuvres, breakfast, or smorgasbord spread. Although they come in sandwich-shaped loaves, they're not ideal for two-slice sandwiches (they break rather than bend), but they *are* an ideal foundation to crown with salted butter and jam, smoked fish and crème fraîche, cheddar and apples, a smashed avocado, smashed egg, or a tuft of chicken salad, i.e. everything I really want to eat.

But I'd always presumed they were not for the uninitiated bread baker—you know, people who don't keep a sourdough starter that dates back to the 1847 Oregon Trail on the counter or who only stock, say, all-purpose and whole wheat flour and not a veritable granary in their pantry. While the flavor of these breads is complex, the ingredient list is long and daunting. But one day when I was at the grocery store trying to work up the courage to buy everything I'd need to try my hand at home, I noticed instead a bag of hot 7-grain breakfast cereal and was surprised to find that it contained many of the ingredients I was supposed to use (rye, flaxseed, and more). At home, I used this instead of all the ingredients I don't usually keep around, and I have never felt so triumphant over what emerged from the oven: a tangy, sour, nutty, and complex bread that tastes like a much fancier bakery than your oven made it. With a few tweaks, I managed to find a one-bowl, no-knead way to get the same result, which meant that I could make it often enough that it was a daily thing.

1⅓ cups (315 ml) lukewarm water

1 tablespoon (15 grams) granulated sugar

1¼ teaspoons (from a ¼-ounce or 7-gram packet) instant or active dry yeast

1½ cups (175 grams) rye (dark or light) or whole wheat flour

⅔ cup (85 grams) all-purpose or bread flour

3⅓ cups (475 to 500 grams) store-bought 7- or 9-grain hot cereal mix, dry

1 tablespoon coarse or kosher salt

⅔ cup (155 ml) beer, any variety

⅔ cup (155 ml) buttermilk, well shaken

Rolled oats or mixed seeds (such as poppy, sesame, flax, or dried millet) for sprinkling

1 egg, beaten with 1 teaspoon water (optional)

one to two days before you would like to eat your bread Combine water, sugar, and yeast in the bottom of a large mixing bowl. Let rest 5 minutes. Add the remaining ingredients (except for oats or seeds for sprinkling) and stir to combine. Stir 20 times with a spoon or the dough hook of a stand mixer, then cover with plastic and leave at room temperature for 24 to 48 hours—preferably the latter, which will give it much more of a sourdough vibe.

to bake When you're ready to bake the bread, heat the oven to 350 degrees. Either coat a standard loaf pan with nonstick spray or line the bottom and sides with parchment paper.

Scoop the dough into the prepared pan and smooth the top. Brush or dab with water, then sprinkle with oats or seeds. (You can also brush with a beaten egg, which will help the seeds stick better.) Bake the bread for about 90 minutes, until the temperature in the center of bread is about 194 to 198 degrees. It will ideally not feel gluey inside—that is, doughy and underbaked. Remove from the oven and let it cool in the pan.

to eat Slice very thin.

note I don't want to pretend that this is going to fill any kind of authentic Vollkornbrot, Schwarzbrot, or Rugbrød void in your life—this is milder, a little more tender with no burrowed seeds or nuts to crunch on (or offend you, if you prefer not to crunch)—but it is, for me, perfect and habit-forming.

do ahead Keeps well at room temperature for 1 day, but for longer periods it's best to keep it in the freezer, pre-sliced.

vegetable mains

halloumi roast with eggplant, zucchini, and tomatoes

makes 2 hearty servings, or up to 6 as a side

My go-to cooking method is roasting. No matter what the stack of grievances—kitchen too small, day too long, terrible oven, little motivation, subpar ingredients—few things are not improved by a well-seasoned bowl of gently charred vegetables, something that even restaurants rarely get as right as we do at home. Four hundred or 450 degrees, 30 minutes on the first side, 10 on the second—I could do it in my sleep. Considering the way my first kid slept, I probably have.

Halloumi has always felt like a bit of a luxury, mostly because the price indicates that a person should not eat the whole block at once—but if you've tried it, you'd know that is impossible. In an effort to stretch it further, I began dotting trays of roasted summer vegetables with it—like salty, pillowy croutons from heaven—and all of a sudden what was already good became exceptional, a full summer meal you could scoop up with flatbread, scatter over salad greens, or pile on top of grains. This became a favorite way to use vegetables in any season, but we like the lemon-oregano marinade I give here the most in the mid-to-late summer, when it often feels like the vegetable population will soon outpace us if we don't make this regularly.

3 tablespoons (45 ml) olive oil, plus a glug or two for the trays

3 garlic cloves, minced

2 teaspoons dried oregano, crumbled, or 1 tablespoon fresh, chopped

Finely grated zest of ½ lemon, plus juice of 1 lemon

2 teaspoons kosher salt

Many grinds of black pepper

1 medium zucchini or summer squash (about 14 ounces or 400 grams)

1 medium eggplant (about 11 ounces or 315 grams)

2 cups grape or cherry tomatoes (about 10 ounces or 285 grams)

One 8-ounce (225-gram) block halloumi

Heat the oven to 450 degrees. Coat one large (13-by-19) or two small (9-by-13) baking sheets lightly with olive oil. In a large bowl, combine 3 tablespoons olive oil, the garlic, oregano, zest (save the juice for the end), salt, and pepper.

Cut the zucchini in half lengthwise, then into about ½-inch half-moons. Do the same with your eggplant, unless it has a globe shape, in which case first cut it into quarters. Halve the cherry tomatoes. Cut the halloumi into 1-inch cubes. Add everything to the marinade, and stir to coat evenly. Spread it out on the roasting tray(s), and roast for 20 to 30 minutes on the first side, then flip and roast for 10 to 15 minutes more on the second, until the vegetables are browned in spots and tender. Drizzle the trays with lemon juice to taste, and scoop onto plates.

parmesan dutch baby with creamed mushrooms

makes 2 hearty or 4 smaller servings

I used to make Dutch-baby pancakes—the crêpe's tousled, melodramatic cousin—all the time as a treat: gingerbread-spiced at the holidays; with cherries and toasted almonds in June; with lemon and powdered sugar the rest of the year. Nothing made one feel like more of an Instagram/Pinterest/Snapchat–ready domestic diva than pulling one of these fluffy, crispy-edged beauties out of the oven and shrugging off how easy they are to make—and telling the truth. You take the milk, eggs, and flour you'd use to make a crêpe but move the melted butter directly to the skillet, and generously. There's no ladling or brushing pans with melted butter or fragile high-stakes flipping techniques, only oohs and aahs when the timer rings. The oven does all the work; you get all the credit.

Eventually, though, the reality of dinnertime got me plotting a savory version that would be just as special. This became our instant favorite. Where there was nutmeg, there's salt and pepper. Powdered sugar becomes Parmesan, and instead of lemon juice, we make a rubbly sauce of mushrooms that have been sautéed with shallots in butter before being swirled with cream. Suddenly what seemed like the highest calling of a breakfast pancake becomes the most luxurious calling of a weeknight dinner, easily split between two people with a side salad, or among four perhaps with some grilled sausages or an additional vegetable on the side.

mushrooms

2 tablespoons (25 grams) unsalted butter

1 shallot, minced

½ pound (225 grams) cremini (small brown) mushrooms, cleaned, chopped into small bits

Kosher salt and freshly ground black pepper

1 tablespoon (15 ml) dry white wine or white vermouth

3 tablespoons (45 ml) heavy cream

pancake

4 large eggs

½ teaspoon kosher salt

Freshly ground black pepper

½ cup (120 ml) milk (whole is ideal, but any kind will work)

½ cup (65 grams) all-purpose flour

3 tablespoons (45 grams) unsalted butter

3 tablespoons (25 grams) finely grated Parmesan

1 tablespoon finely chopped fresh chives

make the creamed mushrooms In a 12-inch cast-iron or other ovenproof skillet, over medium heat, melt the butter. Add the shallot, and cook until soft, 1 to 2 minutes. Add the mushrooms and salt and pepper to taste, and increase the heat to medium-high. Cook, stirring frequently, for about 5 minutes, during which the mushrooms will release and then cook off their liquid and brown a little at the edges. Add the wine, reduce the heat to medium-low, scrape up any stuck bits, and cook off the wine, 1 to 2 minutes. Add the cream, and as soon as it simmers (i.e., almost immediately), scrape the whole mixture into a bowl and set aside.

make the pancake Heat the oven to 425 degrees. Wipe out the pan, add the butter, and place in the oven to melt until very hot and sizzling.

Meanwhile, in a medium bowl, beat the eggs with the salt and pepper. Add the flour, and whisk until mostly smooth. Whisk in the milk. Lumps are fine.

to finish Remove the skillet from the oven, swirl the butter around to evenly coat and pour in the batter all at once, and return the skillet to the oven. Cook for 15 minutes, after which the pancake should be browned in places and rumpled. Sprinkle with Parmesan, and return to the oven for 1 to 2 minutes, until it has melted. Remove it from the oven, and immediately dollop the mushroom sauce in pockets all over the pancake, and scatter with chives. Divide onto two or four plates.

crispy tofu and broccoli with sesame-peanut pesto

makes 2 giant servings or 4 smaller ones

I fell in love with deliciously inauthentic peanut-sesame noodles when I was 13. I had recently decided, most likely thanks to listening to the Smiths' *Meat Is Murder* too much, that I wouldn't eat meat anymore, but also hadn't quite figured out what I would subsist on instead. (Vegetables? Don't be ridiculous.) A friend introduced me to this magical dish at our local strip-mall shopping center Hunan Palace, and I haven't looked back since. The mix of sesame-seed paste, peanut butter, sugar, vinegar, and chile oil remains my takeout weakness, although these days you're much more likely to receive something kind of . . . gloopy.

At home, though, you can fix anything. I found that if I bypassed the sesame-seed paste and peanut butter for actual sesame seeds and peanuts, I could grind them to a fine rubble and end up with a sauce with much more texture and interest. I've always joked that the sauce is so good, the noodles are just wasting your time, but I never actually attempted to prove it until I started putting it on crisp-roasted vegetables and tofu, which I've otherwise found to be a hard sell with my family (because they are wrong). Not this time, though. This time, we were fighting over the last cube.

tofu and broccoli

1 block (12 to 15 ounces or 340 to 425 grams) extra-firm tofu

1 pound (455 grams) broccoli

3 tablespoons (45 ml) olive, peanut, or neutral oil such as sunflower/safflower

Salt and freshly ground black pepper

1 tablespoon (15 ml) low-sodium soy sauce or tamari

1 tablespoon (10 grams) cornstarch

pesto

1 tablespoon (10 grams) toasted sesame seeds

¼ cup (35 grams) shelled peanuts (salted are fine), roasted

1½ teaspoons (10 grams) minced fresh ginger

1 small garlic clove

2 tablespoons (30 ml) low-sodium soy sauce

2 tablespoons (30 ml) toasted sesame oil

1 tablespoon (15 ml) unseasoned rice vinegar

¼ teaspoon granulated sugar, dark-brown sugar, or honey

to finish

3 scallions, thinly sliced

Chile-garlic or another hot sauce (optional)

prepare the tofu Drain the tofu, and place it on a few paper towels; place a few more towels over it. Place a heavy object—like a big frying pan—over the tofu, and let it rest for 10 minutes (and up to 30, if you have the time), to press out as much excess liquid as you can.

Meanwhile, heat the oven to 400 degrees. Line one large baking sheet with parchment; leave another one bare. (Tofu really wants to stick; for broccoli, you'll miss out on crunchy bits if you use parchment, which would be a travesty.)

prepare the broccoli Trim and chop the broccoli into chunky florets. Don't let the stems go to waste: I peel off the tough outer skin and knots and cut the stems into ½-inch segments. Drizzle 1 tablespoon oil over the parchment-paper-free baking sheet, and brush or roll it around so the sheet is evenly coated. Scatter the broccoli chunks over it, drizzle with a second tablespoon of oil, and season it well with salt and pepper.

Remove the tofu from the towels, and cut into 1-inch cubes. Toss the tofu with the remaining tablespoon of oil, the soy sauce, and the cornstarch until evenly coated, and spread out on the parchment-lined baking sheet.

cook the tofu and broccoli Place both baking sheets in the oven and roast for 20 minutes, then toss the pieces around for even coloring and roast another 10 minutes. At this point, the tofu is usually done, which is to say golden at the edges and lightly crisp; remove the pan from the oven. I like to toss the broccoli around and roast it for another 10 minutes to get an extra char on it.

while the broccoli and tofu roast, make the pesto Pulse all the ingredients together in a food processor until ground. Adjust the flavors to taste.

to finish In a large bowl, combine the broccoli and tofu, and toss with the sauce. Garnish with the scallions and with hot sauce, if using. Don't forget to share.

fried green plantains with avocado black bean salsa

feeds 4 as a meal or 8 as an appetizer

Once upon a time, a college boyfriend was obsessed with making fried plantains the way his mother always had, and insisted he could do it from memory in his dorm-room kitchen. I bet you can tell that things did not go very well. Among the problems were that his only utensil was a butter knife he'd probably stolen from the cafeteria, and this led to 45-plus minutes of our sawing pitifully away at this green beast banana with the leathery skin. Needless to say, it didn't get much better from there. Because of this, I'd always assumed that *tostones* were very difficult to make—if a person who'd been eating them his whole life couldn't pull them off, there wasn't much hope for the likes of me.

Silly Deb. A single trip to the store made it clear that plantains are not hard to peel—we just had an exquisite combination of cluelessness, a particularly tough plantain, and definitely the wrong knife. And a quick trip down a YouTube rabbit hole made it clear that *tostones* are not hard to make at home at all, which led to two additional problems: I needed them right that very second (like all terrible ex-girlfriends, I waited until after we broke up to see what the *tostones* fuss was about), and I wasn't sure how I could pass them off as dinner. I found my excuse in the dipping sauce. In Puerto Rico, fried green plantains are most often served with a garlicky green sauce called mojo (although "mojo" means other kinds of sauces in other countries, just to make things complicated). If you add lemon or lime juice, it becomes more of a vinaigrette, which, if you toss it with a great big chunky salsaish salad of black beans, avocado, and mango, is not only a happy complement to these salted fried discs but the perfect justification to make them often. Salad with a *side* of *tostones*? Do excuse me while I applaud my own brilliance.

salad

Juice of 1 lime or ½ lemon

1 large or 2 small garlic cloves, minced

¼ cup (60 ml) olive oil

1 tablespoon chopped fresh cilantro

Salt and freshly ground black pepper

1 large avocado, diced

1 cup (about 175 grams) diced papaya, mango, or pineapple

1 cup (250 grams) cooked black beans, drained and rinsed

plantains

3 firm green plantains

Vegetable oil, for frying

Salt

make the salad Whisk the lime juice, garlic, olive oil, cilantro, and salt and pepper in a small bowl. Put the avocado, papaya, and black beans in a larger bowl. Season with salt and pepper, and toss with half of the dressing. Taste for seasoning and set aside.

prepare the plantains Cut off the ends of each plantain so that a small amount of the inner vegetable is exposed. From here, there are many ways to remove the skin. You might be able to peel it with your fingertips, first making a slit from top to the bottom and opening the plantain from the side. You might find it easier to remove the skin in neat sections if you make a few slits down the side. Or, if you have a really tough one, you might just use a sharp knife to pare the peel away. If any green skin remains, scrape it off with your knife. Cut each plantain into six to eight 1-inch pieces.

cook the plantains Heat 1 inch of oil in a medium-sized heavy skillet over medium-high heat to 325 degrees. If you don't have the right kind of thermometer, I find plantains forgiving of inexact frying temperatures. As long as they're not taking more than 5 minutes in the first frying, or not blackening before 2 minutes, you're probably in a good-enough range.

Add about one plantain's worth of pieces to the oil, and cook, turning as needed, until they are just a little bit darker in color and hollow-sounding when lifted from the oil and tapped, 3 to 5 minutes. Drain them on a large paper-towel-lined plate. Repeat with the remaining plantains in two batches.

Using a heavy skillet or the underside of a can, press down on the still-hot fried plantain chunks until they make 2-to-3-inch flattish discs. Return these to the frying pan a handful at a time, and fry until lightly bronzed, about 1 minute more per side. Drain again, and immediately season with salt.

to finish Serve the warm plantains with the salad, with the extra dressing on the side to drizzle over the plantains.

broccoli, cheddar, and wild rice fritters

makes 4 large servings, or more as a snack or side

Thanks to the peculiar kind of shame that comes with ordering takeout for three people and receiving an amount of rice and/or chopsticks that would feed ten, and because I come from a long line of frugal people and cannot just throw it away, we fairly often have leftover rice in our fridge. Since my answer to almost all of life's problems (or at least life's excess-ingredient problems) is to make fritterlike pancakes—they're easy, portable, kid-friendly, and a good balance of vegetables and indulgence—it was inevitable that I'd try my hand at rice fritters. I realize that when most people think of frittered rice they imagine the breadcrumbed and deep-fried luxury that is *arancini*, but I'm not that fancy on a weeknight.

Even unbattered, nonrisotto cooked rice, vegetables, cheese, and eggs together make a spectacular-enough pancake, so I wish I'd done it much sooner. It's delicious not only for predictable reasons (cheese) but because of this miraculous thing that rice does when it hits a well-oiled frying pan, which is to puff ever so slightly and crisp. These are so, so good. I want this to be your new back-pocket recipe.

---

3 large eggs, lightly beaten

1 teaspoon kosher salt

Freshly ground black pepper

2 cups (about 330 grams) cooked wild-rice blend or other leftover rice

1 cup (100 grams) finely chopped parcooked broccoli florets, cooked

2 scallions, finely chopped

¾ cup (80 grams) coarsely grated sharp cheddar

Butter and olive oil, for frying

make the batter Using a fork, beat the eggs with the salt and pepper in a bowl until combined. Add the rice, broccoli, scallions, and cheddar, and stir to combine.

cook the fritters Heat a large frying pan over medium-low heat. Once it's hot, add a tablespoon of olive oil and a pat of butter; let them warm. Using a soupspoon, scoop about 1½ tablespoons of the rice mixture into the pan, and lightly press the top so it flattens to about ½-inch thickness. Here's the essential bit: keep the heat low enough so that it takes a few minutes for the undersides to brown; if you move a fritter sooner, it will fall apart easily. But once the fritters are brown, the eggs have cooked, and the cheese has melted, it's much easier to flip and repeat on the other side. Make the rest of the fritters with the remaining rice mixture, giving it an occasional stir.

note I make these in a seemingly small size (2 inches), because that makes them easier to flip. Larger, they're much more fragile until the egg sets up.

do ahead Keep the fritters warm in the oven or eat them immediately. The fritters will keep in the fridge and reheat well; you can also freeze them. But there aren't usually leftovers.

wild mushroom shepherd's pie

makes 6 to 8 servings

One of the truly terrible things almost all food writers like to do is take a beloved comfort-food classic and change it in the name of modernism, seasonality, or so-called sophistication. Lobster potpie with a crème fraîche pastry lid, heirloom-potato latkes with caviar, fried eggs with a pinch of truffle salt . . . I've done it all, too. To me, the sin isn't wanting a different flavor balance or approach, but the accidental tinge of condescension in suggesting that the original wasn't good enough, especially comical given my own affection for weeks-long lunch jags of peanut butter and jelly on store-bought sandwich bread.

But I have always wanted to make a shepherd's pie with a wild-mushroom stew underneath that had a depth of flavor that would reverberate from all of your taste buds—not as a criticism of the stick-to-your-ribs ground-beef-and-mashed-potatoes gold standard, but because, around here, we consider the intersection of mushrooms and potatoes *our* comfort-food happy place. Amping up the flavor with rehydrated porcini, a dark broth, dry sherry, a tiny bit of tomato paste, and sherry vinegar takes a simple mushroom sauté and makes it so sublime, we're not sure we ever want to go back to the original. Did I put a little crème fraîche in the mashed potatoes? On this, too, guilty as charged.

filling

½ cup (15 grams) dried mushrooms, such as porcini or a mix

1 cup (235 ml) boiling water

2 tablespoons (30 ml) olive oil

1 large onion, diced

2 medium carrots, diced

Salt and freshly ground black pepper to taste

3 garlic cloves, minced

2 pounds (roughly 1 kilogram) fresh mushrooms, in chunks (I use a mix of shiitake, elephant ear, and cremini; all cremini is also fine)

2 tablespoons (30 ml) dry sherry

1 tablespoon (15 grams) tomato paste

1 cup (235 ml) vegetable, chicken, or beef stock

lid

1¾ to 2 pounds (800 to 900 grams) russet potatoes, peeled and cut into large pieces

6 tablespoons (85 grams) unsalted butter, in chunks

1 teaspoon kosher salt

Freshly ground black pepper

¼ cup (55 grams) crème fraîche or sour cream

⅔ cup (115 ml) milk or buttermilk

to finish

Smoked or regular paprika and/or
1 tablespoon roughly chopped fresh flat-leaf parsley, for garnish

prepare the mushrooms In a small bowl, combine the dried mushrooms and boiling water. Set aside for 30 minutes (while you continue with the other steps), then drain, reserving the soaking water, and chop the rehydrated mushrooms into small bits. If the soaking water has any sand or grit at the bottom, pour it through a fine-mesh strainer.

meanwhile, prepare the lid Place the potatoes in a medium pot, and cover them with a couple inches of salted water. Bring to a boil, and then simmer over medium heat for 10 minutes, until the potatoes are easily pierced in the center with a knife or skewer. Drain, and either rice the potatoes into a large bowl, or place them in the bottom of a large bowl and mash with a fork or potato masher. Add the butter, salt, and pepper, and stir. The heat from the potatoes should melt the butter. Add the crème fraîche and the milk, and stir to combine. Taste, and adjust the seasonings if needed.

Heat oven to 400 degrees.

cook the vegetables In a large pan (4-quart, or an 11-inch deep skillet or braiser), heat the olive oil over medium heat. Add the onion, carrots, salt, and pepper, and sauté until the vegetables begin to color, about 10 minutes. Add the garlic, and cook for 1 minute more. Add fresh mushrooms, salt, and pepper, increase the heat to high, and cook the mushrooms until they brown and soften, releasing their juices, 5 to 10 minutes. Add the sherry, and scrape up any stuck bits. Add the tomato paste, and stir to combine. Add the rehydrated mushrooms and their liquid, plus the stock. Season again if needed, and simmer over medium heat for about 10 minutes, or until the mushrooms are coated in a thick sauce.

bake the pie If your skillet is oven-safe, you can bake the pie in it. If not, transfer the mixture to a 2-to-3-quart baking dish. Scoop the potatoes in large spoonfuls all over the top of the mushrooms, then use the back of your spoon to spread them smooth all the way to the edges, forming a seal.

Bake for 25 to 30 minutes, until lightly browned on top. Garnish with a dusting of paprika and/or parsley. Scoop and serve.

do ahead This keeps for 5 days in the fridge and longer in the freezer. Rewarm it in a 350-degree oven for 20 to 25 minutes.

spring fried barley with a sesame sizzled egg

makes 4 servings

I realize this sounds worrisome, but some of the best fried rice I've made at home was via a French chef's recipe. Yet Jean-Georges Vongerichten's ginger fried rice has legions of fans for the two best reasons: elegance and simplicity. In his version, far from the heaviness and soy-sauce assault of bad takeout, garlic and ginger become toasty confetti. Softened leeks disperse through the rice. The only soy sauce and sesame oil you use are the tiny amounts drizzled over the fried egg that you top it with, leaving their flavor uncluttered.

But even Jean-Georges cannot be blamed for what I did to it next: I used it to re-dress a mishmash of leftovers, and we liked them so much that it became a thing. Cooked barley, with (what I think of as) a fluffy sheep look, is made for a frying pan, where those soft edges take on some texture and the barley grains happily absorb any flavors you throw at them. Because it was May, and May in New York means you've finally seen the first glimpses of spring produce, I could not resist speckling the barley with asparagus, favas, and sugar snaps, instead of just the usual peas and carrots—but any seasonal vegetable, cooked only until crisp, then cooled and chopped, will work well. What I retained from the dish that inspired me was the egg on top (my way, so, extra-crispy) and the finish of soy and sesame, plus extra crunch from seeds.

fried barley

4 to 5 tablespoons (60 to 75 ml) peanut oil

2 large garlic cloves, minced

1 tablespoon minced fresh ginger

3 scallions, thinly sliced

4 cups cooked (600 grams) barley (from 1 heaped cup, about 225 grams, uncooked), cooled

Salt

2 cups (about 255 grams) mixed spring vegetables, such as favas, peas, chopped asparagus or sugar snaps, cooked until firm-tender

to finish

4 large eggs

4 teaspoons (20 ml) soy sauce, plus more to taste

2 teaspoons (10 ml) toasted sesame oil

2 teaspoons (5 grams) sesame seeds, toasted, or a mix of white and black seeds

make the fried barley and vegetables Heat 3 tablespoons of the oil in a large heavy skillet or wok over medium-high heat. Add the garlic, ginger, and scallions and let them sizzle for 30 seconds. Add the barley, spreading it out and sprinkling it with salt, and then don't move it for 5 to 10 minutes; you're looking to get a little color underneath, but you should keep a close eye on it to make sure it doesn't burn. Once it's a bit brown underneath, stir the mixture around, attempting to give a little more texture to the barley. Finally, add the vegetables, and stir for 1 minute, just to get them to heat through. Transfer to a serving bowl.

cook the eggs Wipe out the skillet, and heat over high heat with the remaining oil, creating a good slick. When it's piping, smoking hot, drop in 2 eggs (or 4, if they fit) and step back, because this is going to be violently splattery. When the eggs are lacy brown underneath, carefully shimmy a thin spatula under each, loosening and flipping the eggs, cooking on the other side for 20 to 30 seconds. Repeat with the last 2 eggs, if they didn't fit in the first batch.

to finish Place each egg atop a portion of fried rice, and drizzle each with 1 teaspoon soy and ½ teaspoon sesame oil, then sprinkle with ½ teaspoon seeds. Break the eggs so that they pour over the barley.

romesco, chickpea, and smashed egg bowl

makes 4 meal-sized bowls

I spent years trying to master the art of the poached egg. I spilled eggs from small dishes into teeming pots of water, I used both drops and splashes of white vinegar, I made whirlpools, I threw money at rings and silicon cups that promised success. And though I even got it right in the end about 75 percent of the time, I never enjoyed it, because who wants to play cooking roulette when you're hungry? Then, one day, I peeled a soft-boiled egg—and I haven't poached an egg since.

I don't limit these eggs to breakfast toast anymore, however. These days, my favorite thing to squeeze between the smashed egg and toast is the Catalan sauce known as romesco. There are about as many versions of it out there as there are people who make it, but the core elements are typically some sort of roasted pepper, tomato, and chile pepper; almonds and/or hazelnuts; garlic; parsley; sherry vinegar for pop; and olive oil for richness. Most versions also grind in a slice of bread fried in olive oil, but I leave it out so I can enjoy it on the side. That's the simple approach here, and the one I'd intended to share with you: a smashed egg atop romesco atop a piece of fried bread. But from the moment I checked that recipe off the list, a nagging voice showed up in my head, begging me to stretch this sauce further into a bowl with chickpeas, spinach, charred scallions, and yogurt. I tried to ignore it—I tried for nine months, even. But here we are, and do you know, I would never, ever tell you to take on so much cooking—a sauce, a roast, a sauté, and a simmer, all quick, but *I know, I know*—unless the reward was so much greater than the investment. Do as we do and double up on everything to assemble a week of outstanding meals.

romesco sauce

¼ cup (60 ml) olive oil

3 plum tomatoes (about 250 grams), peeled (canned is fine; chopped if fresh)

Red pepper flakes to taste, or 1 dried ancho chile, rehydrated, seeded, and finely chopped

1 large or 2 small garlic cloves, smashed

¼ cup (35 grams) roasted almonds, Marconas if you can find them

2 red bell peppers, roasted, peeled, and seeded

1½ teaspoons Spanish smoked paprika (pimentón), hot or sweet

2 teaspoons (10 ml) sherry vinegar

1 tablespoon roughly chopped fresh flat-leaf parsley

Salt to taste

assembly

2 tablespoons (30 ml) olive oil

Bunch of scallions (roughly 8 ounces or 100 grams), root ends trimmed

Salt

1 garlic clove, pressed or minced

10 ounces (285 grams) fresh baby spinach

4 large eggs

1¾ cup (from a 15-ounce can) rinsed chickpeas

(*cont.*)

the other direction in the same way, creating a grid pattern. Rub the cut and skin sides of the potatoes lightly with olive oil. Drizzle a little oil on a baking sheet and place the potatoes on it.

cook the vegetables Roast the potatoes, cut side down, for 15 to 20 minutes, then flip them over and brush them lightly with cider vinegar. Pat them with 1 teaspoon of the spice rub, and roast them for an additional 30 to 35 minutes, with the now rubbed cut side facing up, or until a knife inserted into the sweet potato meets no resistance and the rub has melted into the potatoes. If desired, you can run these under the broiler for 2 minutes to increase the caramelization on top.

Meanwhile, cook the beans in boiling salted water for 2 to 3 minutes, until crisp-tender, then plunge them in ice water to cool quickly. Drain and pat dry, then cut into 1-or-so-inch lengths on the bias.

to assemble and finish Mix the dressing ingredients, and season to taste. Stir half the dressing with green beans to dress them right before serving or the slaw may discolor or become watery.

Serve the sweet potato steaks with a small pile of green bean slaw; pass the remaining dressing on the side.

tomato and gigante bean bake / pizza beans

makes 8 servings

M ost of us know the number one rule of cooking for a crowd: don't make anything new or scary. Not the rack of lamb you've been eyeing, not the soufflé or anything else that's going to send you into a vibe-ruining tizzy. This rule is probably doubly important if you're invited to a potluck at a big-deal editor's apartment with a dozen food writers you're totally intimidated by, each of whom will arrive with his or her own signature dish. But this is not what I did. I'd like to pretend that it's just because I've got an unshakable confidence in my cooking, or, at the least, kitchen, uh, "meatballs" of steel. Alas, it would be more accurate to say that I decided to make this dish you see here—a mash-up of a giant-beans-in-tomato-sauce dish from Greece and American-style baked ziti, with beans instead of noodles—because, well, it was really what I was in the mood to cook that day, and cravings trump rationality pretty much always around here, and especially when I am 6 months pregnant.

Before I left, I baked off a smaller amount for my husband and son for dinner, and my son—perhaps predictably for the kindergarten set—threw a fit. *"I do not like beans."* "You're going to love these." *"I won't eat them."* "You should try them! You'll see! There's tomato sauce, and look at all of that cheese on top. . . . It's just like pizza." *"Pizza beans!!"* (Do I even need to tell you that this did the trick?)

And thus this is the story of how I showed up to a potluck with a dish tagged "Tomato-Braised Gigante Bean Gratin," but there isn't a person there who will remember them (fondly, I hope) as anything but "Pizza Beans."

2 tablespoons (30 ml) olive oil

1 large onion, chopped

2 celery stalks, diced

1 large or 2 regular carrots, diced

Salt and freshly ground black pepper or red pepper flakes

2 large garlic cloves, minced

¼ cup (60 ml) dry white or red wine (optional)

4 ounces (115 grams) curly kale leaves, chopped or torn

2¼ cups (550 grams) crushed tomatoes (28-ounce or 800-gram can minus 1 cup; reserve the rest for another use)

1 pound (455 grams) cooked firm-tender giant white beans

Up to ¾ cup (175 ml) vegetable broth

½ pound (225 grams) mozzarella, coarsely grated

⅓ cup (35 grams) grated Parmesan

2 tablespoons (5 grams) roughly chopped fresh flat-leaf parsley, for garnish (optional)

prepare the beans and vegetables Heat the oven to 475 degrees. In a 2½-to-3-quart (ideally oven-safe) deep sauté pan, braiser, or shallow Dutch oven, heat the olive oil on medium-high. Add the onion, celery, and carrots.

Season well with salt and black or red pepper. Cook, sautéing, until the vegetables brown lightly, about 10 minutes. Add the garlic, and cook for 1 minute more. Add the wine, if using, to scrape up any stuck bits, then simmer until it disappears, 1 to 2 minutes. Add the kale, and cook for 1 to 2 minutes, until collapsed, then add the tomatoes and bring to a simmer. Add the beans, and, if the mixture looks too dry or thick (canned tomatoes range quite a bit in juiciness), add up to ¾ cup broth, ¼ cup at a time. Simmer the mixture together over medium for about 10 minutes, adjusting the seasonings as needed.

If your pan isn't ovenproof, transfer the mixture to a 3-quart baking dish. If it is, well, carry on.

bake Sprinkle the beans first with the mozzarella, then the Parmesan, and bake for 10 to 15 minutes, until browned on top. If you're impatient and want a deeper color, you can run it under the broiler. Finish with parsley, if desired.

notes

These beans are called *fagioli corona* (in Italy), *gigante/gigandes* (in Greece), Royal Corona (by Rancho Gordo, where I ordered mine), and other names.

For a meaty variation, brown some fresh sweet or spicy Italian sausages (about ¾ pound or 340 grams) with the vegetables.

bean cooking note This recipe was originally designed as a long oven-braise that began with dried beans. I recommend you cook your beans in advance. Because they're very big, I usually soak them for 12 to 24 hours in salted water, then simmer them for a couple hours; you could also use a slow cooker on HIGH (usually 4 to 6 hours, but it will vary), or a pressure cooker (about 20 minutes, with variance), or bake them in the oven at 325 degrees for approximately 70 to 90 minutes after bringing them to a simmer on the stove.

my go-to garlic bread

1 large (about 12 ounces), not *too* firm seeded baguette

8 tablespoons (4 ounces or 115 grams) unsalted butter, cut into chunks

4 medium garlic cloves, minced

A few pinches of red pepper flakes, to taste

½ teaspoon coarse or kosher salt

½ teaspoon dried oregano (optional)

⅓ to ½ cup (34 to 50 grams) finely grated Parmesan or aged Pecorino Romano (optional)

1 tablespoon finely chopped herbs, such as parsley and chives

Heat your oven's broiler. Line a large baking sheet with foil to limit the mess you make. Cut the baguette lengthwise and arrange the pieces cut side up in a pan. Put the butter, garlic, red pepper flakes, and the salt in a small saucepan and melt over medium-high heat, stirring, until the garlic is sizzling in the butter (but not browning). Remove from the heat and stir in the oregano, if using. Spoon evenly over the bread. Sprinkle the bread with Parmesan, if using, and broil until lightly browned—keeping a close watch on it and turning it as needed for even coloring.

Remove from the oven, sprinkle with parsley and chives, if using, and cut into segments.

do ahead We keep extras in foil in the fridge and rewarm them in the oven, but you know it's always best on the first day.

cacio e pepe potatoes anna

makes 8 servings

G oing to Rome turned me into an insufferable snob about *cacio e pepe*. I'm not proud of this. There's no excuse for my attitude in relation to one of the world's least pretentious dishes, but I understand that this is a common side effect of twirling tonnarelli (that's the squared-off fresh spaghetti used for *cacio*, sometimes called spaghetti alla chitarra, after the strings of the guitar-resembling instrument it is cut on) tossed with nothing but *cacio* (usually an aged, preferably black-rind Pecorino Romano) and black pepper, in cobblestoned alleyways, drinking wine at 10:00 p.m. Unsurprisingly, little has compared since. There's also no excuse for this because, as of the publication date of this book, approximately 4 years and 22 rounds of *cacio e pepe* since I was last in Rome, I have yet to unlock any level of mastery—that is, a magically creamy sauce—just a lot of clumping and sloshing and rarely any cohesion.

Needless to say, these are not traditional flavors for this galette, which I think of as a poor man's *pommes Anna. Pommes Anna* is nothing but potatoes and a significant amount of clarified butter, layered to form a cake that's flipped in a pan on the stove every 10 minutes until the outside is golden and crispy. A potato galette is for people who live their lives outside restaurant kitchens—or, perhaps, have a curly-haired tyrant named Anna in their lives.

This version is far more hands-off but doesn't skimp on the best part, which is that it looks like a crown of potatoes and tastes a bit like a potato chip casserole, with deeply bronzed and crisp edges and a baked-just-so center, infused with salty cheese and a warming kick of pepper. With a salad of lightly dressed greens, it makes a pretty luxurious simple dinner.

½ cup (65 grams) finely grated aged Pecorino Romano

1 tablespoon (10 grams) potato starch or cornstarch

½ teaspoon fine sea salt, or to taste

½ teaspoon finely ground black pepper, or a larger amount coarsely ground

2 to 3 tablespoons (30 to 45 grams) butter, melted, or olive oil

2 pounds (roughly 1 kilogram) Yukon Gold potatoes, peeled, cut into ⅛-inch-thick rounds, ideally on a mandoline

salad

8 cups (5⅔ ounces or 160 grams) loosely packed arugula

1 tablespoon (15 ml) olive oil

2 teaspoons (10 ml) white wine vinegar

assemble the potatoes Heat the oven to 375 degrees. Combine the cheese, potato starch or cornstarch, salt, and pepper in a small dish. Taste a pinch; you want it to have a strong salty-peppery kick, because it's going to be distributed all over the galette.

Pour 1 tablespoon butter or oil into the bottom of a 9-inch-diameter cast-iron or ovenproof pan, and swirl it up the sides. Arrange the potatoes in overlapping concentric circles in a single layer at the bottom of the pan. (This will use approximately a quarter of your sliced potatoes.) Drizzle with 1 teaspoon butter or oil, and sprinkle with 2 tablespoons of the cheese-pepper mixture. Repeat four times, or until the potatoes are used up; you should have about 1 tablespoon cheese-pepper mixture left over; reserve this.

to bake Lightly coat a piece of foil with nonstick spray and tightly cover the pan with it. Put in a heated oven for 35 minutes, at which point the potatoes will be almost tender. Using pot holders, press firmly on the foil to compact the potatoes a bit. Remove and reserve the foil and bake for 25 to 30 minutes more, until lightly brown all over. Press again with the foil, remove, then briefly run under the broiler for an even golden brown finish.

to finish and serve While the galette bakes, toss the arugula with the olive oil and vinegar, keeping the dressing very light.

Once the galette is out of the oven, let it rest in the skillet for a few minutes before running a knife around to ensure that it is loose. Gently tip the skillet over your sink to drain any excess butter or oil. Invert it onto a plate or cutting board, then flip right side up. Cut the galette into wedges, then top with the dressed greens, and sprinkle with the reserved cheese-pepper mixture.

do ahead This galette can be made up to 3 days in advance. Rewarm at 350 degrees for 15 minutes with foil on top.

caramelized cabbage risotto

makes 4 main servings or 6 appetizer portions

I cannot think of one time I ate cabbage when I was growing up; I have no lingering childhood trauma incident with cabbage stewed forever into some mysterious heap; I am not repelled by the scent of it braised or fermented, which means I love it with the openhearted abandon of someone who chose it. So when I first learned about Marcella Hazan's "smothered" cabbage, I knew it would be heaven. A lot of shredded cabbage and a small amount of diced onion are cooked together for 1½ hours to a collapse that you are encouraged to stretch into a rustic soup with rice. It's amazing, but I never stopped there. Since the rice has a tendency to drink up most of the soup anyway, I prefer making it intentional and approaching it like a risotto, just a very hearty and vegetable-loaded one. And because I'm me, I want it to taste even more like caramelized onions than it does—that is, I wanted something halfway between smothered cabbage and caramelized onions.

I use a few shortcuts. At the beginning, I cook the onions and cabbage together at a low temperature with the lid on, a trick from a Julia Child recipe, which reduces the amount of time it takes for onions to caramelize because the trapped steam helps them collapse and sweeten. (Thank you, Julia.) I also don't heat my broth before ladling it in as you usually would do for risotto. I find that, as long as the liquid is at or close to room temperature, the heat in the pan from that sautéed rice is enough, and using smaller amounts splashed from a spouted measuring cup helps, too.

5 tablespoons (70 grams) butter

1½ tablespoons (20 ml) olive oil

2 medium yellow onions, thinly sliced

½ small-medium green cabbage (about 2½ pounds or 1⅛ kilograms whole), cored, halved, and thinly sliced (6 cups or 570 grams)

1 teaspoon coarse or Diamond kosher salt, plus more to taste

6 cups (1¼ liters) vegetable or chicken stock, at room temperature (you may find you need less)

1½ cups (280 grams) Arborio or other starchy short-grain white rice

⅓ cup (70 ml) dry white wine

½ cup (65 grams) finely grated Parmesan or aged Asiago, plus more in shavings for garnish

Freshly ground black pepper, to taste

Freshly chives, minced, for garnish

caramelize the cabbage Melt 1 tablespoon butter and the olive oil together in a large deep skillet or Dutch oven over medium heat. Add the onions and cabbage to the pan, toss them gently with the butter and oil, reduce the heat to medium-low, and cover the pan. Let the mixture cook for 15 minutes, stirring once or twice to avoid overcooked spots, then remove the lid, stir in the salt, and cook, stirring, for 20 to 25 minutes, bumping up the heat slightly if necessary, until the cabbage is soft and the onions are moderately caramelized and have taken on a golden color. Keep the closest watch on it in the second half of the cooking time, when it is most eager to scorch and stick. Deglaze with a splash of broth, then scoop the mixture into a bowl.

make the risotto Wipe out the pot, and heat 1½ tablespoons butter in it over medium-high heat. Add the rice, and cook, stirring, for 1 minute. Add the wine, and stir until absorbed, about 1 minute more. Pour in about 1 cup broth, and cook at a strong simmer, stirring, until absorbed, about 2 minutes. Continue simmering and adding broth a splash or two at a time, stirring frequently, and letting each addition be absorbed before adding the next, until the rice is just tender (al dente) and looks creamy but loose, 18 to 20 minutes. Add the cabbage mixture, and, if needed, thin the risotto with another splash or two of broth. Good risotto doesn't stand in a heap, but likes to spill out into a bit of a puddle in a shallow bowl.

to finish Remove from the heat, and stir in the cheese, remaining 2½ tablespoons butter, and salt and pepper to taste. Serve garnished with a few shavings of cheese and some snipped chives.

mujadara-stuffed cabbage with minted tomato sauce

makes 6 servings of 2 rolls each

On Lexington Avenue near East Twenty-eighth Street, there's a five-story redbrick row house that I adore for two reasons: (1) On September 20, 1881, in a delicious tidbit of New York City history unacknowledged except on a lobby plaque, Chester Arthur was sworn in here—his family home—as president. (2) Sixty-three years and a few changes of ownership later, Kalustyan's, the great specialty foods emporium, opened, and it remains one of my favorite places to shop.

Of all the magical things the store sells—pretty much every spice, rice variety, and dried legume on earth—one of my favorites is mujadara,* a rice-lentil mash that tastes so much better than those three words would imply, thanks to a hidden heap of fried onions. I ate this salad for lunch (along with their excellent vegetable soup) many times a week when I worked nearby. It didn't dawn on me until later, however, that what I love about mujadara—the way the rice and lentils play off each other, the spices, the killer onions—might also hold the vegetarian key to another dish: stuffed cabbage. I've always wanted to make a meat-free variety but never could come up with a filling that isn't, well, just filler. But this—rice, lentils, and onions wrapped in cabbage leaves, braised in a minty, lemony tomato sauce and dolloped with plain yogurt—we love not in spite of its being meat-free, but because it is hearty and has so much flavor.

* Aka majadra, mejadra, moujadara, mudardara, and megadarra, koshary, and khichri.

crispy onions

¾ cup (175 ml) olive oil, or another oil you like, for frying (sunflower, safflower, or peanut), plus more if needed

2 medium onions, thinly sliced

Kosher salt

lentils and rice

¾ cup (150 grams) green or brown lentils, picked over and rinsed (to yield about 2 cups cooked)

1 teaspoon cumin seeds

¼ teaspoon coriander seeds

¼ teaspoon mild pepper flakes, such as Aleppo

1 teaspoon kosher salt

A pinch or two of ground allspice (optional)

A pinch or two of ground cinnamon (optional)

½ cup (100 grams) basmati rice

assembly

1 large savoy cabbage

2 garlic cloves, minced

One 28-ounce (800-gram) can puréed plum tomatoes

Salt

Freshly ground black pepper

Zest and juice of ½ lemon, plus wedges to serve

2 sprigs of fresh mint, plus a few extra leaves for garnish

Plain yogurt (optional)

fry the onions Heat the oil in a large sauté pan over medium-high heat. Add the onions, and cook until they become dark brown, stirring as needed to keep the color even, about 15 minutes. Remove them with a slotted spoon, and drain on paper towels. Season with salt quickly, while they're still hot, and set aside.

meanwhile, parcook your lentils Place the lentils in a small saucepan, cover with plenty of water (at least triple the volume of lentils), bring to a boil, then reduce it to a simmer and cook for 15 to 20 minutes, until the lentils are firm-tender but *not* fully cooked. Let cool for 5 minutes, and then drain. Set aside.

make the rice Strain your onion-cooking oil into a bowl or jar, because you'll use some of it for the rest of the dish. Add 1 tablespoon back to the large sauté pan that you used to cook the onions, and reheat it over medium-high heat. Add the cumin and coriander seeds, and cook for 1 minute, stirring. Add 4¼ cups water, the pepper flakes, salt, allspice (if using), and cinnamon (if using), the parcooked lentils, and the uncooked rice. Bring to a boil, reduce to a very low simmer, then cover with a lid. Cook for 15 minutes. You're not supposed to peek, but since rice and lentils will vary, it cannot hurt to do a quick look-see to make sure it hasn't run out of cooking liquid before it's done. Let it rest for 5 minutes in the pot off heat. Scatter three-quarters of the onions (reserve the rest for garnish) over the top, and gently mix them in. Taste, and adjust the seasonings if needed.

prepare the cabbage You can do this while the rice is cooking, if you can bear to dirty another pot. I cannot; I wait, give it a quick rinse, and use it to wilt the cabbage. Bring a large pot of salted water to a boil. Discard any messy or broken outer cabbage leaves, and carefully peel 12 nice large leaves. Blanch a few leaves at a time for about 1 minute to wilt them, then drain and spread them out on towels so they dry. Trimming any thick veins will make it easier to roll the cabbage. Place ¼ to ⅓ cup mujadara inside each cabbage leaf, and roll it tightly. Place the leaves, with seam side down, on a plate and set aside while you prepare the sauce.

make the sauce Drain the pot, and wipe it out. Heat 1 tablespoon of the onion-cooking oil over medium heat. Add the garlic, and let it sizzle for 30 seconds or so, then add the tomatoes, salt, pepper, lemon zest, and sprigs of mint. Let it simmer for 5 minutes, then gently lower the cabbage packets into the pot, arranging them so that they all fit. Simmer with the lid slightly ajar (I like to put a spoon across the top and the lid on top of that, to keep it propped ajar) for 20 to 25 minutes. Fish out the mint sprigs.

to serve Squeeze lemon juice over the top, dollop with yogurt (if desired), and scatter with mint.

notes

You can use bulgur or another grain instead of rice; the chef Michael Solomonov uses freekeh, for example.

This makes 12 cabbage rolls, or the amount that should fit in a standard Dutch oven (5 quarts) or a deep sauté pan (12 inches across). But it also makes enough mujadara for two batches. As this is a bit of a project for *only* 12 rolls, you might go ahead and make double, to freeze half for a future use, or to eat plain, outside of the cabbage rolls. You'll thank yourself later.

spaghetti *pangrattato* with crispy eggs

makes 4 servings

I spent my first pregnancy quietly bemused by all of these wild notions people had about what pregnant women do and do not eat—I didn't have a speck of morning sickness, and my singular cravings were lemonade and green vegetables. I bet you know what happens next: the second time, I finally got it. Food was revolting, something inconvenient under the best of circumstances, and borderline debilitating if you're supposed to be cooking or writing about food all day. Later in my pregnancy, when I finally got even marginally hungry again, the only things I wanted were my old friends green vegetables and lemonade . . . and runny eggs. Is there some rule about runny eggs? Whoops.

One boing-boing-curled moppet and this dish were the two best things to come out of that time. I spied a version of this first on the Food52 website, where the author, Rhonda Hesser Thomson, took inspiration from a version from Arthur Schwartz and Jamie Oliver. *Pangrattato*—which means "grated bread" or "breadcrumbs," when treated like this, which is to say, toasted in olive oil with herbs, seasonings, and everything from anchovies to lemon zest, capers, or olives—is often referred to as the poor man's Parmesan, because it adds remarkable texture and complex flavor to pasta without the expense of the cheese. These crumbs would be incredible on many things—steamed mussels, warm roasted vegetables, or green salads—but when they were tangled through al dente spaghetti with a fried egg on top that you broke up with your fork, my otherwise MIA cravings fastened themselves to this dish; 2½ years later, I'd still easily reject 90 percent of pasta preparations to have this one instead.

crumbs

2 tablespoons (30 ml) olive oil

1 large garlic clove, minced

½ cup (30 grams) plain breadcrumbs, such as panko

Salt and red pepper flakes, to taste

1 teaspoon minced fresh rosemary

A few fine fresh gratings of lemon zest

pasta and assembly

8 ounces (225 grams) dried spaghetti

1 tablespoon (15 ml) olive oil

2 teaspoons (10 grams) drained capers (rinsed if salted), chopped

Handful of fresh flat-leaf parsley, chopped

⅓ cup (45 grams) grated Pecorino Romano (optional)

crispy eggs

1 glug of olive oil per egg

1 egg per desired portion

Salt and freshly ground black pepper

make the crispy breadcrumbs Heat the olive oil in a medium skillet over medium heat. Once it's hot, add the garlic, and let it sizzle for barely a minute, just until it begins to turn a pale-golden color. Add the breadcrumbs, salt, pepper flakes, rosemary, and lemon zest, and reduce the heat to low; cook the mixture slowly until all of the crumbs are an even golden color, about 5 minutes. Set aside.

cook the pasta Bring a pot of well-salted water to a boil, and cook the pasta until it's al dente, 1 to 2 minutes shy of the package directions. Reserve a little pasta-cooking water, then drain.

meanwhile, make the crispy eggs Wipe out the bread-crumb skillet. Return it to the stove over high heat, and add a generous glug of olive oil per egg. Once it's hot enough so the oil begins to smoke, add the eggs. They're going to hiss and splatter, so step back as soon as you do. Spoon some of the cooking oil over the eggs, care-fully. Season with salt and pepper. In 1 to 2 minutes, the eggs will be brown and very crisp underneath and around the edges. Shimmy a thin spatula underneath the eggs (a flexible fish spatula works great here), being careful not to break the yolks. If you're cooking for someone who shouldn't be eating runny yolks (ahem), you can flip the eggs over and cook them for another 30 seconds or so before removing them. Transfer the cooked eggs to paper towels to drain.

assemble the dish Once the pasta is drained, return it to the empty pot or a large skillet with 1 tablespoon olive oil and a splash or two of the reserved cooking water. Over high heat, toss with the capers and parsley for 1 minute. Divide among bowls or plates. Sprinkle a portion of the breadcrumb mixture over it, then the cheese (if using). Place an egg over each dish, and break it up with a fork. Eat immediately.

note There is no one correct way to make *pangrattato*, only the way you like it. Nobody is going to know if you skip the parsley or try sage or thyme instead of rosemary. I couldn't resist adding a little Pecorino here anyway, but you'd be fine without it if you'd like to keep the dish dairy-free.

brussels and three cheese pasta bake

makes 4 servings

I'm never one to turn down a chance to eat a deep scoop of creamy, stretchy, crunchy-lidded macaroni and cheese, especially if it's the world-famous Martha Stewart version. However, almost 100 percent of the time, a nap is required afterward, and almost 100 percent of our evening routine of washing dishes, finding all the bits of food the baby has flung throughout the day, wrangling two kids into baths and pajamas, and engaging in bedtime-story negotiations that could rival the Paris peace talks doesn't particularly allow for naps, so most of the time when the cravings for baked cheesy pasta dishes hit, I'm making some adjustments.

I usually replace the macaroni shape with a more twisty, ruffly, or chunky pasta, so there's more crags to catch the sauce. Because I like to bring as few side dishes to the table as possible, I usually add an equal or greater amount of a sautéed fresh vegetable to the pasta. For years, I used a béchamel sauce—that flour, butter, and milk wonder that forms the creamy foundation of traditional macaroni and cheese—but when I began replacing the milk with broth or stock, I ended up with a rich but unheavy sauce that managed to showcase the vegetables without smothering them. This is our current favorite version: It holds back on none of the cheese of a good baked ziti (there are three different types; you're welcome), but includes a great heap of lightly sautéed brussels sprouts, lemon, and garlic, and has all of the important parts played up—browned, crunchy edges for miles—with absolutely no hedging on comfort, luxury, or alertness.

½ pound (8 ounces or 225 grams) pasta of your choice; I really like gemelli or something twisty here

2 tablespoons (30 grams) unsalted butter, plus more for the baking dish

1 tablespoon (15 ml) olive oil

2 garlic cloves, minced

10 ounces (4 cups) thinly sliced or shredded brussels sprouts (12 ounces untrimmed)

Salt and freshly ground black pepper

Finely grated zest of ½ lemon

3 tablespoons (25 grams) all-purpose flour

1¾ cups (415 ml) vegetable broth

Juice of ½ lemon

½ cup (50 grams) finely grated Parmesan

1 cup (80 grams) coarsely grated Gruyère

1 cup (80 grams) coarsely grated fontina (see note)

Bring a pot of well-salted water to a boil. Add the pasta and cook until very al dente, a full 2 minutes before perfect doneness. Drain and set aside.

Heat the oven to 400 degrees. Butter a 2-quart or 9-inch round baking dish.

Heat the olive oil in a large, deep skillet (or in the bottom of the pot where you just cooked your pasta) over medium-high heat. Once it's hot, add the garlic and let it sizzle for 10 to 20 seconds, then add the brussels sprouts. Season well with salt and pepper and sauté for 2 to 3 minutes, until brighter green but barely wilted. Add the lemon zest and stir to mix. Add 2 tablespoons butter and stir until melted. Sprinkle the flour in and stir until you no longer see it. Add the broth a glug at a time, stirring constantly. Once all the broth is added, simmer the sauce for 2 to 3 minutes. Remove from the heat and stir in the lemon juice, then the cooked pasta; stir to evenly coat. Combine the cheeses in a bowl and stir all but ⅔ cup of them into the pasta and sauce. Taste and adjust the seasonings; don't hold back on black pepper here. Scrape the pasta mixture into the prepared baking dish and sprinkle with the reserved cheese. Bake for 25 to 30 minutes, until browned on top.

notes

I'm using somewhat untraditional cheeses here. I love the nuttiness of the Gruyère, but you can swap in another cheese you prefer, either in the same family (Swiss, Comté, etc.) or fontina. Italian fontina (which is aged and has a stronger flavor) is the more logical choice, but I've found I like the funkier, smoother Danish fontina, if you can find it. It often has a red rind, is inexpensive, and melts beautifully.

My favorite way to trim sprouts: Trim any discolored leaves. Thinly slice (either with a knife or adjustable-blade slicer/mandoline) the brussels sprouts into very thin ribbons. Alternatively, Trader Joe's sells shredded brussels in 10-ounce bags.

This dish is also good with asparagus and other spring vegetables, parcooked, when brussels are out of season.

one-pan farro with tomatoes

makes 2 hearty main course or 4 side servings

I once fell for a one-pan pasta recipe in which the dried noodles and all the other ingredients went right into a small amount of water (your *nonna* would never approve), so that by the time it was done, it had self-sauced and you'd, ostensibly, saved on time or dishes. It was gloppy. It was not my thing. But I loved the approach so much that I applied it to farro—the kind of grain that takes well to a little extra softness and cohesion—and I never looked back.

Farro arriving from its saucepan already perfectly balanced and ready to eat is something of a weeknight miracle, the kind of rare dream of a dish that we made once and immediately added to our permanent, laminated, framed, forever-and-ever repertoire. It requires little work or forethought (I mean, isn't there always an onion and some freakishly ne'er-rotting tomatoes around?), and it makes an almost complete meal. "Studies" have shown that it will increase your farro intake by a minimum of 300 percent in the first month, and by studies I mostly mean: buy extra of everything.

2 cups (475 ml) water

1 cup (210 grams) uncooked semi-pearled farro

½ large onion (I usually use a white one, for mildness)

2 garlic cloves

9 ounces (255 grams) grape or cherry tomatoes

1¼ teaspoons kosher or coarse sea salt

Up to ¼ teaspoon red pepper flakes, to taste

1 tablespoon (15 ml) olive oil, plus extra for drizzling

A few fresh basil leaves, cut into thin ribbons

Grated Parmesan, for serving (optional)

Place the water and farro in a medium saucepan to pre-soak (I find just 5 to 10 minutes sufficient) while you prepare the other ingredients. Adding each ingredient to the pot as you finish preparing it, cut the onion in half again, and very thinly slice it into quarter-moons. Thinly slice the garlic cloves as well. Halve or quarter the tomatoes. Add the salt, red pepper flakes to taste, and 1 tablespoon olive oil to the pan, and set a timer for 30 minutes. Bring the uncovered pan to a boil, then reduce to a gentle simmer and continue to cook, stirring occasionally. When the timer rings, the farro should be perfectly cooked (tender but with a meaty chew) and seasoned, and the cooking water should be almost completely absorbed. If needed, though I've never found it necessary, cook it for 5 additional minutes, until the farro is more tender.

Transfer it to a wide serving bowl. If there's enough leftover cooking liquid to be bothersome, simply use a slotted spoon to leave behind whatever liquid you don't want. Drizzle the farro lightly with additional olive oil, and scatter with basil and Parmesan (if desired). Eat immediately. Repeat tomorrow.

note When you put the ingredients in, you will surely think, "This is too much onion!" But in 30 minutes of simmering time, the onion becomes the foundation of a dreamy, loose tomato sauce whose flavors root deeply into each farro bite.

meat mains

brick hens with charred lemon

each bird serves 2

W hen I go out, all I want to try is new stuff, so you can understand why I rarely order things like chicken. Thank goodness, I don't only go out to eat with myself. At dinner with my parents one night, someone suggested we also order the chicken dish to share, and what came out was one of the most exquisite I've had.

It was actually a Cornish hen, cooked flat, seasoned with little more than lemon and salt. In the days and weeks that followed, I described it, basically to anyone who would listen, as having "potato-chip skin" and being doused in a "salty lemon vinaigrette," and "If it were fully boneless, we'd have put it between two pieces of sandwich bread with a schmear of aioli and a tuft of arugula, and called it a day." And then, one day, the restaurant started serving half-chickens instead, and it wasn't the same, so it was time for me to get it right at home. Because we all need this.

This was also when I remembered that I covered flat-roasted chicken in the last book. With lemon, even! Am I in a rut? And yet this is such an important progression to me. Last time, I channeled the slow-cooked *poulet rôti* in Paris, with potatoes to catch the drippings; but my goal was to make it faster by taking out the backbone. I was always in a rush. Life is busier now than ever, and yet every year I become more incapable of racing through things, or trying to speed up that which does not want to be rushed.

Chicken *al mattone* (a *mattone* is a heavy tile), or chicken under a brick, my inspiration here, originated in Tuscany, and it was always intended for tiny chickens. You don't need to rush them; you celebrate this, and your reward is a better dish, and faster, too. It takes 5 minutes to prepare and cooks in 15 minutes on my stove, which is to say that it's a weeknight dream—and no potatoes needed.

---

2 (1¾-pound or 800-gram) Cornish hens

Salt

Glug of olive oil

1 lemon, ends trimmed, then cut in half

A few sprigs of fresh thyme and/or rosemary

Freshly ground black pepper or red pepper flakes

Chopped fresh parsley

2 bricks wrapped in foil, or a slightly smaller frying pan on which you can stack other heavy objects

Pat the hens dry. Place them breast side down on a cutting board and, using kitchen shears, cut along either side of the backbone of each to remove it. Turn the hens over and open them up. Press each one's breastbone firmly to flatten and open the chicken like a book. (You can also trim off the wingtips if you desire. Save these, and the backbones, for your next chicken soup, page 87, please.)

Pat dry and season extremely well with salt, inside and out. If you can spare the time, leave the bird skin side up for 30 minutes (or up to 1 hour in the fridge) to help it dry more. Heat a large heavy skillet (cast iron is ideal here)

over medium-high heat, and add a glug of olive oil to the pan. Once it's hot, place one chicken skin side down in the pan, arrange a piece of lemon in an empty space right on the frying pan's surface, and place your thyme and/or rosemary on top. Add your heavy weight(s) on top, and let the hen cook until it is a very deep golden brown underneath, 7 to 10 minutes. Don't skimp; don't move it around. The color you get here will carry the whole dish.

When it is bronzed and crispy, flip the hen (tongs make this easier) and the lemon slice, and cook on the second side without the weight for 3 to 5 more minutes, until a thermometer inserted into the deepest part of the breast registers 160 degrees. Repeat with the other hen.

Transfer to a serving platter. Remove the thyme and/or rosemary. Squeeze all over with the charred lemon from the pan, then sprinkle with pepper. Scatter with parsley.

siberian pelmeni

makes about 65 pelmeni, serving 6 to 8

S hortly before my 30th birthday (you know, last week, if anyone is asking), Peter Meehan wrote in *The New York Times* about a Russian dumpling shop in Brighton Beach, using some of my favorite turns of word to this date, such as "as light as carbs wrapped in carbs drenched in melted fat can be." I thought my husband, being Russian, would be up for checking it out, but his reaction was the opposite: Go out to eat dumplings? They're something you keep in the freezer and boil up when nobody wants to make dinner. But I kept at it, ultimately pulling the birthday card, and in the end he concluded that they were indeed the best Russian dumplings he'd ever had. We became, if not regulars, then people who went as often as we could squeeze in a trip, even in the summer months (thanks to its beach proximity). This is where the story should end—have dumpling source, eat dumplings there. But that's not how I roll, is it?

At home, I became obsessed with reverse-engineering them, a little bit for me but a lot for you, because all varieties of Russian dumplings are wonderful things, and I want you to have them. I could never make them as well as the ladies who have been doing it since they lived in the old country, but I was delighted to find that we can manage a pretty good job at home. The ingredients are simple. No pasta machine is required; the dough is a cinch to roll out. They freeze like a dream, so go ahead, take an afternoon and make a massive batch of them, and they'll be ready when you need them. Which, realistically, will be often.

dough

2 cups (260 grams) all-purpose flour, plus more for your work surface

½ teaspoon fine sea or table salt

2 large eggs

4 tablespoons (60 ml) water, plus a teaspoon or two more if needed

filling

½ pound (225 grams) ground meat, such as pork, beef, veal, or chicken (pork and veal are traditional)

1 tablespoon (15 grams) unsalted butter

½ small onion, finely chopped

¼ teaspoon fine sea or table salt

Freshly ground black pepper

to serve

White vinegar

Salt

Freshly ground black pepper

Sour cream (shh)

make the dough Combine the flour and salt in the bottom of a large bowl. Make a well in the middle, and add the eggs and 4 tablespoons water. Break up the eggs with your fingers or a fork, and blend the flour mixture into the wet center until you've formed a shaggy mass. Knead it together a few times inside the bowl to form a rough ball (messy and sticky is fine), and then knead it on the counter for 10 minutes, until it's cohesive and no longer sticky. Place the dough in a lightly floured spot, upend the empty bowl over it, and let it rest for 30 minutes to 2 hours at room temperature.

in the meantime, make the filling Place the meat (or mixture of meats) in the work bowl of a food processor or blender. In a medium sauté pan, heat the butter over medium heat until it's sizzling. Add the onion, and cook, stirring, for 3 to 4 minutes, until it's beginning to brown lightly at the edges. Let it cool for 1 minute off heat, then add it to the work bowl with the salt and pepper to taste. Blend until you can no longer see the coarse bits of onion. Set aside.

assemble Divide the dough and roll half of it on a lightly floured surface as thin as you can get it into a 15-to-16-inch circle—it should roll well and not give you a lot of trouble. (Leave the other half of the dough covered in a bowl.) Cut into 2¼-to-2½-inch rounds. Place ½ teaspoon filling in the middle of each round, and fold the sides together over the filling, creating half-moons. Pinch the corners together to form a napkin shape; then you can bend the round edge out, a bit like a flying saucer. The first will feel awkward; by the tenth, you will be a natural, and, as such, appalled by my suggestion of sour cream above.

Place the formed dumplings on a tray or plate that has been lightly sprinkled with flour. Repeat with the remaining dough and filling. You can cook the dumplings right away, or freeze the tray of dumplings until they are solid and then transfer them to a freezer bag.

cook the pelmeni Bring a large pot of salted water to a boil. Add the dumplings, and cook them until they float, and then 2 to 3 minutes more. (If your dough is thicker, you might need more time to get them tender, but not more than 5 minutes.) Scoop them right from the pot with a slotted spoon, shake off the excess water, and drop into your serving dish. Serve, and pass the vinegar, salt, pepper, and (shh) sour cream. Did I sprinkle chive blossoms all over mine? I regret nothing.

notes

A little Russian-dumpling primer here: Vareniki, those featherweight carbs mentioned above, are most commonly filled with potatoes and sometimes fruit, so they're like pierogi but always seem lighter to me. Pelmeni are almost always filled with meat or fish, and the dough is even thinner; they're usually small—larger than tortellini but smaller than a potsticker. Siberian pelmeni usually contain a mix of beef, veal, and pork, but we've taken some liberties here, and I've even had all-chicken versions that were excellent.

Traditionally, potato vareniki are served with browned or caramelized onions and sour cream, and meat pelmeni are served with vinegar, salt, and black pepper. I have tried to maintain these strict lines and repeatedly failed—in short, I want all of these things on all varieties of dumplings, but mostly the sour cream, so I've included it above. Proceed as you wish. We won't tell my mother-in-law.

The dough is close to an Italian pasta, but not as close as it might seem, with a lower proportion of eggs to the flour and water, yielding a less firm dough; there's nothing al dente here.

Twice-ground meat is not essential, but it is my preferred texture here, because it's more smooth.

crispy short rib carnitas with sunset slaw

makes 8 small tacos, serving 3 or 4

was first introduced to carnitas by my friend Lisa Fain's *Homesick Texan Cookbook,* through a recipe inspired by the great Diana Kennedy. The cooking method, to me, was nothing short of revolutionary. Take a pork shoulder, add a little liquid to a pot, cook it with the lid on for a few hours at a low temperature, until the meat is soft, the fat has rendered out, and the liquid has cooked off, and then crisp the edges of the meat in that fat. It's a shatteringly brilliant way to cook a fatty piece of meat, and from the moment I first made it with pork, I became obsessed with trying the same with one of *my* favorite cuts of meat, short ribs. Shame on me for taking so long to finally make it happen, because shreddingly soft pieces of meat with dark crunchy edges are a rarity to pull off at home, and to do it as easily as this—not one bit of cooking voodoo is required—is a miracle in and of itself. Rather than hovering about the stove for an afternoon, I found that I could tuck the whole thing into the oven and ignore it. It takes a while (you'll need 3 hours—I think we should watch a movie), but you're in for some of the best tacos of your life.

carnitas

2 teaspoons kosher salt

1 teaspoon chile powder, or to taste

3 pounds (1⅓ kilograms) meaty short ribs, with bone

Juice of 1 orange

Juice of 1½ limes;
save the last ½ lime for garnish

5 garlic cloves, unpeeled

sunset slaw

3 cups (190 grams) finely shredded red cabbage
(from about ½ large cabbage)

1 carrot, coarsely grated

Coarse salt

Juice of ½ lime

2 scallions, thinly sliced

Dollop of mayonnaise, sour cream, or plain yogurt

Dash of hot sauce (optional)

¼ cup (10 grams) roughly chopped fresh cilantro
or flat-leaf parsley leaves

to serve

Corn tortillas

Minced white onion or thinly sliced scallions

Chopped fresh cilantro

Pickled jalapeños

Hot sauce

Heat the oven to 275 degrees. Combine the salt and chile powder in a dish. Spread the short ribs out on the butcher paper they came in or on a tray, then rub them all over with the salt mixture. Arrange them in a deep roasting pan (the walls should be higher than the ribs; it doesn't matter which side is down), and pour the orange and lime juice into the bottom. Scatter the garlic cloves throughout. Cover the dish tightly with foil, and slow-bake it for 2 to 2½ hours. The meat should be tender and beginning to separate from the bone but pretty ugly-looking (it's been steam-roasting, after all). Remove the foil, and increase the heat to 425 degrees. Basting the meat with the pan juices once or twice, roast the meat for 15 to 20 more minutes, until the edges are crispy and browned and the residents of your home are pawing at the oven door, asking what time dinner is.

when the ribs are almost done roasting, make the slaw Toss the cabbage, carrot, salt, and lime juice together in a bowl; set aside for 5 minutes, during which the slaw will shrink down a bit and become easier to season. Stir in the scallions, then the mayo and hot sauce (if using). Adjust the seasonings or other ingredients to taste, then stir in the cilantro leaves.

Discard the bones, pick off any large chunks of visible fat, then lightly shred the meat right into a dish, pouring the extra pan juices over it. You can squeeze out the garlic cloves from their skin and keep them on the side for those who want to eat them.

Heat the corn tortillas in a dry skillet for 20 to 30 seconds per side. Pile a small amount of shredded short-rib meat on top, then season with your desired fixings—minced white onion and chopped cilantro are the most traditional, followed by hot sauce or pickled jalapeños. Serve with slaw on the side.

quick sausage, kale, and crouton sauté

makes 2 large or 4 small servings

There's always been a completely pointless divide between people for whom cooking is a bother and people who luxuriate in the kitchen, who find it enjoyable after a long day even to do crazy things like crank out pasta—it's their escape. On one side, there are 18-minute meals, 4-ingredient fixes, ingredient delivery services, and cookbooks devoted to meals you can make with supermarket rotisserie chicken; and on the other is basically every other cookbook, ever. But as for me—and maybe most of you—I'm a cook with no island. I (clearly) love it, but I often need just to get it done. I know that if I'm tired enough I can always order something (a trade-off for living in a crowded space within a bigger crowded space), but what I really want (and, I don't know, doesn't everyone, really?) most days are meals that taste special, that we can eagerly anticipate, but that we can prepare in a reasonable amount of time—i.e., before two hangry children have melted down into the floor and must be stepped over to reach the Microplane grater, or before two hangry adults are snipping at each other because the children need to go to bed soon and nobody has eaten, not that my (clearly) perfect life ever resembles that.

One of my longtime favorites from this never-big-enough category comes from Jacques Pépin, a 6-minute sauté of chorizo, asparagus, almonds, and croutons to which I also add beans. This new recipe is the next chapter. Italian sausages are much easier for us to get, and so is, realistically, kale, especially the washed, trimmed, and ready-for-salad variety. Because we are starting with fresh sausage, it takes longer than 6 minutes but not much. Make this just before you are ready to eat, because it comes together quickly.

Olive oil

2 cups (60 grams) 1-inch cubes of sturdy white bread (such as sourdough, ciabatta)

½ pound (225 grams) fresh sweet Italian sausages, casings removed

1 garlic clove, minced or pressed

¾ cup (200 grams) cooked white beans (about half a 15.5-ounce can)

2 big handfuls (or more, to taste) torn curly kale leaves

Kosher salt and freshly ground black pepper and red pepper flakes, to taste

2 tablespoons (30ml) red wine vinegar

Grated Parmesan (optional)

Heat two glugs of oil in a large heavy skillet over medium-high heat. Add the bread cubes and toast, stirring, until lightly browned and mostly crisp, 3 to 4 minutes. Push the croutons aside and add another glug to the pan, then the garlic and sausage meat. Cook, breaking up sausage into small bits, until browned all over. Add the greens and cook until they begin to wilt, then add the beans and warm through. Season well with salt, black pepper, and red pepper flakes. Add vinegar to the pan and use it to scrape up any stuck bits. Scrape the sauté into bowls, finish with cheese if desired, and inhale.

smoky sheet pan chicken with cauliflower

makes 4 servings

've really gotten into sheet pan cooking in the last couple of years, although I know it sounds ridiculous. I mean, sheet pans? What else would you use those banged-up old things for? But really it's this idea of throwing all your dinner components onto a pan, putting the pan into the oven, and cooking them together until they're done. It shouldn't be a Thing at all, but in these days of chef-driven home cooking, subrecipes, and dinners that use ten bowls, the sheet pan meal is your friend.

Here, I was eager to play off the flavors of a good smoky, salty cured chorizo with chicken, potatoes, cauliflower, green olives, red onion, carrots, and smoked paprika but also bits of chorizo itself. I thought we'd get cute and finish it with some lightly pickled red pepper strips, and maybe dollops of a garlicky aioli. I had *plans*. And then it was actual dinnertime (versus the dinnertime I imagine when I'm on my laptop, typing up recipe ideas), and one by one, elements were axed. Goodbye, carrots! Goodbye, aioli! Goodbye . . . chorizo? Somehow, the central ingredient fell off the list, and we didn't miss it nearly as much as I'd expected. If you have it, about 8 ounces (225 grams), dried, in chunks, definitely brings more of a salty, smoky emphasis to the pan, but if you don't have it or don't eat it, you wouldn't know you were missing anything unless you read this paragraph.

for the chicken

2 tablespoons (30 ml) olive oil

1 tablespoon (15 ml) white wine vinegar

4 garlic cloves, minced

1 tablespoon (10 grams) sweet smoked paprika (you can replace any portion of this with hot paprika if you wish)

1½ teaspoons kosher salt

2 pounds (roughly 1 kilogram) chicken thighs, drumsticks, or halved chicken breasts (all skin-on, bone-in)

for the vegetables

1¼ pounds (565 grams) Yukon Gold potatoes (about 4 medium)

1¾ pounds (795 grams) cauliflower (1 small or ½ very large head)

½ large red onion

⅔ cup (120 grams) green olives, pitted

2 tablespoons (30 ml) olive oil, plus more for the pan(s)

2 teaspoons fresh thyme leaves, minced

Salt and freshly ground black pepper

to finish

A few juliennes of red bell pepper

1 tablespoon (15 ml) white wine vinegar

½ teaspoon kosher salt

Pinches of granulated sugar

2 tablespoons roughly chopped fresh flat-leaf parsley

marinate the chicken Combine the olive oil, vinegar, garlic, paprika, and salt in a bowl. Add the chicken parts, and toss to coat. Set aside to marinate while you prepare your vegetables (or leave it in the fridge for up to 1 day).

assemble the chicken and vegetables When you're ready to cook the dish, heat your oven to 400 degrees and line a half sheet pan (13-by-18-inch) or two quarter sheet pans (9-by-13-inch) with foil and coat with 1 tablespoon olive oil.

Peel your potatoes if you wish, and cut them into approximately ¾-inch chunks. Cut the cauliflower to about 1-inch florets. Cut your onion half into eight thin wedges. Spread the vegetables on the prepared tray(s), and use your hands to toss them with 2 tablespoons olive oil, the thyme, and salt and pepper. (If you'd like to add the chorizo, scatter it over the vegetables now.)

Make spaces throughout the pan of vegetables, and add the chicken pieces, skin side up. Cook for 30 minutes, at which point check the tray and toss the potato and cauliflower to ensure they're cooking evenly, then return the pan to the oven for 10 to 15 minutes more, or until the chicken and vegetables are cooked through.

to finish Toss the pepper strips together with the wine vinegar, salt, and a pinch or two of sugar in a small dish, and set aside until needed.

When the chicken and vegetables are cooked, top with the pepper strips and parsley.

chicken and rice, street cart style

makes 4 servings

Tourists may associate street food in New York City with dirty-water dogs and stale pretzels, but that's not all there is. The best halal street carts prepare chicken-and-rice or lamb-and-rice platters that, in my opinion, are not just a rite of passage, but one of the greatest meals to be had, regardless of price point. This doesn't mean I took quickly to them; I'd always more or less ignored them until about a decade ago, when my daily walk to work up Park Avenue South took me by a Rafiqi's cart each morning, and the aroma wafting off the griddle as the guy prepared for the lunch rush consumed me in a way that made me question everything: "Why can't I have spicy chicken and rice for breakfast instead of this overpriced coffee and mediocre muffin I'm carrying? Would that mean I'm not vegetarian anymore?" I could feel a dozen notions I had unraveling at once.

You're probably expecting me to tell you here that I'd built it up too much, that when I finally tried it, it was just okay. In fact, it was everything. Even now, I can be completely full from a meal and yet get hungry to the point of distraction all over again when that aroma sneaks up on me. Making it at home feels almost heretical: Where's the line and chaos? Where's the clank-clank of the giant spatulas chopping the meat on the griddle? Isn't it much easier to get the level of white sauce on top right (a lot, that is) when someone else is pouring it and you can pretend it was just a moderate dollop? But the truth is, our version might be even better, and since you cannot get it on Seamless anyway, it quickly became one of our favorite weeknight meals (and even more fun to scale up for a dinner party).

---

marinade and chicken

Juice of ½ lemon

2 garlic cloves, minced

1 teaspoon kosher salt

1 teaspoon paprika, sweet, hot or smoked

¾ teaspoon ground coriander

1½ teaspoons ground cumin

Pinch of ground cloves

1 teaspoon dried oregano

2 pounds (roughly 1 kilogram) boneless, skinless chicken thighs (about 6)

1 tablespoon (15 ml) olive oil, plus more to coat the pan

rice

1 tablespoon (15 ml) olive oil

½ teaspoon ground turmeric

¾ teaspoon ground cumin

2 cups (360 grams) basmati or another long-grain white rice

3½ cups (840 ml) chicken stock

1 teaspoon kosher salt

sauce

1 cup minus 2 tablespoons (200 grams) plain yogurt

2 tablespoons (25 grams) mayonnaise

(cont.)

1 tablespoon (15 ml) distilled white vinegar

½ teaspoon granulated sugar

½ teaspoon kosher salt

assembly

½ head iceberg lettuce, chopped

2 medium tomatoes, chopped

½ small white or red onion, chopped

Kosher salt and freshly ground pepper, to taste

1 tablespoon (15 ml) hot sauce

1 tablespoon (15 grams) harissa

1 tablespoon (15 ml) olive oil

Chopped fresh cilantro, for garnish (optional)

3 large pocketless pita breads, toasted, halved

marinate the chicken Combine the ingredients for the marinade, and pour into a large ziplock bag. Add the chicken, seal, and slosh it around so that it coats evenly. Let the chicken marinate in the fridge for 30 minutes or up to 2 days.

cook the chicken Heat a large, deep skillet with a lid over medium-high heat. Coat lightly with olive or vegetable oil. Arrange the cutlets (usually three at a time) in one layer, and do not move them until they're brown and don't want to stick anymore, 5 to 8 minutes. Flip, and brown well on second side, which will take 4 to 5 minutes more. Transfer to a plate. Don't worry if they're not 100 percent cooked through yet; you're mostly prepping them so that when that line of nonpaying customers known as your family appears, you'll be able to finish the meat and have it hot. Repeat with remaining chicken, then wipe out the pan.

make the rice Add 1 tablespoon olive oil to the pan, and heat it, then add the spices and rice and toast together for a minute, stirring. Add the stock and salt, and bring

to a simmer; then reduce the heat to its lowest setting, cover with a lid, and let cook for about 15 minutes, until the water has absorbed and the rice is tender. Let it rest for 3 to 5 minutes off the heat, then scoop onto half of a serving platter.

While the rice cooks, make the sauce, combining all the ingredients in a medium bowl. Adjust seasonings to taste.

Combine the lettuce, tomatoes, and onion in a large bowl to make the salad. Season with salt and pepper. The sauce will be your dressing.

Stir the hot sauce and harissa together to make your hot sauce.

to finish Chop the chicken into bite-sized, uneven pieces. The griddle guys do this with a bench scraper right on the griddle, but you can do it on your cutting board. Reheat the empty pan from the rice over medium-high, add a little olive or another oil, just to coat the pan lightly, and then add the chopped chicken. Cook, stirring and breaking up the meat with spatula into smaller pieces if desired, until it is fully cooked through, 2 to 4 more minutes. Add more salt to season, if desired. Scrape it on top of the rice.

Pile the salad in the remaining part of the platter. Dress the dish with sauce, to taste, and garnish with cilantro. Serve with halved pitas.

notes

If you like your chicken extra-spicy, double up on the hot sauce.

At street carts, you'll be served a lot more rice than you get from this recipe, which is more of a home-cooking proportion. Ditto for the white sauce, so if you're worried you will need more, well, you probably will (heh).

grilled squid with chickpeas, chiles, and lemon

makes 2 large or 4 small servings

M y seafood palate is limited. My husband, always trying to convince me I should eat more than I am naturally inclined to, insisted I try a bit of grilled octopus at a restaurant one night, and I became instantly converted, not just by the meaty flavor of the large legs but by the preparation—charred with lemon, olive oil, olives, and chiles. The next place we tried it, another restaurant, served it on a bed of chickpeas with garlic. This, too, became added to my imaginary grilled seafood dish. However, when I went to get octopus legs to make this recipe, I was faced with the reality that, sure, I can special-order them, but they're hardly the most accessible thing. Almost everywhere I looked, however, I saw ample quantities of squid, defrosted or still frozen. I turned to my go-to on all seafood-cooking matters, my friend Angie Moore, and she said that grilled squid is equally amazing as long as you don't overcook it.

She showed me how she'd seen it prepared in Japan, where cuts are made across the top of the squid, almost as if to Hasselback it. (We did this with kitchen shears.) On the grill, these create extra surfaces to char against the heat, and more opportunities for the squid to absorb the olive oil, salt, pepper, and lemon juice that make it sing. Because Angie is from Texas, she voted for fresh chiles over red pepper flakes, although the ones in my garden were about 1 inch long at the time. Eating it (with sparkling rosé, of course, because when friends come over to cook it's a party) almost makes you feel like you're on a Mediterranean vacation—not bad for about 15 minutes of work on a Tuesday night.

---

1 pound (455 grams) whole squid bodies, cleaned

3 tablespoons (45 ml) olive oil

Salt and freshly ground black pepper

¼ teaspoon finely grated lemon zest

Juice of 1 lemon, divided

1 small garlic clove, minced

5 firm green olives, pitted and finely chopped

2 teaspoons minced fresh red chile pepper, or more to taste, or a few pinches of dried red pepper flakes

1¾ cups (from a 15.5-ounce or 440-gram can) canned or cooked chickpeas, drained and rinsed

Chopped fresh parsley, to finish

Extra lemon wedges, for serving

Spread the cleaned squid out on a layer of paper towels, and cover it with another paper towel to dry the surface as much as possible.

In the bottom of a medium bowl, whisk 2 tablespoons olive oil, salt and pepper, the lemon zest, half the lemon juice, the garlic, olives, and chiles together. Add the chickpeas, and toss to coat. Adjust seasonings to taste, then spill out the mixture onto a small platter.

Light a charcoal grill, or turn a gas grill to the highest temperature. Give it 5 minutes to get very hot.

Your squid will naturally want to flatten in one direction; press it the opposite way (i.e., squeeze the sides so it's vertically flat), and use kitchen shears or a knife to make cuts halfway (i.e., rings will stay connected) into each squid ¼ to ½ inch apart. After you cut it, it should return to its original shape. Toss the squid with 1 tablespoon olive oil, plus salt and freshly ground black pepper to coat. Oil your grill, then place the squid on it, with the intact side down, for 2 to 4 minutes, until it's lightly charred but not rubbery—the latter is more important than grill marks. Flip the squid so that the rings are perpendicular to the grill lines (i.e., unlikely to get caught in them), and grill for another 2 to 4 minutes, again until lightly charred.

Transfer the squid to the platter with the chickpeas. Finish with the remaining lemon juice and scatter with chopped parsley. Serve with extra lemon wedges.

note Pictured here is ½ pound squid with all of the chickpea salad. To get this balance, you should double the chickpeas called for in the recipe. For more of a grilled-fish-with-a-chickpea-side dinner balance, use the recipe as written here.

meatballs marsala with egg noodles and chives

makes 4 servings

A funny thing happens when you have a reputation for being a person who knows her way around the kitchen, which is that you get asked more often than most people what your desert-island foods would be, and they're hoping you're going to say something awesome. I try not to disappoint. I talk about duck fat fries or a perfect steamed artichoke with a lemon-aioli dip, or hanger steak, served with salsa verde. Do know that if a desert island—or even, perhaps, this densely populated island on which I actually reside—contained these three foods, I would never leave.

What is actually closer to the truth, though, is buttered egg noodles, the really wide ones. I like egg noodles that are like pages, harder to separate when they so naturally want to stack; there is no spearing fewer than four noodles at once. I like them with not an avalanche of butter or anything, but enough so you might have a little runoff puddle at the bottom of the bowl for that last, lucky noodle, then finished with a shower of chives. But I rarely tell people this, because it's turned out to be a total conversation thudder. You cannot explain the bliss of buttered egg noodles to people who do not derive bliss from buttered egg noodles. Not all beloved things elicit, or need to elicit, popular fervor.

Bear with me here. These are not just buttered noodles, but what happened when I was dreaming about Swedish meatballs but wanted something a little different: First, a chicken meatball, because ground chicken gets no love, but I think it can be wonderfully light. I wanted the sauce to be flavored with dry Marsala, because I think more things should be. And although I love a good mash, with pickles and lingonberry jam, my first love, those wide noodles, called to me, and I ended up making a kind of Central European meatballs and spaghetti. Nobody needs to be talked into this kind of bliss.

meatballs

1 pound (455 grams) ground chicken

2 tablespoons (30 ml) olive oil

2 tablespoons (30 grams) unsalted butter

1 small yellow onion, minced

1 teaspoon kosher salt, plus more for the onion

½ cup (30 grams) panko breadcrumbs

1 large egg

¼ cup (60 ml) milk or water

Freshly ground black pepper

sauce

¼ cup (60 ml) dry Marsala, sherry, or Madeira

3 tablespoons (45 grams) unsalted butter

3 tablespoons (25 grams) all-purpose flour

1¾ cups (420 ml) chicken stock or broth

¼ cup (60 ml) heavy cream

Salt and freshly ground black pepper

assembly

12 ounces (340 grams) wide egg noodles

1 tablespoon (15 grams) butter

4 teaspoons minced fresh chives

make the meatballs Place the chicken in a large bowl. Heat a large heavy sauté pan over medium heat. Once it's very hot, add half the olive oil and butter, and once they are also very hot, add the onion and a pinch or two of salt. Cook, stirring, until the onion is a deep golden brown, 5 to 7 minutes. Cool slightly, then add to the bowl with the chicken, along with the panko, egg, milk or water, 1 teaspoon salt, and many grinds of black pepper. Stir to combine evenly (I use a fork).

Scoop up about 2 tablespoons of the meatball mixture at a time, and then roll back and forth briefly in your wet palms to form a smoother spherical shape. Arrange on a plate. Repeat with the remaining meat mixture.

Add the remaining butter and oil to your frying pan over medium heat. Arrange the meatballs in one layer. They will seem very soft and you'll worry that this isn't going to work, but as soon as they've cooked for a couple minutes they will begin to hold together better. Don't move them until they're browned underneath, then nudge and roll them around the pan until they're as evenly brown all over as possible. Remove the meatballs with a slotted spoon, and drain on paper towels.

make the sauce Pour in the Marsala, and simmer until it's almost completely cooked off, scraping up any browned bits that have stuck to the pan. Add the butter to the pan and let it melt, then whisk in the flour; cook the mixture, stirring, for 1 minute. Slowly add the broth, whisking the whole time. Add the cream, and bring the mixture to a simmer, then add salt and pepper to taste. Return the meatballs to the pan, turn to coat them in the sauce, reduce the heat to medium-low, and cover; let them simmer in the sauce for 10 minutes. Check a meatball; they should be cooked through, but if not, give them a couple more minutes.

meanwhile, cook the noodles Bring a large pot of salted water to a boil, and cook the noodles according to package directions, although please check early anyway, because many seem to advocate way too much cooking time; I find 6 to 8 minutes is usually right. Drain.

to finish Place the noodles in a bowl and toss with butter. Add meatballs and pan gravy on top. Garnish with chives.

beefsteak skirt steak salad with blue cheese and parsley basil vinaigrette

makes 4 servings

If steak salads may have gone out of style with the other nineties staples—grunge, Doc Martens, baby-doll dresses, and overalls—forgive me as I welcome their return with far more anticipation. Around here, though, we never got the memo anyway, because there are so many great things about them: they're naturally gluten- and bread-free, which means at least 50 percent more people I know at any given time can have them to eat; a single steak can be stretched to feed four people; you can use pretty much any great vegetables you have around, and if you're one of those people (well, me) who are more Team Chimichurri than Team Béarnaise in steak sauces—that is, you prefer herby, bright finishes to richer ones—the vinaigrette will be your not-so-secret favorite part.

This is the skirt-steak salad to eat as long as the tomatoes last. These days, we're all about the marble-sized rainbow tomatoes—me, too, in my balcony garden—but, when I was growing up in New Jersey, my garden tomato choices were plum or beefsteak. Plum were for sauces; beefsteak, often clocking in at nearly 1 pound each, were for everything else: thick slices on burgers and sandwiches and, if you were being fancy, stacked salads. Here, I like to celebrate the beefsteak tomato's heftiness, not hide it, by matching it up with slices of steak. The blue-cheese crumbles—which, really, are more like boulders—are not optional around here, but you could use a salty feta or soft chèvre. The parsley-basil pesto vinaigrette is the happiest lightweight complement; the salad wouldn't be right without it.

vinaigrette

1 large or 2 small garlic cloves

1½ cups (55 grams) packed coarsely chopped fresh basil leaves

½ cup (20 grams) packed fresh flat-leaf parsley leaves

⅓ cup (80 ml) olive oil

1 tablespoon (15 ml) plus 1 teaspoon (5 ml) white wine vinegar

2 teaspoons (10 grams) smooth Dijon mustard

Salt and freshly ground black pepper

Pinches of crushed red pepper flakes, to taste

salad and assembly

2 to 3 cups (40 to 60 grams) mixed salad greens (optional)

1½ pounds (680 grams) beefsteak tomatoes, in thick half-moon slices

½ cup (4 ounces or 115 grams) thickly crumbled blue cheese

½ medium red onion, very thinly sliced

1 pound (455 grams) skirt steak, trimmed of excess fat if necessary, at room temperature

1 tablespoon (15 ml) olive oil

make the dressing In a blender or food processor, pulse the garlic, basil, and parsley together until they're chopped as finely as you can get them. With the machine running, drizzle in the olive oil, then the vinegar and mustard, scraping down the sides as needed. Season with salt, black pepper, and red pepper flakes to taste.

No machine? Mince the garlic and herbs as finely as you can with a knife, transfer them to a bowl, and, whisking the whole time, slowly drizzle in the olive oil and vinegar before seasoning with salt and peppers.

make the salad If using salad greens, place them first on a platter. Arrange the tomatoes on top, fanned out and slightly overlapped. Scatter half of the blue cheese and onion over the tomatoes.

Pat the steak dry, and season on both sides with ½ teaspoon salt and many grinds of black pepper.

to cook the steak on the stove Heat your largest, heaviest skillet over medium-high to high heat, and add 1 table-spoon olive oil. When the oil is very hot, place the steak in the skillet, and do not move it for 5 minutes. Turn it once, and cook for another 3 minutes for medium-rare. If your steak is larger than your biggest skillet, cut it in half and cook it in two pieces.

to cook the steak on a grill Prepare a hot charcoal or high-heat gas grill for cooking. Lightly oil the grill rack, and grill the steak, turning once, 4 to 6 minutes for medium-rare. If you're using a gas grill, it's best to keep the lid on while grilling, to prevent heat loss.

to finish Transfer the steak to a cutting board, and cover it loosely with foil while it rests for 5 minutes. Thinly slice the steak on the diagonal, across the grain, and arrange over the tomatoes. Scatter with the remaining blue cheese and onion. Drizzle vinaigrette on top, or serve it on the side.

pork tenderloin *agrodolce* with squash rings

2 to 4 servings (this doubles easily for a crowd)

My husband and I endlessly disagree on the presence of sweet ingredients in savory dishes. He: Nope! Me: You're wrong. In case you can't tell, we've been married for some time now. He thinks sweet things—apricots with chicken, cherries with duck, prunes anywhere—ruin a dish. I argue that if the sweetness was too far forward the dish wasn't made well. A dish that is sweet before it is savory tastes, to me, like dessert; a dish with some sweetness behind a front of sour and salty nuance is delightful, I think: barbecue sauce, spareribs, the ripeness of summer tomatoes in a fresh marinara sauce—and the sweet-sour delight that is Sicilian *agrodolce*.

As with many Italian dishes, there is disagreement on the one correct way to make it. It's not uncommon to see versions made with balsamic vinegar, tomato sauce, and garlic; but most versions are a little more straightforward—just olive oil, a wine vinegar, and sugar. You can evoke so much flavor from these three things that there's little reason to add clutter. Red onions slowly cooked *agro-dolce* are as common as the sauce itself, for good reason. Against naturally sweet vegetables like winter squash, the sauce is piquant; and with pork, a meat as commonly served with a faintly sweet sauce (my favorite) as it is with pickled hot peppers (my husband's favorite), it's both at once. Pork tenderloin seems to go in and out of style, but around here it's a mainstay. It feels fancy—because of that and since this doubles easily, it makes a great fall dinner-party dish—but it also comes in sizes perfect for a small family, is ready in less than 30 minutes, and picks up any sauce you lay on it really well.

sauce

2 tablespoons (30 ml) olive oil

1 small red onion, thinly sliced

¼ teaspoon kosher salt

2 teaspoons (10 grams) tomato paste

2 tablespoons (25 grams) granulated sugar

½ cup (120 ml) red wine vinegar

squash

One 2-pound (about 1-kilogram) delicata or acorn squash

1 tablespoon (15 ml) olive oil

Salt and freshly ground black pepper

tenderloin

1 teaspoon fennel seeds, crushed with mortar and pestle

2 teaspoons finely chopped fresh rosemary

¾ teaspoon kosher salt

Freshly ground black pepper

One 1-to-1¼-pound (455-to-565-gram) pork tenderloin

1 tablespoon (15 ml) olive oil

Heat the oven to 425 degrees.

make the sauce Heat the olive oil in a large skillet over medium heat. Add the onion and salt, and cook, stirring frequently, until the onion is softened and beginning to brown, about 10 minutes. Add the tomato paste, and stir to combine, then add the sugar and vinegar. Bring to a simmer, then reduce the heat to medium-low, and cook until slightly syrupy but still loose enough that there is a small puddle around the onion, 5 to 7 more minutes. Remove from the heat and set aside.

make the squash Cut the ends off the squash and scrape out the seeds with a spoon. Slice the squash into ½-inch rings. Coat a baking sheet with olive oil. Spread the squash rings on the baking sheet in one layer, and sprinkle with salt and pepper. Roast for about 30 minutes, until bronzed underneath, then flip and roast for another 10 minutes, until browned at the edges and tender in the center.

meanwhile, prepare the pork tenderloin Combine the fennel, rosemary, ¾ teaspoon salt, and a generous amount of black pepper. Pat the tenderloin dry, then rub the spice mixture onto all sides. Heat a large ovenproof skillet over medium-high heat, and add 1 tablespoon olive oil. When the oil is hot, add the pork, and sear the tenderloin until it is brown on all sides. Brush some of the liquid from the onion pan all over the tenderloin before transferring the skillet to the oven. Roast for 10 to 15 minutes, or until the internal temperature of the meat reaches 145 degrees or the juices run clean when pricked with the tip of a knife. Let it rest on a cutting board for 5 minutes before thinly slicing.

to serve Pile the squash rings on a platter, and drape them with three-quarters of the onion and the sauce. Top with sliced pork tenderloin, and add the remaining onion mixture on top to finish.

sizzling beef bulgogi tacos

makes 8 small tacos, serving 3 or 4

When the city gets as hot as it inevitably does each summer, I cannot bear the idea of being anywhere but neck-deep in the ocean. Alas, we haven't yet shaken enough coins out of the sofa cushions to summer-as-a-verb in the Hamptons, on Fire Island, or even in Greenport, so instead we head to Asbury Park, like the Jersey kids that we will forever be. Plus, there's a lot about it that I secretly love: the fact that neither Bon Jovi nor Bruce Springsteen ever went out of style, a dilapidated boardwalk, a vague run-down carnival town vibe, and inexplicably annoyed lifeguards. But if I told you those were the reasons we went there almost every weekend, I'd be lying—it's actually the fact that there are Korean fusion tacos at the boardwalk.

For four summers, we've been obsessed to the point of annoying everyone we know with our gushing over the stand, which goes by the name MOGO. There are the shrimp tacos with a crunchy cucumber salad, the crispy tofu with the soy-sesame slaw, and the marinated pulled pork with a citrus-mayo slaw. But the one I pine for long after beach season is over is always the beef bulgogi, which has all of the deliciousness you'd expect from something that translates as "fire meat" and replaces the thinly sliced short ribs you'd grill at your table in Flushing with ground beef, shoved in a soft flour tortilla.

It was a glorious not-yet-summer day when I realized I could easily replicate these at home. As in, it takes 30 minutes, from beginning to end. As in, 10 minutes on the stove. As in, even if you let everyone assemble their own, you still only have four things to bring to the table. Every one of these numbers counts almost as much as the all of I-can't-admit-it minutes it takes for us to inhale these, and then plot how long we must wait to make them again.

filling

1 pound (455 grams) ground beef

1 large garlic clove, minced

One 1-to-2-inch-piece fresh ginger, minced

¼ cup (60 ml) low-sodium soy sauce

3 tablespoons (45 ml) rice vinegar

2 tablespoons (25 grams) brown sugar

1 tablespoon (15 ml) Asian toasted sesame oil

Red pepper flakes, gochujang, or sriracha

to serve

2 cups thinly sliced iceberg lettuce

1 tablespoon (15 ml) lime juice
plus extra lime wedges for serving

1½ tablespoon (10 ml) toasted sesame oil

Salt

1 scallion, thinly sliced

8 small flour tortillas

Diced tomatoes

Prepared kimchi

Chopped fresh cilantro

Toasted sesame seeds

prepare the filling Heat a large skillet over medium-high heat. Once it is hot, add the ground beef and use a spoon or spatula to break it up, cooking the beef until browned, 7 to 10 minutes. Drain any excess grease that has collected. Add the garlic, ginger, soy sauce, rice vinegar, brown sugar, and sesame oil to the pan and let simmer, stirring, for 2 minutes. Add red pepper flakes, gochujang, or sriracha to taste.

Toss the lettuce, lime juice, sesame oil, and scallions in a medium bowl to evenly coat. Season to taste with salt.

assemble the tacos Warm the flour tortillas individually in a dry skillet, lightly blistering them. Scoop the beef onto each tortilla with a slotted spoon, draining any excess juices as you do. Garnish with the salad mixture, tomatoes, kimchi, cilantro, and toasted sesame seeds.

note These are equally wonderful in lettuce cups. Boston and Bibb lettuce are my favorites. If you're using lettuce cups, skip the lettuce in the salad.

miso maple ribs with roasted scallions

makes 4 to 6 servings

Remember the first time you added a pinch of espresso to dark chocolate and realized that they are exquisite together, and then proceeded to combine chocolate and coffee in every possible way you could find for a good few years, until you moved on to the next thing, maybe chile powder in chocolate or Earl Grey steeped in chocolate? No? Just me? I do this a lot. For a few years, I found it impossible to make a peach dessert without bourbon, because they were so lovely together. In another phase, it was brown butter and toasted nuts in cookies and cakes. The last book's honey-harissa farro salad came at the end of a long period of applying this combination as often as I could to everything I could (sorry about your carrot baby food, kid). I've been kicking the miso-maple combination around in my mind for just as long, since I saw a *Top Chef* contestant brush it thickly over bacon, to the judges' nonstop gushing.

At home, I liked it okay on bacon, but we liked it even more on a rack of baby back ribs. I make ribs in the oven; at first I did it as a compromise I didn't choose, because my East Village balcony is decidedly lacking in a smoker, but over time I've come to admit that even if I had one I don't think I'd bother, when the ribs are so low-maintenance and perfectly cooked, every time, from the oven. As a thin wash (at first) and a thick burnished glaze (at the end), the salty umami flavor of the miso against the cool sweetness of maple makes for an unforgettable combination. We don't just wait for summer; we make these ribs all year round.

---

2 racks of baby back ribs (around 2 pounds or 1 kilogram each)

½ cup (145 grams) white (shiro) miso

½ cup (120 ml) maple syrup

½ cup (120 ml) rice vinegar

Salt and freshly ground black pepper

2 bunches (about 4 ounces or 115 grams each) of scallions, trimmed

1 glug of a high-smoke-point cooking oil, such as peanut or sunflower

Heat the oven to 300 degrees. If you have them, place one baking or cooling rack on each of two large baking sheets. If you don't, you'll still be fine, but the racks help the heat to circulate. Place each rack of ribs on a very large (oversized width, if you have it) sheet of aluminum foil.

Combine the miso, maple, and vinegar in a small saucepan, but don't cook it yet. Brush about ½ cup of the mixture over both sides of the ribs, then season them well with salt and pepper. Seal each rack of ribs in its own packet, tightly. Transfer to the prepared racks or trays. Bake for 2½ hours, until tender.

At some point in the baking time, bring the ingredients left in the saucepan to a boil, then simmer over medium-low heat until thick and glossy; this takes 20 to 25 minutes. Stir frequently, and then constantly near the end, because it will be the most likely to burn when it is thickest.

When the ribs are done, arrange them in one layer on a large, foil-lined baking sheet. Heat the broiler. Thickly brush the sauce over the ribs, including on the edges, then flip the rib rack over and coat the second side. Arrange the scallions around the ribs on the sheet, and drizzle them very lightly with cooking oil. Run them under the broiler until charred, about 5 minutes, keeping a close watch on them so that they do not burn.

Remove the ribs from the oven to a cutting board, and slice between the ribs to separate. Arrange on a serving platter with the scallions, and pass them around.

notes

White (shiro) miso is the least salty and intense; the darker the color, the more salty it is. The recipe will work with other types of miso, but it might be saltier. If you only have a darker miso, you might try using a little less.

Conversely, ½ cup maple syrup makes for a sweetish barbecue sauce; 6 tablespoons will give you a more salt-forward sauce.

bacony baked pintos with the works

makes 6 servings

I totally get why the prospect of beans for dinner is a hard sell. Even if they weren't the source of endless jokes, they'd still have to live down their culinary reputation as something that takes "forever" to cook, and then, when they're done, they still need to be made into something else like soup or a stew or a mash to line tacos or a sweet and smoky side to barbecue. But I think a world in which we have a trick or two for turning a few cans or a bag of dried beans (still only $2, even in Manhattan) into a solid and satisfying dinner would be a better place, and this recipe is mine: pink, anonymous-seeming beans, baked with spices and served with all the fixings worth eating, eaten with our hands.

This meal is *fun*. The bacon assuages any meat-free-meal skeptics, but anyone who doesn't eat meat can recognize its superfluousness here; it imparts a sweet smoky flavor, but there are so many tastes that if you were to skip it, you wouldn't know it was gone. The fixings make it busy: a little kicky relish, juicy tomatoes, buttery avocado, a dollop of sour cream, extra lime and hot sauce for those who cannot get enough, and a great heap of oven-baked tortilla chips. You don't need to share a table with an opinionated 7-year-old to know that dinners that are scooped up with chips are 100 percent more fun than those that are not.

beans

1 pound (455 grams) dried pinto beans (pink beans)
or four 15-ounce cans cooked pinto beans

¼ pound (115 grams) bacon, chopped

1 medium yellow onion, chopped

3 garlic cloves, peeled and minced

2 tablespoons (35 grams) tomato paste

2 teaspoons ground cumin

½ teaspoon ground coriander

2 teaspoons chili powder (the spice blend)

½ teaspoon cayenne, or shakes of your favorite hot sauce or chipotle purée to taste

2 teaspoons coarse sea or kosher salt
(for lightly salted broth; use more for unsalted broth, and less for salted or canned beans)

4 cups (945 ml) vegetable broth (for dried beans)
plus 1 cup (235 ml) water (if beans weren't presoaked),
or 1½ cups (355 ml) vegetable broth (for precooked/canned beans)

fixings

Soft corn tortillas for tortilla chips
(estimate 2 tortillas per person)

Fine salt, to taste

½ medium-large white onion, minced

1 jalapeño, seeded and minced

2 tablespoons finely chopped fresh cilantro

1 tablespoon (15 ml) olive oil

Juice of ½ lime, plus more lime wedges

1 large avocado, diced or sliced

1 cup chopped fresh tomatoes

Sour cream, Mexican crema, or plain yogurt

Hot sauce

soak dried beans Do you have to soak beans before you cook them? No, nope. But it will save a lot of cooking time, making this more of a 1-hour weeknight meal. So, if you can plan ahead, soak the pintos in an ample amount of water at room temperature for 24 hours. Don't have 24 hours? I soaked mine for 3. Using canned beans? Skip this step entirely.

prepare your beans Heat the oven to 375 degrees. Put the bacon in a large ovenproof pot or Dutch oven or a deep sauté pan, and place over medium heat. Cook, stirring, until the bacon is brown and crisp and the fat has rendered out, 5 to 7 minutes. Scoop the bacon bits onto paper towels to drain, spooning off all but 2 tablespoons bacon fat. Add the onion to the pan and cook (still over medium) until soft and lightly golden at the edges, 3 to 4 minutes. Add the garlic and cook for 1 minute more. Add the tomato paste, spices, and cayenne or chipotle, and cook for 1 minute. Add the salt and the canned or drained soaked beans. Then:

- For precooked or canned beans, add 1½ cups broth.
- For soaked dried beans, add 4 cups broth.
- For unsoaked dried beans, add 4 cups broth and 1 cup water to start.

Bring the mixture to a boil and cook for 1 full minute. Place a lid on the pot and transfer it carefully to the oven.

bake your beans Please keep in mind that cooking beans isn't a perfect science, and the amount of liquid absorbed if the beans are presoaked, the age and freshness of the beans, and even the softness of beans from a can are all going to affect how much cooking time and liquid are needed. But these estimates are fairly solid in my experience.

- Already cooked or canned beans: Bake for 15 minutes.
- Soaked dried beans: Bake for 45 minutes (estimate for 24 hours or longer soaking) to 75 minutes (estimate for 2 to 3 hours soaking).
- Dried beans that have not been soaked: Bake for 1 hour 30 minutes, but after 50 minutes, start checking every 10 to 15 minutes to see if more liquid or cooking time will be needed.

The beans are done when they're firm-tender and moist, with most of the liquid absorbed.

about 30 minutes before the beans are done, bake the chips Brush the tortillas lightly with oil. Stack them and cut into 8 wedges. Spread the wedges in one snug layer on a large baking sheet or two (because the beans are baking, you may need to do this in two batches). Season lightly with fine salt. Bake for 10 minutes, check for color, and then add more baking time as needed until they're golden and crisp. Let them cool.

make the relish Combine the onion, jalapeño, and cilantro with the olive oil and lime juice. Season with salt to taste. This is easily tweaked with more of any of the three ingredients to your taste.

to serve Beans are served right in their cooking pan. Chips and each fixing go in their own bowls. Everyone assembles their bowls to their taste, and everyone wins.

sweets

cookies

two thick, chewy oatmeal raisin chocolate chip mega-cookies

makes 2 large cookies

This is our house cookie, but it goes much further back, to the house I grew up in. My mother made oatmeal cookies with raisins in them, the way the Quaker Oats canister told you to, and we were perfectly happy with them until we learned that my best friend across the street's mom made them with raisins *and* chocolate chips. This pretty much blew my mind. You didn't have to choose between oatmeal and chocolate-chip cookies?

I realize that to most people the logical intersection of these two cookies would actually be an oat cookie with only chocolate, no raisins, but I implore you to use them both. Together, the dried fruit bits give an essential tangy accent to the flooded pockets of melted chocolate. If you've ever had a Cadbury Fruit & Nut chocolate bar, you'll understand. Formatted with dark-brown sugar, sea salt, only a tiny bit of cinnamon, and vanilla extract, this cookie is everything I have ever wanted in a cookie, and though it is not "healthy" (please), the fact that there are more oats than butter, flour, or sugar mostly convinces us we can make these cookies more often.

So what happened here? I made the "accidental" (read: I was tired of scooping cookies and threw the rest down in one massive blob) discovery that these are even more amazing in an unnaturally large format. More crunch at the edges, more thick chewiness throughout. Because an entire batch of massive cookies would be unsafe around me, I trimmed the recipe down until it only made two, which means you can indulge when the craving strikes and then move on. Well, that is presuming you share the second cookie. I trust you'll do the right thing.

---

2 tablespoons (30 grams) unsalted butter, melted

3 tablespoons (35 grams) packed light-brown sugar

1 large egg yolk

¼ teaspoon vanilla extract

3 tablespoons (25 grams) all-purpose flour

Heaped ⅛ teaspoon baking soda

A pinch of ground cinnamon

2 pinches of sea salt

½ cup (40 grams) rolled oats

3 tablespoons (30 grams) chocolate chips

2 tablespoons (20 grams) raisins

Heat the oven to 350 degrees, and line a small baking sheet with parchment paper.

In a bowl, combine the butter, sugar, egg yolk, vanilla, flour, baking soda, cinnamon, and salt. Stir in the oats, chocolate chips, and raisins. Divide the dough into two big mounds, and bake for 15 to 17 minutes, until quite golden brown on top but—don't worry—still soft and chewy inside. Let the cookies cool on a tray for 5 minutes, then transfer to a nearby mouth.

strawberry cloud cookies

makes 14 to 16 cookies

Y ou remember when you were a kid and you got your best ideas at breakfast, sitting at the kitchen table, chomping through a bowl of something crunchy in milk, reading whatever wonders were splashed across the back of the cereal box? And then you became an adult, and you traded cereals for yogurt, muesli, and green smoothies, and back-of-the-box games for depressing news headlines scrolling through on your phone? One summer, we rented a beach house with friends who got us started on a certain boxed cereal with dried strawberries throughout. We tried to shake the habit when we got home but could not, which led to a few months of feeling like kids again, thoughts drifting off as we chomped away, except that, being me, I couldn't stop thinking about freeze-dried strawberries.

What were these things? Surely, total garbage riddled with artificial color and flavorings, probably not even strawberries, and best not considered too long. Surely, they weren't the kind of thing available to a normal grocery shopper, who could buy actual fresh strawberries in Aisle 1. Instead, I learned that they contained a single ingredient (strawberries) and were readily available at many big stores; from that point on, I couldn't stop grinding them into the most fragrant pink powder and working them into everything.

Our hands-down favorite experiment resulted in crisp-exteriored, marshmallow-interiored pink cookies my son calls "clouds." Hear me out. Meringues are generally way too sweet, and there's not much you can do about this; you cannot reduce the sugar without compromising the structure. In fact, their structure can be so persnickety that cream of tartar, an acid, is usually added to help them keep their height. Berries may do an exceptional job of balancing out sweetness, but you cannot just add fresh fruit to meringues without having them fall to mush, because liquid pretty much makes meringue dissolve. Enter strawberry dust for the fruit, and lemon juice for the acid. The resulting cookies are as tart as they are sweet, which alone is something of a meringue miracle. They're unquestionably—not artificially—strawberry-ish, and yet still remind us of grown-up cotton candy, of strawberry lemonade, of pink-tinged clouds at sunset. We get carried away with them, and I hope you do, too.

⅔ cup (135 grams) granulated sugar

¼ teaspoon fine sea salt

2 tablespoons (15 grams) strawberry powder from freeze-dried strawberries ground into a powder

2 large egg whites, at room temperature

1 teaspoon (5 ml) lemon juice

Heat the oven to 300 degrees. Line a baking sheet with parchment paper or a nonstick baking mat.

Stir the sugar, salt, and strawberry powder together in a small dish. In a large bowl, beat the egg whites until they're thick and hold soft peaks. Add the strawberry-sugar mixture gradually, beating the whole time. Continue to beat until the batter is stiff, then mix in the lemon juice. Spoon the batter onto the prepared baking sheets. Bake for 30 to 35 minutes, until they feel slightly dry to the touch and are no darker than a golden color underneath or at the edges. Let them cool on the baking sheets for 10 to 15 minutes, so that they're a little easier to remove.

double coconut meltaways

makes 24 (1¼-inch round) cookies

I have been told that I have old-lady taste in cookies, which I of course take as a compliment. I will never turn down a marshmallow-stuffed, salted-caramel-dolloped, peanut-butter-cup-crushed cookie hybrid, but I have a very serious soft spot for the plainest, most tender cookies; I love short-bread and meltaways, and those ground-nut cookies that I've seen called everything from "Russian tea cakes" to "Mexican wedding cakes" to "butter balls" and, when pressed into half-moons, "walnut crescents."

In this case, an excess of coconut chips led me to a mildly coconut-flavored butter cookie that was easy to like, but when I replaced the butter with coconut oil, it got even better, with a coconut intensity that won't scare away the people put off by the scratchiness of the flaked stuff. Add some lime zest for a more tropical vibe; add some vanilla bean seeds to make your kitchen smell like heaven on earth, as far as I'm concerned.

¾ cup (60 grams) dried unsweetened coconut (in large or medium flakes)

1½ cups (195 grams) all-purpose flour

½ teaspoon kosher salt

6 tablespoons (45 grams) powdered sugar, for cookie dough, plus 1¼ cups (150 grams) sifted, to finish

¾ cup (170 grams) virgin coconut oil, firm (not melted)

½ teaspoon vanilla extract

in a food processor Blend together the coconut flakes, flour, and salt until the coconut is finely ground. Add the 6 tablespoons powdered sugar, and blend again. Add the coconut oil and vanilla, and run the machine until the mixture balls together.

without a food processor You'll want to start with ½ cup (40 grams) finely ground coconut or coconut flour and stir it together with the flour and salt. Beat the coconut oil with the 6 tablespoons powdered sugar and vanilla. Stir in the dry mixture until just combined.

both methods Should the dough seem too soft to scoop and hold a shape, transfer to the fridge for 5 to 10 minutes.

Heat the oven to 350 degrees. Line two baking sheets with parchment paper.

Scoop the dough into 1-tablespoon-sized balls (I use a #70 scoop and then roll them in my palms briefly), and arrange on the prepared baking sheets an inch or so apart. Then transfer the trays to the freezer until the dough is firm to the touch, about 10 minutes. Bake for 15 to 16 minutes, until the cookies are golden brown underneath and relatively pale on top, but dry to the touch. Let them cool on the baking sheets just until you can pick them up; then, while they're still quite warm, roll them in the 1¼ cups sifted powdered sugar. Let cool completely on racks. I like to refresh the finish with powdered sugar—either roll the cookies one more time in it, or sprinkle it over the tops, once the cookies are cool.

The cookies keep in an airtight container at room temperature for up to 2 weeks.

olive oil shortbread with rosemary and chocolate chunks

makes about 2 dozen cookies

The landscape of butter-free cookies is usually filled with stories of compromise. Whether you're kosher and need pareve desserts, allergic to dairy, or vegan, the usual butter substitutes of margarine or shortening are rather grim; most are devoid of flavor by design. But I don't have the patience to do things without intention, and when I decided I wanted to make a butterless shortbread, I wanted it to be a shortbread that might taste even better without butter because it celebrated its fat, rather than apologizing for it.

Growing up, I always thought rosemary tasted like pine needles and didn't understand what everyone else saw in it. A trip to Italy fixed that: rosemary crisped in olive oil and sprinkled with sea salt is now one of my favorite flavors, and I've used it to convert many a rosemary skeptic since. Chocolate and olive oil is a less popular combination, but I love the rich earthiness olive oil imparts to it.

1½ cups (195 grams) all-purpose flour

½ cup (60 grams) powdered sugar

2 tablespoons (25 grams), plus 1 teaspoon (5 grams) raw (turbinado) sugar

½ teaspoon fine sea salt

½ cup (120 ml) mild olive oil

1 teaspoon finely minced fresh rosemary leaves

½ cup (85 grams) semisweet chocolate, chopped into small dice

1 egg white, beaten until loose (optional)

Heat the oven to 325 degrees.

In a large bowl, whisk together the flour, powdered sugar, 2 tablespoons turbinado sugar, and salt. Add the olive oil and rosemary, and stir to combine. Add the chocolate chunks and stir again. Gather the dough with your hands into one mass.

Roll out the dough to an 8- to 9-inch roundish slab between two sheets of parchment paper. Remove the top sheet and use the bottom to slide the cookie round onto the back of a large baking sheet.

If desired—it merely provides a little shine—brush the cookie with the egg white. Sprinkle with remaining 1 teaspoon coarse sugar.

Bake for 20 to 25 minutes. Slide the cookie round carefully onto a cutting board while the cookie is still totally hot. Cut with a sharp, thin knife into desired shape(s). Cool completely, then separate.

do ahead This dough keeps well in the freezer. Baked cookies keep for 2 weeks in an airtight tin at room temperature.

note For a milder flavor, replace half of the oil with a neutral/flavorless one. You can cut this into shapes with cookie cutters, too, but the chocolate provides a little resistance.

pretzel linzers with salted caramel

makes 2 dozen linzer sandwiches

One of my favorite things about these cookies—besides, obviously, that they're both pretzels and salted-butter caramel, and thus they're vying at a nerdy-kid-in-the-front-row-with-their-arm-up-hoping-the-teacher-will-pick-them-first level of trying to be your new favorite thing—is that they accumulate many bits and pieces I've picked up over the last decade-plus. Ground nuts in recipes can often be replaced with ground other things—here, salty pretzels. And though jam is great, a soft, salted caramel is even more fun. If you use a food processor you can often skip the pesky step of waiting for the butter to warm up; and if you follow the advice of my friend Gail Dosik, an expert cookie baker and ridiculously talented decorator, you'll never go through the "chill dough, fight dough flat with a rolling pin and a lot of flour" step again. Gail doesn't bother with any of that. The second her dough is mixed, when it's easy and soft, she rolls it between two pieces of parchment paper to the exact thickness she needs and slides it into the freezer until she's ready for it. As soon as 15 to 20 minutes later, the dough is firm, cookie cutters will make clean, neat shapes with just a little extra pressing, and you'll have saved yourself a lot of trouble.

Which is good, because I'm going to insist that we make that caramel filling from scratch, and I won't hear any argument. It's going to be easy, and you're not going to mess it up, because this is a cookie filling, and even if it's a touch soft or firm, it's still going to be amazing in that way that only butter, salt, cream, and sugar boiled together until deeply toasty can be.

cookies

3½ cups (about 165 grams) small pretzel twists

1½ cups (195 grams) all-purpose flour

¾ teaspoon baking powder

½ teaspoon coarse or kosher salt

¼ cup (50 grams) light-brown sugar

1 cup (200 grams) granulated sugar

1 cup (8 ounces or 225 grams) unsalted butter (cold is fine) cut into medium-sized chunks

1 large egg

Powdered sugar, to finish

caramel

½ cup (120 ml) heavy cream

2 tablespoons (30 grams) unsalted butter

½ teaspoon coarse or flaky sea salt

¼ cup (60 ml) golden syrup or light corn syrup

⅔ cup (130 grams) granulated sugar

make the pretzel flour Grind your pretzels in a food processor until very powdery; you cannot blend them too much. Measure from this 1½ cups (155 grams) pretzel "flour." Discard the rest.

make the cookies Return the measured amount to the food processor and add the flour, baking powder, salt, and sugars, and blend them with the pretzels to combine. Add the butter, and run the machine until the mixture is the texture of cornmeal or nut flour. Add the egg, and run the machine just until the dough clumps.

Place a large sheet of parchment or waxed paper on a large board, and drop the clumpy dough on it. Use your hands to quick-mash it into one mound; don't bother kneading the dough. Place another large sheet of parchment or waxed paper on top, and, with a rolling pin, roll the dough out into one thin (about ⅛ inch thick) large sheet. If the sheet is too big for your counter, divide the dough and roll out half at a time. Transfer the board, parchment, and flattened dough to the freezer, and chill until it is firm to the touch, about 15 minutes (or as long as you need to do whatever you were going to do next).

Heat the oven to 350 degrees.

Peel back the first layer of parchment, use it to line a large baking sheet, and begin cutting out your cookie shapes. I use a ½-inch and a 2-inch round cookie cutter, and although it would be logical to cut the 2-inch round first, I find that cutting the interior circles first, then the exterior of the cookie second, allows the dough to keep its shape better. You want to keep your dough cold or it will be hard to lift the pieces from the parchment and keep them in shape; if it begins to warm up or soften, just slide the dough back into the freezer for a couple minutes. Reroll the extra scraps. Arrange the cookies an inch or two apart on the prepared baking sheet.

bake the cookies For 10 to 12 minutes, until golden at edges, then cool completely on racks.

meanwhile, make the filling Warm the cream, butter, and salt together until the butter melts. (I use the microwave for this.) Over medium heat, stir the syrup and sugar together in a medium saucepan and let them cook until they are a deep amber color (305 to 310 degrees

on a thermometer, but you can also eyeball it). Add the warmed cream mixture, and stir to combine. Cook until the caramel is a copper color, 245 to 250 degrees, and then pour into a heatproof spouted cup for easy pouring. Let it cool until it thickens a little, but not so much that it would be hard to pour, 25 to 30 minutes.

assemble the cookies Arrange all of the linzer lids (the cookies with the holes in them) in one layer, and sift some powdered sugar over them. Arrange all of the bases (the cookies without holes) upside down. Give the caramel a stir and pour about a teaspoon slowly, carefully, onto each base, making sure to stop when the puddle is ¼ inch from the edges. You can always add a drop more or remove a smidge if needed. Repeat with the remaining bottom cookies. Should the caramel cool so much that it's not pouring well, you can rewarm it in the microwave. Carefully lift the powdered lids on top. I like to put them in the fridge just long enough so the caramel can firm up, 5 to 10 minutes. If any lids slide out of alignment, you can nudge them back into place.

do ahead Well-wrapped frozen sheets of cookie dough keep for months.

notes

I prefer using thinner rather than thicker pretzels here, my rationale being that the pretzel flavor is mostly at the dark-brown salty edges.

If you don't have a food processor, you'll want to bang up the crumbs some other way, so that they're powdery. Get the butter to room temperature, and beat it with the sugars, then the egg. Add the dry ingredients, and mix just to combine. Roll it right away, just as you would in the main recipe; you'll need a little longer to get it firm, but probably just 5 extra minutes.

Cookies keep for 1 week at room temperature, 2 in the fridge, and longer in the freezer.

bakery-style butter cookies

makes 36 cookie sandwiches

When I was in high school, I worked at a local bakery several times a week, after school, but on the wrong days. The best day to work was Tuesday, otherwise known as Cookie Day. The bakers would bake off all of those long and star-shaped butter cookies before they left and leave out piping bags loaded with jams and chocolates and trays of sprinkles, chopped nuts, and dried coconut, and whichever two people were lucky enough to have the afternoon-to-closing shift would get to spend most of their time in the back, filling and dipping and rolling. But never me. Two girls, sisters, had the Tuesday shift, and never, ever missed or traded an afternoon; believe me, I tried, I pleaded. In the 2-plus years I worked there, I got to cover only once, but I remember every second of it, because it was the best Tuesday of my life.

You can still get cookies like this at a lot of bakeries, and our nostalgia for them may be strong, but the reality of them these days is by and large underwhelming. They're usually ordered from a central supplier, and, if that isn't bad enough, artificially flavored. Still, these are not the kind of cookies I'd ever felt the need to make at home, because it's quite a production. Recently, however, something snapped—perhaps the last, frayed tether on my sanity; don't read ahead if you don't want to know this—when I realized they're astoundingly easy to make at home with real butter, good vanilla, and sea salt. The dough is ready to bake right away, so it's about 15 minutes from mixing to baking, 30 minutes to cool, and then you're just some jam in a sandwich bag with the corner snipped off, melted chocolate chips, and all the sprinkles you can get your hands on from making every day like Tuesday. This time, my assistants are shorter and cuter, and, because even they know how awesome Cookie Day is, 100 percent as unlikely to miss their shift.

cookies

1 cup (8 ounces or 225 grams) unsalted butter, softened

⅔ cup (135 grams) granulated sugar

2 large egg yolks

1 teaspoon (5 ml) vanilla extract

½ teaspoon fine sea salt

2 cups (260 grams) all-purpose flour

to finish

½ cup (160 grams) jam of your choice

1 cup sprinkles, chopped nuts, or finely shredded dried coconut

10-to-12-ounce (285-to-340-gram) bag semisweet chocolate chips or chopped chocolate

make the cookies Heat the oven to 350 degrees. Line two large baking sheets with parchment paper.

Combine the butter and sugar until well blended and light. Add the egg yolks, vanilla, and salt, and beat to combine. Scrape down the bowl and beaters. Add the flour, and mix just until the flour disappears. Fit a piping bag with a medium (5/8-inch) closed star tip, or you can use a large plastic bag with the corner snipped off.

Pipe the dough into about 1/2-inch-wide, 1 3/4-to-2-inch-long segments, spaced about 1 inch apart, on your baking sheets. It's possible a professional would have a better way to do this, but since I am not a professional, I use a knife or scissors and simply snip off the dough for each cookie, giving it a clean finish. Bake the cookies for 11 to 13 minutes, or until they are golden at the edges.

You can cool these completely on the baking trays, or for at least 2 minutes, to make them easier to lift to a cooling rack. Let the cookies cool completely. Repeat with the remaining dough.

assemble Meanwhile, place your jam in a sandwich bag, but don't snip off the corner until you're going to need it, to limit messes. Place the sprinkles on plates with rims or in shallow bowls. Melt the chocolate chips in the microwave or in a small saucepan until they're three-quarters melted, then stir to melt the rest. (This will keep the chocolate from burning or overheating.) Place the melted chocolate in a bowl with a good depth for dipping. Line two large baking sheets with parchment, or just use the cookie trays you baked on, wiping off any excess crumbs.

Once the cookies are completely cool, flip half of them over, to become the bottom half of your sandwiches. Snip a little corner off your jam bag, and squeeze a little down the center of each flipped cookie, but not so much that it will squeeze out when sandwiched. Sandwich with the other half of the cookies. Dip each a third to half of the way into the chocolate and (trust me) let it drip off, wiping away any excess. (I know we all love chocolate, but the sprinkles will slide off if it's too thick.) Roll the cookies in sprinkles, then return them to the baking sheets to set. You can pop them in the freezer for 5 minutes to hasten this process along.

note For more of that Italian bakery flavor, you can add 1/4 teaspoon almond extract and a little bit of lemon zest to the dough. You can use this same dough to make round star cookies, piping them accordingly. In bakeries, these are often baked with sprinkles on top or sold with a candied cherry pressed into the center; they're less often dipped or filled.

do ahead These keep at room temperature in an airtight container for a week.

tarts and pies

wintry apple bake with double ginger crumble

makes 8 servings

Please don't tell her, because it would be very embarrassing, but when I make this I like to pretend that I am Nigella Lawson. I mean, we all do this sometimes in the kitchen, right? Right, don't tell me. I can't help it—the flavors here, loosely inspired by mince pies, are unquestionably associated with British cookery, even though each is just as popular here. Crumbles feel impossibly other-side-of-the-pond to me, too, especially when served with a trickle of double cream. And ginger—well, it's pretty much tied for me with the word "schedule" for my favorite to hear when delivered in an English accent. I know, I know, I should just keep this stuff to myself.

More specific to Ms. Lawson, I began putting baking powder in my crumble toppings after I used it in a recipe of hers more than a decade ago and loved the effect—the results felt more cookielike. Cookies are never a bad idea. What I was really going for here, however, was brightly spiced, saucy apples absolutely smothered in crumbs. If it seems like you've tucked a few pieces of fruit into a pan just to make it seem more acceptable to eat a tray of buttery ginger cookie crumbs, well, this was not an accident. When you scoop it into a bowl, it's basically begging for a melty scoop of ice cream or the aforementioned drizzle of cream. I say we listen to it.

filling

3 large, firm, tart baking apples
(1½ to 1¾ pounds total or 680 to 775 grams)

Zest and juice of ½ lemon

¼ teaspoon ground cinnamon

A few gratings of fresh nutmeg

A pinch of ground cloves

2 teaspoons (10 ml) brandy, or 1 teaspoon (5 ml)
vanilla extract

3 tablespoons (40 grams) granulated sugar

Pinch of salt

topping

⅔ cup (about 10½ tablespoons, 5⅓ ounces,
or 150 grams) unsalted butter

¼ cup (50 grams) raw (turbinado) sugar

¼ cup (50 grams) granulated sugar

¼ teaspoon coarse or kosher salt

1½ teaspoons baking powder

½ teaspoon ground ginger

2 cups (260 grams) all-purpose flour,
or more if needed

1 tablespoon (10 grams) minced candied ginger,
or more to taste

Heat the oven to 375 degrees.

Peel, halve, and core your apples. Cut each piece into 1-inch wedges. Arrange these in the bottom of a 9-by-13-inch baking dish.

In a small bowl, combine the lemon zest and juice, cinnamon, nutmeg, cloves, brandy, sugar, and salt. Pour mixture over the apples, and toss the pieces so that they're coated.

make the crumbs Melt the butter in a large bowl or saucepan. Stir in the sugars, then add the salt, baking powder, and ground ginger. Stir in the flour and candied ginger. Clumps of dough should easily form; if not, add another tablespoon of flour, and stir again.

Sprinkle the crumble on top of the prepared apples.

bake the crumble Bake for 40 to 45 minutes, until the crumble is lightly browned and apples poked with the tip of a knife have no resistance.

to serve Let cool for 10 to 15 minutes before serving with a dollop of whipped cream, a trickle of cold cream, or some ice cream.

note You can replace ⅓ of the flour in the topping with an equal volume of ground or finely chopped nuts. You can also add a handful of rolled oats for more texture.

julie's punked strawberry tart

makes a 9½-inch tart, serving 8

My friend Julie grew up in Paris, and when I met her (a funny story involving a friend's bringing her to a party but ditching her for someone/something better, to the opposite effect: we lost him and kept her) I was deep, deep in my French-cooking-by-way-of-Julia-Child phase. When we went away for a weekend to a friend's house on the Chesapeake Bay and found some great strawberries along the way, I talked Julie into making tarts with me, the kind with the buttery cookielike shell, vanilla-bean-flecked pastry cream, and fresh berries on top. I pulled out three cookbooks. She grabbed a pot and eyeballed everything, pinching and tasting as she went. I measured quarter-teaspoons of salt and got flummoxed over whether 8 or 9 tablespoons would be the right amount of flour. She dumped her strawberries on top and piled them high. I painstakingly arranged mine in thin slices in a floral pattern. She laughed at how complicated I made everything. I was awed that a person could make *crème pâtissière* and *pâte sucrée* without a recipe.

Our friends liked her tart better. I liked her tart better, and all of my previous cooking goals became redirected to this: to become the sort of cook who could throw together a fresh strawberry tart in a strange kitchen for friends, *au pif*.

Ten years and two cookbooks later, I'm still a recipe cook and she's the kind of person who can reel it off over Skype from Germany, where she now lives, but I went back and made it her way, and it's as perfect as I remember. Please, don't be intimidated by the fancy French words, though. The crust is basically a cookie, the custard a pudding, and the fruit . . . Well, the messier you make it, the more laid-back and cool everyone will know you are.

crust

1⅓ cups (175 grams) all-purpose flour

⅓ cup (40 grams) confectioners' sugar

¼ teaspoon fine sea salt

½ cup (4 ounces or 115 grams) unsalted butter, cubed, chilled

1 large egg yolk

2 tablespoons (30 ml) cold water

custard

⅔ cup (135 grams) granulated sugar

⅓ cup (45 grams) all-purpose flour

¼ teaspoon fine sea salt

4 large egg yolks

2⅓ cups (560 ml) milk

½ vanilla bean, split lengthwise

1 tablespoon (15 ml) kirsch, Cognac, or brandy

1 pound (455 grams) strawberries, the tinier the better, trimmed (for larger berries, you may need up to an extra ½ pound)

to make the crust in a food processor Pulse the flour, sugar, and salt until combined. Add the butter, and pulse in the machine until it is in pea-sized bits. Add the egg yolk and water, and run the machine until the dough clumps a little.

if you don't have a food processor Combine the flour, sugar, and salt together in a large bowl. Add the butter, and, using your fingertips or a pastry blender, work it in until it almost disappears and the mixture resembles corn-meal. Combine the yolk and water in a small dish, and pour this over the top; stir the mixture together with a spoon, then knead gently, as little as possible, with your hands until it forms large clumps.

bake the crust Butter a standard pie dish or 9-inch removable-bottom tart pan. Scatter clumps of dough all over the bottom, and press them across the bottom and up the sides. Poke holes all over with a fork. Place the pan in the freezer for 15 to 25 minutes, until fully solid.

Meanwhile, heat the oven to 350 degrees. Butter a large piece of foil, and press it tightly against the frozen inside surface of the crust. Bake for 25 minutes, then carefully remove the foil. Return to the oven and bake for 5 to 10 minutes more, until the crust is golden. Let cool completely.

meanwhile, make your custard Whisk the sugar, flour, salt, and egg yolks together in the bottom of a large saucepan. Drizzle in the milk, whisking the whole time so that no lumps form. Add the ½ vanilla bean. Place over medium heat on the stove and bring up to a simmer, stirring constantly until the custard thickens, 4 to 7 minutes. Remove from the heat and whisk in the kirsch.

Let the custard cool completely in the fridge, or you can hasten this along by placing the bowl in a larger bowl of ice water.

to finish and serve Spread the cooled pastry cream in the cooled crust. Pile your berries on top. Cut the tart into wedges, and make plans to repeat tomorrow.

chocolate pecan slab pie

makes 12 to 18 servings

Considering how annoyed I get about fairly inconsequential stuff, such as decorative paper straws (mmm, wet paper fibers), single giant ice cubes in cocktails (that thwack you in the face when you take a sip), or a single granule of playground sandbox matter in my bed (always the bed; *always the bed!*), I am sure someone finds it illogical that I find it difficult to get worked up about the evils of corn syrup. My gut feeling is that it shows up mostly in things that nobody is eating for underlying health benefits, and that we all understand we're only supposed to enjoy in moderation (candies, caramels, etc.); shouldn't that be enough?

What *does* bother me about it, however, is that it's just plain bland—it tastes like sweet nothingness, and though I can shrug this off in small quantities, in larger amounts it's a real bummer. With this in my mind, I went from assuming that everyone who wanted to make pecan pie already had a go-to recipe for it, to creating my own, with as much nuanced, deeply toasted, luxurious flavor as I could pack in there. But first I have five rather bossy rules for making an excellent pecan pie:

1. Toast your nuts! You must, you must. Untoasted pecans taste sweet but faintly waxy. Toasted pecans taste like toffeed pecan pie before they even hit the caramel. Just do it.

2. Dark-brown sugar trumps light-brown: more molasses, more flavor. By the same logic, both maple syrup and golden syrup taste better to me in pecan pie than corn syrup. The latter, a lightly cooked cane sugar syrup from the U.K. that is basically their maple syrup (i.e., beloved on pancakes), does contain a bit more sodium than corn syrup, however, so hold the salt back slightly if you're using it. (I learned this the hard way.) I have also used honey in the past, but prefer using it for only half the volume of liquid sweetener here; otherwise, I find its flavor takes over.

3. A tiny bit of cider vinegar (trust me) really helps balance out the aching sweetness of a gooey caramel pie.

4. Good pecan pie causes a commotion, so you're going to want to make a lot. Go slab or go home (and have to make more).

5. Finally, if you want to gild the lily (of course you do), add some chocolate.

crust

3¾ cups (490 grams) all-purpose flour, plus more for your work surface

1½ teaspoons fine sea salt

1½ tablespoons (20 grams) granulated sugar

1½ cups (12 ounces or 340 grams) unsalted butter, very cold

¾ cup (175 ml) very cold water

filling

3⅓ cups (330 grams) pecan halves

8 ounces (225 grams) bittersweet chocolate, coarsely chopped, or about 1¼ cups chocolate chips

½ cup (120 ml) heavy cream

10 tablespoons (145 grams) unsalted butter

1⅔ cups (215 grams) packed dark-brown sugar

1 cup (235 ml) maple syrup or golden syrup (see headnote)

¼ teaspoon coarse sea salt

1½ teaspoons apple cider vinegar

1 tablespoon (15 ml) vanilla extract

1½ tablespoons (25 ml) bourbon (optional)

5 large eggs

to finish

1 egg, beaten with 1 teaspoon (5 ml) water

to make the pie dough by hand, with my one-bowl method In the bottom of a large bowl, combine the flour, salt, and sugar. Work the butter into the flour with your fingertips or a pastry blender until the mixture resembles a coarse meal and the largest bits of butter are the size of tiny peas. (Some people like to do this by freezing the stick of butter and coarsely grating it into the flour, but I haven't found the results as flaky.)

with a food processor In the work bowl of a food processor, combine the flour, salt, and sugar. Add the butter, and pulse the machine until the mixture resembles a coarse meal and the largest bits of butter are the size of tiny peas. Turn the mixture out into a mixing bowl.

both methods Add the cold water, and stir with a spoon or flexible silicone spatula until large clumps form. Use your hands to knead the dough together a few times right in the bottom of the bowl. Divide the dough and wrap each half in a sheet of plastic wrap or waxed paper, and refrigerate until firm, at least 1 hour or up to 72 hours, or

you can quick-firm this in the freezer for 15 minutes. If you plan to keep it longer than 3 days, it will have the best flavor if you freeze it until needed.

prepare the filling Heat the oven to 375 degrees. Line the bottom of a 10-by-15-by-1-inch baking sheet or jelly-roll pan with parchment paper.

Spread the pecans on a rimmed baking sheet and toast in the oven for 10 to 12 minutes, stirring once or twice so that they toast evenly. Set aside until needed. If you like smaller bits, you can chop some or all of the nuts to your desired size.

Melt the chocolate chunks with the heavy cream, and stir until smooth. Spread over the bottom of the frozen crust. Freeze the crust again until the chocolate is solid, about another 10 minutes.

assemble the pie On a lightly floured surface, roll one of your dough halves (the larger one, if you have two different sizes) into an 18-by-13-inch rectangle. This can be kind of a pain, because it is so large. Do your best to work quickly, keeping the dough as cold as possible and using enough flour so it doesn't stick to the counter. Transfer the dough to your prepared baking sheet, and gently drape some of the overhang in, so that the dough fills out the inner edges and corners. Some pastry will still hang over the sides of the pan; trim this to ½ inch. Freeze the piecrust in the pan until it is solid.

In a large saucepan, combine the butter, brown sugar, maple or golden syrup, and salt. Bring to a simmer over medium heat, and cook for 2 minutes, stirring regularly. Remove the pan from the heat and stir in the pecans, cider vinegar, vanilla, and bourbon (if using). Pour into a bowl (so that it cools faster), and set the mixture aside to cool a little, 5 to 10 minutes. Then whisk in one egg at a time until combined. Pour the mixture into the prepared pie shell.

Roll the second of your dough halves (the smaller one, if they were different sizes) into a 16-by-11-inch rectangle.

You can drape it over in one piece (cutting slits to vent the top), or cut it into wide strips to form a lattice; pinch or crimp the upper and lower crusts together, and fold the bottom crust's overhang, if you wish, over the top crust to seal it. (The lattice is always a bit of a mess, but no matter how much you hodgepodge it, people will freak out when they see it.) Lightly beat the egg with water, and brush this over the top crust and edges.

bake the pie Bake at 350 degrees until the crust is golden and the filling is bubbling, about 30 minutes. Transfer to a wire rack until just warm to the touch, about another 30 minutes, before cutting into squares.

caramelized plum tartlets

makes 6 tarts

n my fantasy recipe-writing league, every recipe would be as flexible as a yogini: an all-purpose pie that works with every filling; a cake formula that conquers all cake hopes and dreams, a dead-simple fruit tart that works with any fruit you can get your hands on and always looks amazing. Of course, I'd also write about one recipe a year. So, while I cannot promise that this will work for all stone fruits and all apples, pears, and beyond, do know that this is a really lovely thing to do with fresh plums and a wonderful template that I encourage you to try with anything in season. Tossing thinly sliced fruit with sugar makes it macerate, leaving you with softer fruit that cooks faster and also juices you can reduce until thick and syrupy. Now that you have just made a plum caramel sauce—go you!—you can brush it all over that tart for a burnished finish.

4 firm-ripe red plums, pitted and very thinly sliced (5 to 5¼ ounces each)

⅓ cup (65 grams) granulated sugar

2 tablespoons (30 grams) unsalted butter

2 pinches of sea salt

1 sheet frozen puff pastry (from one 14- or 17-ounce package), thawed according to package directions

prepare the plums In a medium bowl, toss the plum slices with the sugar. Let them macerate together for 30 minutes, until the slices are soft and a puddle of juices has formed. Set a strainer over a small saucepan and strain the plums, letting the juices land in the pan. (You'll have about 6 tablespoons, but don't worry if you have less or more.)

make the glaze Heat the saucepan over medium-high heat and bring the juices to a simmer. Continue to cook, stirring, until they reduce to a thick syrup. You'll know it's ready when you drag your spoon briefly across the bottom of the saucepan and it makes a clear path. Add the butter and sea salt. Once the butter has melted, cook the mixture together until thickened but still syrupy, about 2 minutes. Remove from the heat and set aside.

prepare the pastry Heat the oven to 400 degrees. Cut the puff pastry into six 4-inch squares, then place them on a large parchment-lined baking sheet. Dock the squares all over with a fork. Divide the plum slices between the tartlets, either arranging the slices in overlapping tiles or fanning them out like overlapped flower petals.

to finish Bake the tarts for 12 to 14 minutes, until lightly golden. While they bake, if the plum caramel glaze has cooled so much that it has set, briefly rewarm it on the stove to loosen it again. Brush or dab (with a spoon) the caramel glaze over the whole tartlets, both the fruit and the exposed crust, trying not to nudge the fruit out of place, and return them to the oven for 5 to 7 more minutes, until they are bronzed and shiny.

Let the tartlets cool on a rack. Eat warm or at room temperature.

note The tartlets keep best in the fridge for up to 3 days.

apricot pistachio squares

makes 16 to 25 bars

When I was younger, I always thought that, as you got older, you had a choice as to whether you were going to *act* or *dress* or *do things* the way old people do. For example, you didn't have to pick a year—we'll say 8 years after you graduated from college—to stop listening to new music and start complaining that none of today's music is good. It was a choice! I also thought you didn't have to pick a year to stop buying new jeans and to start wearing mom/dad jeans instead.

Alas. You can listen to all the new music (and like it) and wear all the new jeans (and like them) and your jeans/jams are still ultimately going to be considered by your kids Mom Jeans/Old People Music. It was never about the jeans.

But sometimes getting older has its benefits, like ostensibly becoming wiser. For example, in another era of my life, this recipe would have been a tart. I would have made a tart shell and pressed it into a fluted, removable-bottom tart pan, trimmed the overhang, pricked it all over with a fork, filled it with pie weights, and parbaked it before filling it elegantly. This all felt way too fussy for my current lifestyle—and by "lifestyle" I mean "barely managed chaos"—and so I made bar cookies instead. Bar cookies are your friend. The crust can be whizzed up in a food processor and pressed into the bottom. You parbake it with no docking and no pie weights, and while it's in the oven, you use the bowl of your food processor, which you didn't even wash (because, la-di-da, it doesn't matter), to grind the pistachio-frangipane filling.

And then you get these wonderful, buttery, rich but not-too-sweet squares. For bar cookies, they are downright elegant. And if either of my kids grows up to have an interest in baking, I can't wait to see what he or she will do with these "mom-style bars" to make them fresh again. (A tart, right?)

crust

1 cup (130 grams) all-purpose flour

¼ teaspoon table salt

¼ cup (50 grams) granulated sugar

½ cup (4 ounces or 115 grams) cold unsalted butter

filling

¾ cup (a scant 4 ounces or 110 grams) shelled unsalted pistachios

6 tablespoons (75 grams) granulated sugar

1 tablespoon (10 grams) all-purpose flour

A few pinches of sea salt

5 tablespoons (70 grams) unsalted butter (cold is fine)

1 large egg

¼ teaspoon almond extract, 1 teaspoon (5 ml) brandy, or another flavoring of your choice (totally optional)

1 pound (455 grams) firm-ripe apricots

to finish

Powdered sugar or ¼ cup (80 grams) apricot jam

Heat the oven to 350 degrees. Cut two 12-inch lengths of parchment paper, and trim them both to fit the 8-inch width of an 8-by-8-inch square baking pan. Press parchment paper into the bottom and sides of your pan in one direction, then use the second sheet to line the rest of the pan, perpendicular to the first sheet. (If you have an 8-inch square springform, you can skip this step, and just butter it really well.)

make the crust Combine the flour, salt, and sugar in the bowl of a food processor. Cut the butter into chunks, add it to the bowl, then run the machine until the mixture forms large clumps. That's right, just keep running it; it might take 30 seconds to 1 minute for the dough to come together, but it will. Transfer the dough clumps to your prepared baking pan, and press them evenly across the bottom and ¼ inch up the sides. Bake for 15 minutes, until very pale golden. For the sake of speed, transfer to a cooling rack in your freezer for 10 to 15 minutes while you prepare the filling.

(Don't have a food processor? You might have an easier time using softened butter and preparing this cookie-style: cream the butter with the sugar with a hand mixer, then spoon in the salt and flour, beating until just combined. It might help to chill this mixture a bit before pressing it into the pan, or it might feel too greasy to spread easily.)

make the filling In your food-processor bowl (which I never bother cleaning between these steps), grind your pistachios, sugar, flour, and salt together until the nuts are powdery. Cut the butter into chunks, and add it to the machine. Run the machine until no buttery bits are vis-

ible. Add the egg and any flavorings, blending until just combined.

Spread the filling over the mostly cooled crust (warmth is okay, but we hope that the freezer will have firmed the base enough so you can spread something over it). Cut the apricots in half (or you might find that you can tear them open at the seams with your fingers) and remove the pits. From here, you have a few decoration options. You can place the apricot halves facedown or faceup, all over the pistachio base. You can do as I did, which is cut them into strips, then slide each cut half onto a butter knife or offset spatula, tilt it so that it fans a little, and slide it onto your pistachio filling decoratively. (With this method, I ended up not using all of my apricots.) You could also arrange the strips like flower petals around the pan, for maximum pretties.

bake the bars Bake for 60 minutes, or until they are golden and a toothpick inserted into the pistachio portion comes out batter-free. This might take up to 10 minutes longer, depending on the juiciness of your apricots and the amount you were able to nestle in. Let cool completely in the pan; you can hasten this along in the fridge.

to finish You can make a shiny glaze for your bars by warming the jam in a small saucepan until it thins and brushing this over the top of the cooled tart. Or you can keep it rustic with just a dusting of powdered sugar, as I did.

Cut the bars into squares—chilled bars will give you the cleanest cuts. Keep leftover bars chilled.

bake sale winning-est gooey oat bars

makes 24 to 36 bars

Regardless of whether the prospect of a bake sale strikes dread in your heart or you delight in any and all excuses to bake for good causes, consider this recipe a two-page manual for how to win at them. I don't mean to imply that bake sales are competitions—who said that? Not me!—I just mean that if we're going to break out the eggs and chocolate chips for a good cause, we might as well make the kind of treats that yield dozens, taste like brown butter and caramel and oats and coconut (like an old-school Magic Bar, but possibly even more delicious), and . . . also are liable to sell out first. Take it from the person who once spent hours she didn't necessarily have one night making from-scratch apple hand pies in little squares that were quite brown, flat, and utterly devoid of frosting, sprinkles, gooey chocolate, and other things that reliably make people swoon, and were thus left orphaned at the end of the sale: These are so so much better. For everyone.

crust

Nonstick spray

1¾ cups (230 grams) all-purpose flour

½ teaspoon fine sea or table salt

⅓ cup (65 grams) granulated sugar

¾ cup plus 2 tablespoons (200 grams) cold unsalted butter

filling

½ cup (115 grams) unsalted butter

½ cup (100 grams) granulated sugar

¾ cup (145 grams) dark-brown sugar

¼ teaspoon fine sea or table salt

3 large eggs

1½ teaspoons vanilla extract

1⅓ cups (105 grams) rolled oats

½ cup finely shredded coconut, sweetened or unsweetened

1½ cups chocolate chips, chopped white or dark chocolate, candy bars, dried fruit, or a mix thereof (with the dried fruit, a mix with chocolate is best or the sweetness of the fruit will be overwhelming)

Powdered sugar, to finish

prepare your pan Heat the oven to 350 degrees. Line the bottom of a 9-by-13-inch baking tray (a quarter sheet pan or cake pan is fine) with parchment paper (if using a cake pan, hang the parchment over the sides so the bars are easier to remove). Lightly coat the sides with nonstick spray.

make the crust Combine the flour, salt, and sugar in the bowl of a food processor. Cut the butter into chunks, and add it to the bowl, then run the machine until the mixture forms large clumps—that's right, just keep running it; it might take another 30 seconds for it to come together, but it will. Transfer the dough clumps to the prepared baking pan and press them evenly across the bottom and ¼ inch up the sides. Bake for 15 to 20 minutes, until very pale golden.

meanwhile, prepare the filling Melt your butter in a medium saucepan over medium heat. Continue to cook the butter, stirring frequently, until golden brown bits form at the bottom, about 5 minutes. Remove from the heat and stir in the sugars and salt. Let cool for 5 to 10 minutes, then whisk in the eggs, one at a time, and the vanilla, and stir in the oats, coconut, and chocolate, fruit, and/or candy.

Pour over the parbaked crust, spreading evenly.

bake the bars Bake for 15 to 20 minutes, until the top is firm and golden and the bars are set or, at most, barely jiggle if shimmied. The bars are much easier to cut cleanly from the fridge, but they are gooiest when warm. Dust with powdered sugar before serving or selling for the prettiest finish.

do ahead Store at room temperature for up to 2 days, or in the fridge for longer.

cake

marble bundt cake

makes 12 to 16 servings

A reader recently asked me if I had a recipe for marble cake, and I was (quietly, politely) aghast. People eat it . . . by choice? I'm sorry if it's your favorite and now we cannot be friends, but I'd only experienced it in settings where it was just one step above no cake at all, usually dry and managing to taste like neither chocolate nor vanilla. In life, but in cake baking especially, I think we should all aspire to do one thing really well before making things more complicated.

I'm so glad she pressed me, because it led me to read about the cake's origins in Germany, where it is known as *Marmorkuchen,* a deeply beloved birthday standard. This inspired me to do some fancy fractions with a favorite rich chocolate cake to divide it into vanilla and dark-chocolate parts. It was a very good cake, but this one is even better, thanks to a friend and fellow food blogger. Luisa Weiss—who lives in Berlin and wrote *Classic German Baking,* a book no baker should miss—who, from a neighbor, learned a trick of using melted white chocolate in the vanilla portion instead of leaving it plain. But don't run away if you don't like white chocolate. Here, it adds a complex toastiness, and makes a luxurious textural match for the chocolate swirls—not something you endure just to get to them.

cake

1 cup (8 ounces or 230 grams) unsalted butter, at room temperature

2 cups (400 grams) granulated sugar

2 large eggs

1 teaspoon (5 ml) vanilla extract

⅔ cup (160 grams) sour cream

1½ cups (355 ml) milk, preferably whole

1 teaspoon baking soda

¾ teaspoon fine sea or table salt

2⅓ cups (305 grams) all-purpose flour

2 ounces (55 grams) white chocolate, melted and cooled slightly

⅓ cup (25 grams) cocoa powder (any variety), sifted if lumpy

2 ounces (55 grams) dark or bittersweet chocolate, melted and cooled slightly

to finish

6 tablespoons (90 ml) heavy cream

1 cup (6 ounces or 190 grams) chopped dark or bittersweet chocolate or chocolate chips

Heat the oven to 350 degrees. Coat the inside of a Bundt pan with nonstick spray, or butter and flour every nook and cranny well.

Cream the butter and sugar together with an electric mixer until light and fluffy. Beat in the eggs, one at a time, scraping down the bowl between additions. Beat in the vanilla and sour cream until smooth, then add the milk. Sprinkle the baking soda and salt over batter, and mix until thoroughly combined. Add 2 cups of the flour to the batter, and mix until just combined.

Scoop half of the batter—you can eyeball it—into a separate bowl, and stir the melted white chocolate into it until fully combined; then stir in ⅓ cup flour.

Stir the cocoa powder and melted dark chocolate into the other half of batter.

Drop or dot large spoonfuls of the white chocolate batter into the bottom of your prepared cake pan. Drop or dot large spoonfuls of the dark chocolate batter over that, checkerboarding it a little. Continue until all the batter is used. Use a skewer to marble the batters together in figure-8 motions.

Bake the cake until a toothpick or skewer inserted into the center comes out batter-free, 40 to 50 minutes.

Let cool completely in the pan on a cooling rack, then invert onto a cake plate.

to finish Heat the cream and chocolate together, and stir until just melted. Spoon over the fully cooled cake, and use the back of a spoon to nudge the drippings down in places.

Refrigerate cake to set the chocolate coating; leftovers keep best in the fridge as well.

the *smeteneh küchen* / sour cream coffee cake

makes 20 to 24 servings

Y ou know that thing where you see someone waving at you at a party and you wave animatedly back at them and then realize they're actually waving to the person behind you? And then you have to crawl into a hole and die of embarrassment, because why would you do that / you barely even know that guy / not everything is about you. This is about the time I spied a reference to a *smeteneh küchen* online and leaped a little (waved back, if you will), because it looked and sounded so much like Smitten Kitchen and it turned out to have nothing and everything to do with it.

Except, instead of being embarrassed, I realized I wanted nothing more than to create my own *smeteneh küchen,* one that could actually be *the* Smitten Kitchen signature cake. In Yiddish, *smeteneh* means sour cream and *küchen* means cake; quite often, they're yeasted, too, so I already knew my cake was off to a delicious start. But while cakes like this often have a little streusel on top, I wanted one with an unholy amount—that is, at least as much crumb as cake. The problem, if it could be considered one, is that eating a cake that's approximately 50 percent powdered sugar–covered crumb is a messy affair—crumbs tumble and they're no friend to dark clothing, which means that they're no friend to me.

At the bakery where I worked in high school, they had a trick for this: the cake was baked upside down, allowing the crumbs to become one with the cake. Once the cake is reversed onto a platter, well, it looks a little funny because it's flat instead of rubbly on top. However, when you take your first forkful of cake and not a single buttery brown sugar cinnamon crumb is left behind on the plate, it all makes sense. This is, for me, a sour cream crumb cake's highest calling. I hope it becomes your signature, too.

cake

½ cup (115 grams) unsalted butter, melted and cooled slightly

½ cup (100 grams) granulated sugar

¼ cup (60 ml) milk

1½ cups (360 grams) sour cream, at room temperature

2 large eggs, ideally at room temperature

1 teaspoon (5 ml) vanilla extract

2 teaspoons instant yeast (not active dry; from one ¼-ounce or 7-gram packet)

2⅔ cups (345 grams) all-purpose flour

1 teaspoon fine sea salt

crumbs

1 cup (235 ml) melted butter, no need to cool

⅔ cup (130 grams) granulated sugar

1 cup (190 grams) light- or dark-brown sugar

1 teaspoon ground cinnamon

½ teaspoon fine sea salt

3⅓ cups (435 grams) all-purpose flour

2 teaspoons baking powder

to finish

Powdered sugar

make the cake Combine all of the cake ingredients in a medium-sized mixing bowl, stirring till the mixture becomes cohesive, then stirring for 2 minutes more. In a stand mixer, you can mix this with the paddle attachment at low-medium speed for 2 to 3 minutes. Scrape down the sides of the bowl, cover with plastic wrap, and let rise in a draft-free place for 60 minutes, until it's slightly puffy. (It won't double; this is fine.)

meanwhile, make the crumbs Heat the oven to 350 degrees. Mix the melted butter, sugars, cinnamon, and salt in a bowl. Add the first two cups of flour and the baking powder, and stir. Then add the remaining flour, about ½ a cup at a time. The mixture is going to be very stiff and you're going to think it cannot be mixed, but keep working it in, making the flour disappear, breaking it into the rubble, cutting and mashing it together with a spoon. Press the crumbs into the bottom of your bowl; set aside until needed.

assemble the cake Butter a 9-by-13-inch cake pan and line the bottom with parchment paper. Break up the crumbs with a fork into large and small rubble and sprinkle into the bottom of the pan.

Pour the batter over the crumbs in a thin sheet. Use an offset spatula to smooth it out. Cover again with plastic wrap (don't let it drape in and touch the top of the batter) and set aside for another 30 minutes.

bake the cake For 40 to 45 minutes until the top is lightly browned and a toothpick inserted deep into the cake portion comes out batter-free.

Let the cake cool on a wire rack for 5 minutes, then run a knife along the edge to loosen and flip the cake out onto a serving plate.

to serve Dust generously with powdered sugar.

banana bread roll

makes 9 to 10 servings

Wait, come back. I know how most of us feel about roll cakes, which is that they're the worst—pesky with separated eggs, fragile, cracking, prone to failure—and I know this because every Passover my mother would make a flourless chocolate "heavenly" roll cake and grit her teeth through making it, as the assembly proved to be anything but, leading me to nickname it The [Expletive] Cake. The name stuck, but we've never learned our lesson and continue making and grumbling about it every year.

But this one isn't like that. It's easier. It ditches the whole egg-separation thing in favor of beating the eggs long enough so they get thick and ribbony, a trick I learned from *Cook's Country*. Banana makes the whole thing plush and forgiving, as does flour. And spices, vanilla, dark-brown sugar, and a wee tiny bit of bourbon make it taste like the best banana bread—that is, if your idea of the best banana bread involves cream cheese frosting, a whole inner spiral of it, which if it doesn't already, it will shortly.

cake

Oil, for cake the pan

3 large eggs

⅓ cup (65 grams) dark-brown sugar

⅓ cup (65 grams) granulated sugar

⅔ cup (150 grams) mashed very ripe bananas (from 1 to 1½ medium bananas)

1 teaspoon (5 ml) vanilla extract

2 teaspoons (10 ml) bourbon (optional)

1 teaspoon (5 grams) baking soda

¾ teaspoon ground cinnamon

Freshly grated nutmeg

Pinch of ground cloves

¼ teaspoon kosher salt

¾ cup (100 grams) all-purpose flour

Powdered sugar

filling

8 ounces (225 grams) cream cheese, at room temperature

2 tablespoons (30 grams) unsalted butter, at room temperature

¾ cup (90 grams) powdered sugar, plus more for sprinkling

1 teaspoon (5 ml) vanilla extract

Heat the oven to 350 degrees. Line a 10-by-15-inch rimmed baking pan with parchment paper, and lightly spray it with oil for extra insurance.

make the batter Beat the eggs in a large bowl until foamy, then continue beating while slowly adding the sugars. Beat until very thick and cappuccino-colored, 5 to 10 minutes. Beat in the bananas, vanilla, and bourbon, if using. Sprinkle the baking soda, spices, and salt evenly over the batter, and beat to combine. Add the flour, and beat just until it disappears. Spread the batter into your prepared pan.

bake the cake For 10 to 12 minutes, or until it's lightly bronzed all over and it springs back when lightly touched.

Definitely rotate this one halfway through, because a thin cake is far more harmed by uneven baking.

prepare the cake for assembly Cool for 5 minutes on a rack, then run a knife around the edges to loosen the cake. Sprinkle the top of the cake lightly with powdered sugar. Place a second sheet of parchment paper, this one larger than the cake, over the powdered top, and a cooling rack facedown over it. Flip the cake out onto the now parchment-covered rack. Carefully peel away the parchment paper from the bottom. Lightly powder this side, too. Starting from a short side, roll the cake and remaining parchment together into a log, and rest it, seam side down (so it doesn't unroll), on the rack to cool completely, for about 45 minutes.

make the filling and assemble Meanwhile, beat the cream cheese, butter, ¾ cup powdered sugar, and vanilla together until light and fluffy. Carefully unroll the cake, and spread the top with cream-cheese filling. Slowly, carefully, reroll the cake with the frosting inside, and rest it, seam side down, on a serving platter.

to serve You can serve it right away, but I think it slices better when it's had a chance to cool and set up a little more in the fridge, if you have time to spare. (You can also freeze it at this point.)

Before serving, sprinkle the top with additional powdered sugar, and cut the cake into slices.

marzipan petit four cake

makes two 4-by-8-inch cakes, each with 8 servings

My family is chock-full of marzipan junkies, and the only thing we like more than marzipan is the way it tastes against chocolate, especially if there's a smidge of raspberry or apricot jam involved. Thus, this cake is just for them. I mean, you can make it, too, and you should, but do know I'm just trying to make sure they tell their friends, synagogue and bridge-club members, and various people they chat up in grocery store checkout lines to buy this book.

I'm with them, but I also have a soft spot for well-made, unplasticky petits fours and those rainbow cookies you can get at Italian-American bakeries. This is a celebration of all of the above. And though I realize it looks incredibly fussy, every time I make it I'm delighted with how easily it comes together. The cake is one bowl; it bakes up quickly and dead flat, needing no leveling. A single 7-ounce tube of almond paste will flavor the whole cake and leave a dollop for easy decorations. And that's about where the fussiness ends; we use store-bought jam for the filling and a simple ganache for the icing. Oh, and it makes *two cakes,* which means when you brag and post a picture of your cake on social media and your friends are all "What? Gimme. I'm coming over!" you can brush some imaginary crumbs off your shoulder and say, "Anytime—I made two."

cake

12 tablespoons (175 grams) unsalted butter at room temperature, plus more for the baking pans

½ cup (5½ ounces or 155 grams) almond paste; use the remainder of the 7-ounce (198-gram) tube for decorations

1½ cups (300 grams) granulated sugar

2 teaspoons (10 ml) almond extract

6 large egg whites

1 tablespoon baking powder

½ teaspoon fine sea or table salt

2¾ cups (360 grams) all-purpose flour

1 cup (235 ml) milk, preferably whole

Food coloring

filling, coating, and finishing

¾ cup (240 grams) raspberry and/or apricot jam

½ cup plus 2 tablespoons (150 ml in all) heavy cream

½ pound (225 grams) dark chocolate, chopped, or chocolate chips

1 tablespoon (15 ml) corn syrup (optional, but ensures a shiny finish)

Remaining almond paste (optional; see cake ingredients)

Additional food coloring (optional)

prepare the pans Heat the oven to 350 degrees. Line four 8-inch square baking pans with parchment paper. What? Of course you don't have four. I have two, and do this in two batches. If you have only one, don't worry—you'll be done soon, and the batter will keep just fine while it is waiting. Coat the parchment and the sides of baking pan(s) well with butter (or nonstick spray).

make the batter Using a food processor or stand mixer, cream the almond paste with the sugar at low speed until broken up; add the butter a chunk at a time, letting the machine cream each addition into the paste before adding the next. As you add more pieces, the paste will become creamy and light, whipped with the butter, and you can add the rest at once. Beat in the almond extract and then the egg whites, two at a time, scraping down the bowl after each addition. Add the baking powder and salt, and mix. Add a third of the flour (eyeball it) and half of the milk; repeat this, and then finish with the rest of the flour.

Spoon off 1½ cups (322 grams) batter into each of three bowls (you'll have the same amount left in your mixing bowl, for your fourth cake layer). Tint each with your desired color.

bake the cake Bake each layer until a toothpick inserted into the center comes out batter-free, 10 to 11 minutes. Let cool in the pan for 10 minutes, then run a thin knife around the cake (I find the top edge always likes to stick) and flip out onto a cooling rack. Peel off the parchment square, flip the cake over, and put it back in the cake pan, to which you've given a quick refresh of nonstick spray or butter. Repeat with the remaining cake layers, letting them cool completely before filling. You can hasten this along (and make them easier to lift and trim) by cooling them in the freezer.

to assemble Arrange the first layer on a work surface or plate and spread with ¼ cup jam. Repeat on the next two layers; the top cake layer should have no jam on top. Carefully cut the cake evenly in half, forming two rectangles. Trim the sides if they're not even. Place each cake on a separate plate, and use strips of waxed or parchment paper tucked underneath all around to protect your plate (you'll be glad you did).

to finish and decorate Heat the cream, chocolate, and corn syrup (if using) together in a heatproof bowl over a pot containing an inch of simmering water, or in the microwave in 30-second bursts, stirring frequently until the chocolate is mostly melted. Then, off the heat, stir until fully melted.

Pour some chocolate over the top of the first cake, and nudge it down the sides, using an offset spatula to spread it smooth on the sides. Once the first cake is covered messily in a thin layer of chocolate, place it in the freezer to set quickly, and repeat the process with the second cake. Once the second cake is in the freezer, coat the first cake in a final layer of chocolate, then repeat with the second. You can set the coating in the fridge or freezer.

If you'd like to make flowery decorations out of the remaining knob of almond paste, do so by kneading a tiny amount of food coloring into pieces of about 2 tablespoons. The flowers you see require zero technical skill and no special tools; I simply pulled off pea-sized bits of colored paste, rolled them into balls, squished them flat between my fingers (if they were sticking, I found that damp hands made them stop), and slightly overlapped the flat discs to form three-petaled flowers. Finish with a tiny bead of paste in the middle, and thinner "stems" if you wish.

notes

I played around with classic pastel petit-four colors here, but you can omit them entirely for a snow-white cake, adjust them to the holiday du jour (red and green; black and orange; red, pink, and white), or have fun with them; a gradient/ombré in which you add an additional drop or two of color per layer looks fantastic.

This also works as a two-layer 8-inch square or 9-inch round cake, dividing the batter between two pans instead of four.

chocolate peanut butter icebox cake

makes 8 servings

I didn't grow up eating icebox cakes—what's up with that, Mom, by the way?—but I made up for lost time as often as I could when I discovered them as an adult. The best ones are like cookies and cream went to heaven; the chocolate wafers taste like Oreos, and the cream isn't that sweetened pastelike filling but plumes of freshly whipped cream. Stacked together and chilled, the cookies soften into glorious thin cakes. I never set out to make my own chocolate wafers; I've always claimed I had to because the store-bought ones are harder to find every year, and while this is true, I'm probably not kidding anyone. Homemade wafers, freshly baked and aromatic with good cocoa, butter, and a kiss of vanilla, taste a gazillion times better. I tried many homemade chocolate wafers over the years, but most ended up being too much work for what is supposed to be an easy last-minute dessert before I found perfection, as one often does, from the brilliant bakers at King Arthur Flour.

I changed a few things because don't let the homemade chocolate wafers fool you, I still like to do as little work as possible. I turned them into a one-bowl food processor cookie dough; I also skip the chilling step so we can roll them out straightaway. I avoid the peskiness of floured counters and sticky doughs by rolling them between two pieces of parchment paper, and we then use that same parchment to bake the cookies. I know you're not going to believe me, but this goes very quickly. Then, instead of making 50 small wafers from this, I make 6 large ones. Each becomes a layer of the most stunning icebox cake I've ever made.

Finally, while of course you can use plain whipped cream here or even flavor it with espresso or mint, cocoa, or more, I need to tell you that once I made this with peanut butter whipped cream for my family of chocolate–peanut butter junkies, there was no other way. I had significant doubts about whipped cream's ability to showcase the nuance of peanut butter, and each of them was unfounded. This whipped cream is terrifically peanut buttery with zero textural compromise and a perfect filling for those cake-sized cookies. The result is dead simple to make but manages to exceed all of our icebox cake hopes and dreams.

wafers

1½ cups (195 grams) all-purpose flour

¼ cup (20 grams) Dutch-process cocoa powder

¼ cup (20 grams) black cocoa powder
(use more Dutched cocoa powder if you don't
have black cocoa)

1 cup (200 grams) granulated sugar

½ teaspoon fine sea or table salt

½ teaspoon baking powder

½ cup (115 grams) unsalted butter
(cold is fine if using a food processor)

1 large egg

1 teaspoon (5 ml) vanilla extract

peanut butter whipped cream

3 tablespoons (50 grams) smooth peanut butter

¾ teaspoon vanilla extract

A couple pinches of salt

1½ tablespoons (20 grams) granulated sugar

1½ cups (355 ml) heavy or whipping cream,
cold

to finish

Chocolate sprinkles, shavings, crunchy pearls,
or chopped chocolate-peanut-butter candies

make the wafers in a food processor Combine the flour, cocoa powders, sugar, salt, and baking powder in the work bowl of a food processor, pulsing until mixed. Add the butter and run the machine until the mixture is powdery. Add the egg and vanilla and run the machine until the dough begins to clump and ball together.

make the wafers with an electric mixer Beat the butter and sugar together until combined. Add the egg and vanilla and beat until smooth. Add the baking powder, salt, and cocoa powders and beat until combined. Add the flour and mix just until it disappears.

both methods Heat the oven to 350 degrees. Divide the dough into 6 equal pieces. Roll the first between 2 pieces of parchment paper until very, very thin and just over 7 inches across. Slide onto a board (parchment paper and all) and place in the freezer for 10 minutes, until firm. Once firm, peel back the top piece of parchment paper (it should now come off cleanly when pulled gently) and use a stencil or bowl with a 7-inch rim to trim it into a neater circle. Slide the cookie round and the lower piece of parchment paper onto a baking sheet. Bake for 10 minutes and let it cool completely on paper, which you can slide onto a cooling rack so that you can use the tray again. Repeat with the remaining 5 pieces of dough.

It sounds like a lot of work, but the best thing is to get into a pattern where one piece is being rolled while another is freezing while the third one bakes and a fourth is cooling, so you're never working with more than one piece at a time. By the time one piece bakes, the next is ready to leave the freezer.

while the cookies cool, make the peanut butter whipped cream In a large bowl, beat the peanut butter, vanilla, salt, and sugar until smooth. Beating the whole time, slowly add the heavy cream, one small splash at a time, until the peanut butter cream mixture is loose enough that you can add the rest of the cream without breaking it into clumps. Whip the cream, watching it carefully as it's very easy to overbeat with an electric mixer, until soft peaks form.

assemble the cake Place the first cookie on a cake stand. If it's sliding around, as cookies do, put a dab of whipped cream down first. Once it softens the cookie, it will make it stick. Thickly frost the first cookie all the way to the edges with about ½ cup peanut butter cream. Repeat with the remaining cookies, decoratively swirling the top cookie. Garnish with sprinkles or candy.

Place the cake in the fridge overnight or, ideally, for closer to 24 hours so that the cookies soften into cake layers. A knife dipped in warm water will make clean cuts.

notes

You'll want to make this one day early so the cake can soften overnight in the fridge.

For the darkest, most authentically Oreo/packaged chocolate waferish color, you'll want to swap half the cocoa with black cocoa powder, also sold as onyx cocoa powder. It's available online and at most baking supply shops.

The recipe, as shown, makes a small family-sized cake, 7 inches in diameter. For a larger cake that could easily serve 16, double everything and roll the discs to 10 inches in diameter.

the party cake builder

My party-cake theory is that 98 percent of cakes, especially those intended for the birthdays of loved ones, are made between the hours of 10:30 p.m. and 4:00 a.m. Because the recipe you found on the internet said it would take 1 hour, max, but it neglected to mention butter-softening time and the fact that you cannot put frosting on a cake that's not absolutely cold without it sliding off. Because on Pinterest, the place where all of us temporarily forget that we are not Martha Stewart, you saw this elaborate train cake design, and you know it would make the kid really happy, even if tinting and rolling fondant shapes is never a good way to spend 2:00 a.m. Because the timer dinged on the cake layers and you realize the eggs are still on the counter. From there, it just spirals out, and nobody is having fun anymore.

Party cakes should be fun. Because: party. Because: cake. Because: sprinkles.

What if, instead, you had the last party-cake recipes you'd ever need? You might delete the local bakery from your bookmarks. You might volunteer to make cake. You might actually have more fun at these parties, because you weren't watching buttercream-rose tutorials when the sun came up. Nobody has ever said, "That cake tasted better because of the buttercream roses."

This is party cake the way I think it should be: one-bowl cake, one-bowl frosting, no sifting, no special ingredients, but absolutely no compromise on flavor or texture. The frosting is swooshed and swirled messily over the top and not the sides, because this method is as easy as it is fun, and nothing says love like great big swirls of buttercream. Finally, you can turn these building blocks into celebrations of any magnitude and size. Such as:

- **the just because it's tuesday night / been too long since you had cake cake** One 8-inch square layer cake with a swoosh of frosting

- **it's your birthday / anniversary / first day of your new job today? of course I didn't forget! cake** One 9-inch round cake with a swoosh of frosting

- **the guest most welcome / bake sale vanquisher** Twelve cupcakes!

- **the classic party cake** A single-layer 9-by-13-inch sheet cake or a two-layer 9-inch round cake

- **the show-off party cake** A 3-layer 9-inch round cake

- **the let's invite the whole neighborhood cake** A two-layer 9-by-13 inch sheet cake. Does it sound like we're getting into a wedding-cake zone? This is not an accident.

build your cake

- **1 cake + 1 frosting yield** = A 1-layer frosted 8-inch square cake = A 1-layer frosted 9-inch round cake = 12 frosted cupcakes

- **2 cakes + 2 frosting yields** = A 2-layer frosted 8-inch square cake = A 2-layer frosted 9-inch round cake = A 1-layer frosted 9-by-13-inch cake = 24 frosted cupcakes

- **3 cakes + 3 frosting yields** = A 3-layer frosted 8-inch square cake = A 3-layer frosted 9-inch round cake = 36 frosted cupcakes

- **4 cakes + 4 frosting yields** = A 2-layer frosted 9-by-13-inch cake = 48 frosted cupcakes

- **2 cakes + 4 frosting yields** = A 4-split-layer frosted 8-inch square cake (as seen in the 4-layer square chocolate cake in the spread) = A 4-split-layer frosted 9-inch round cake

- These single-layer cakes are on the thin side, while the frosting on top is slightly on the thick and decadent side. You can use the same volume of frosting to frost your cakes more traditionally, i.e., covering the sides as well as the top.

- While the coconut frosting is a natural fit for the coconut cake and the cream cheese goes impeccably well on the pumpkin cake, all of these frostings are mix-and-match. Yellow cake with chocolate frosting is my favorite, thank you for asking.

bake your cake

- Bake at the same temperature (350 degrees) regardless of size

- An 8-inch square cake layer = as written, anywhere between 20 and 30 minutes

- A 9-inch round cake layer = same as 8-inch square

- Standard cupcakes = 16 to 18 minutes

- A 9-by-13-inch cake layer = 38 to 40 minutes

serve your cake

- 1 generously frosted 8-by-8-inch cake can be cut into 16 snacky squares or 9 more generous ones

- 1 generously frosted 9-inch round cake can be cut into 8 generous wedges or 12 moderate ones

- 1 generously frosted 9-by-13-inch sheet cake layer can serve 20 to 24 in small squares

- A 2-layer frosted and filled 8-inch square cake can serve 16

- A 2-layer frosted and filled 9-inch round cake can serve 12

- A 2-layer frosted and filled 9-by-13-inch sheet cake can serve 24 to 32

frost and decorate your cake

Scared of making a layer cake for the first time? Don't be: All you're doing is exactly what you would for one frosted layer, two or three times. Here are a few more specific tips:

- **level your layers** Cake layers—and these especially—will stack better if the layers are leveled, which sounds scary but just means that you use a long serrated knife to horizontally cut the dome off the cake layers, leaving a flat surface. The next layer will stack neatly (versus being bent and possibly cracking on top) and the resulting cake will look very professional. Another trick of professional decorators is to cool cakes upside down, to help flatten out the tops so they require less trimming to make them flat.

- **fill your layers first** You'll always want more frosting between layers than seems necessary because it will flatten out as the cakes are stacked and you'll want to see a visible strip of frosting in slices.

- **consider a flipped lid** Some people like to flip the top layer of a cake upside down so that the underside of the last layer makes a nice, clean cake top.

- **level again** Once all of your layers are filled, if they aren't perfectly even once stacked, you can use your serrated knife to trim the sides a little, too. This matters more if you're planning on frosting the sides; for exposed side cakes (aka "naked cakes"), don't worry about this unless it bothers you.

- **consider a crumb coat** For the most professional appearance, if you want to frost the sides of your cake—and especially if you're putting, say, a light frosting on a dark-colored cake—you can do a crumb coat first. Simply coat the whole cake in a very thin layer of frosting and pop the cake in the freezer for 10 minutes. This will "set" the frosting and ensure that the crumbs stay attached to the cake and not in your final coat of frosting. Then, frost it generously on top of the crumb coat.

- **tools** You could spend a lot of money on cake decorating tools, but I do everything you see here with a small offset spatula. They cost about $4. For smooth frosting sides, or an even frosting appearance on the sides of a naked cake, the edge of a bench scraper makes it easy.

- **write a message** Finally, if you'd like to write on your cake, hold back a couple tablespoons of light-colored frosting and tint it with food coloring before scooping it into a sandwich bag and cutting the tiniest opening from the corner. Voilà! You've made a piping bag.

do ahead Cake layers freeze fantastically; once firm to the touch, wrap tightly in plastic for up to 3 months. I'm a big fan of working with them while still frozen; they're easier to stack and trim. After an hour at room temperature or half a day in the fridge, they should be fully defrosted. You can make the frosting and chill it in the fridge until needed; it will easily last 1 week. At room temperature, it should be soft and spreadable again.

storage Only the cream cheese frosting *must* be kept in the fridge. The other cakes and frostings are fine at room temperature. However, I find that the cakes last longer in the fridge, so should you hope to have them around for more than 3 days, I'd refrigerate them.

spice cake

6 tablespoons (85 grams) unsalted butter,
at room temperature

¾ cup plus 2 tablespoons (165 grams) firmly packed
light-brown sugar

1 large egg

1 large egg yolk

1 teaspoon (5 ml) vanilla extract

¾ teaspoon baking powder

¼ teaspoon baking soda

½ teaspoon fine sea or table salt

1 teaspoon ground cinnamon

¼ teaspoon ground ginger

A few gratings of fresh nutmeg

⅛ teaspoon ground cloves
(use ¼ teaspoon for a more spicy kick)

¾ cup (215 grams) applesauce, mashed bananas,
pumpkin purée (from about half a 15-ounce can),
or 2 packed cups grated carrot (8 ounces or 225 grams)

1½ cups (195 grams) all-purpose flour

Heat the oven to 350 degrees. Coat an 8-inch square cake pan with nonstick cooking spray and line the bottom with parchment paper.

Beat the butter and sugar together in a large bowl with an electric mixer until fluffy. Beat in the egg, yolk, and vanilla until combined, scrape down the bowl, and then sprinkle the baking powder, baking soda, salt, cinnamon, ginger, nutmeg, and cloves over the batter and beat until very well combined. Add the applesauce, bananas, pumpkin, or carrot, and stir to combine. Stir in the flour until it just disappears.

Scrape the batter into the prepared pan and smooth the top. Bake for 20 to 30 minutes, until a toothpick inserted into the center of the cake comes out batter-free. Let cool in the pan on a cooling rack for 10 minutes, then run a knife around the cake to ensure it is loose, flip it out onto a cooling rack, and then back right side up again onto another. Let cool completely before frosting. You can hasten this process along in your freezer, where it shouldn't take more than 15 minutes to fully cool.

coconut cake

6 tablespoons (85 grams) unsalted butter,
at room temperature

¾ cup (150 grams) granulated sugar

1 large egg

1 large egg yolk

1 teaspoon vanilla extract

¾ teaspoon baking powder

¼ teaspoon baking soda

½ teaspoon fine salt

¾ cup (175 ml) coconut milk, well-stirred,
from a can

½ cup (40 grams) shredded unsweetened coconut

1¼ cups (165 grams) all-purpose flour

Heat the oven to 350 degrees. Coat an 8-inch square cake pan with nonstick cooking spray and line the bottom with parchment paper.

Beat the butter and sugar together in a large bowl with an electric mixer until fluffy. Beat in the egg, yolk, and vanilla until combined, scrape down the bowl, and then sprinkle the baking powder, baking soda, and salt over the batter and beat until very well combined. Add the coconut milk and mix to combine; the batter may look curdly, but this isn't a problem. Add the shredded coconut and flour, and mix until the flour just disappears.

Scrape the batter into the prepared pan and smooth the top. Bake for 20 to 30 minutes, until a toothpick inserted into the center of the cake comes out batter-free. Let cool in the pan on a cooling rack for 10 minutes, then run a knife around the cake to ensure it is loose, flip it out onto a cooling rack, and then flip back right side up again onto another. Let cool completely before frosting. You can hasten this process along in your freezer, where it shouldn't take more than 15 minutes to fully cool.

fudgy chocolate cake

6 tablespoons (85 grams) unsalted butter, at room temperature

¾ cup (145 grams) firmly packed dark-brown sugar

2 tablespoons (25 grams) granulated sugar

1 large egg

1 large egg yolk

1 teaspoon vanilla extract

¾ cup (175 ml) buttermilk

¼ teaspoon baking soda

¾ teaspoon baking powder

½ teaspoon table or fine sea salt

½ cup (40 grams) Dutch-process cocoa powder

1 cup (130 grams) all-purpose flour

Heat the oven to 350 degrees. Coat an 8-inch square cake pan with nonstick spray and line the bottom with parchment paper.

Beat the butter and sugars together in a large bowl with an electric mixer until fluffy. Beat in the egg, yolk, and vanilla until combined, scrape down the bowl, and then sprinkle the baking powder, baking soda, and salt over the batter and beat until very well combined. Add the buttermilk and mix to combine; the batter may look curdly, but this isn't a problem. Add the cocoa and flour, and mix until the flour just disappears.

Scrape the batter into the prepared pan and smooth the top. Bake for 20 to 30 minutes, until a toothpick inserted into the center of the cake comes out batter-free. Let cool in the pan on a cooling rack for 10 minutes, then run a knife around the cake to ensure it is loose, flip it out onto a cooling rack, and then flip back right side up again onto another. Let cool completely before frosting. You can hasten this process along in your freezer, where it shouldn't take more than 15 minutes to fully cool.

golden vanilla cake

6 tablespoons (85 grams) unsalted butter, at room temperature

¾ cup plus 1 tablespoon (160 grams) granulated sugar

1 large egg

2 large egg yolks

2 teaspoons (10 ml) vanilla extract

¾ teaspoon baking powder

¼ teaspoon baking soda

½ teaspoon table or fine sea salt

¾ cup (175 ml) buttermilk

2 tablespoons (15 grams) cornstarch

1¼ cups plus 2 tablespoons (180 grams) all-purpose flour

Heat the oven to 350 degrees. Coat an 8-inch square cake pan with nonstick spray and line the bottom with parchment paper.

Beat the butter and sugar together in a large bowl with an electric mixer until fluffy. Beat in the egg, yolks, and vanilla, until combined, scrape down the bowl, and then sprinkle the baking powder, baking soda, and salt over the batter and beat until very well combined. Add the buttermilk and mix to combine; the batter may look curdly, but this isn't a problem. Add the cornstarch and flour, and mix until the flour just disappears.

Scrape the batter into the prepared pan and smooth the top. Bake for 25 to 27 minutes, until a toothpick inserted into the center of the cake comes out batter-free. Let cool in the pan on a cooling rack for 10 minutes, then run a knife around the cake to ensure it is loose, flip it out onto a cooling rack, and then flip back right side up again onto another. Let cool completely before frosting. You can hasten this process along in your freezer, where it shouldn't take more than 15 minutes to fully cool.

chocolate buttercream frosting

½ cup (115 grams) unsalted butter,
at room temperature

1½ cups (180 grams) powdered sugar
(sifted if lumpy)

Pinch of fine sea salt (optional)

2 ounces (55 grams) unsweetened chocolate,
melted and cooled

1 tablespoon (15 ml) cream or whole milk

½ teaspoon vanilla extract

make the frosting in a food processor Place the frosting ingredients in a food processor and run the machine to mix. Scrape down the bowl, then process for another 1 to 2 minutes just until smooth and somewhat fluffed.

make the frosting with a hand or stand mixer Beat the butter, powdered sugar, and salt, if using, in a large bowl with electric beaters (for a hand mixer) or the paddle attachment, not the whisk (for a stand mixer), until fluffy. Pour in the chocolate, cream or milk, and vanilla, and beat until combined, then 1 more minute to whip it further.

vanilla buttercream frosting

½ cup (115 grams) unsalted butter,
at room temperature

1¼ cups (150 grams) powdered sugar
(sifted if lumpy)

Pinch of fine sea salt (optional)

1 tablespoon (15 ml) cream or whole milk

½ teaspoon vanilla extract

make the frosting in a food processor Place the frosting ingredients in a food processor and run the machine to mix. Scrape down the bowl, then process for another 1 to 2 minutes just until smooth and somewhat fluffed.

make the frosting with a hand or stand mixer Beat the butter, powdered sugar, and salt, if using, in a large bowl with electric beaters (for a hand mixer) or the paddle attachment, not the whisk (for a stand mixer), until fluffy. Drizzle in the cream or milk and vanilla, and beat until combined, then 1 more minute to whip it further.

coconut buttercream frosting

6 tablespoons (85 grams) unsalted butter,
at room temperature

2 tablespoons (26 grams) virgin coconut oil
(if your kitchen is warm and the coconut oil has
liquefied, refrigerate it until firm)

Pinch of fine sea salt

1¼ cups (150 grams) powdered sugar
(sifted if lumpy)

1 tablespoon (15 ml) coconut milk, heavy cream,
or whole milk

½ teaspoon vanilla extract

Toasted dried, unsweetened coconut chips
(optional garnish)

make the frosting in a food processor Place the butter and coconut oil in a food processor and run the machine to mix. Add the salt, sugar, coconut milk, and vanilla and process for 1 to 2 minutes, scraping down the bowl as needed, until the frosting is smooth and somewhat fluffed.

make the frosting with a hand or stand mixer Beat the butter and coconut oil in a large bowl with electric beaters (for a hand mixer) or the paddle attachment, not the whisk (for a stand mixer), until fluffy. Add the salt, sugar, coconut milk, and vanilla and beat for 1 to 2 minutes, until somewhat fluffed and smooth.

note This frosting may seem worrisomely soft when first whipped, but that has no effect on how well it frosts. If you'd like, you can let it set up a bit in the fridge.

cream cheese frosting

4 ounces (half an 8-ounce package/115 grams)
cream cheese, softened

4 tablespoons (2 ounces or 55 grams) unsalted butter,
at room temperature

⅔ cup (80 grams) powdered sugar
(sifted if lumpy)

Pinch of fine sea salt (optional)

1 tablespoon cream or whole milk

½ teaspoon vanilla extract

make the frosting in a food processor Place the frosting ingredients in a food processor and run the machine to mix. Scrape down the bowl, then process for another 1 to 2 minutes, just until smooth and somewhat fluffed.

make the frosting with a hand or stand mixer Beat the cream cheese, butter, powdered sugar, and salt, if using, in a large bowl with electric beaters (for a hand mixer) or a paddle attachment, not the whisk (for a stand mixer), until fluffy. Drizzle in the milk and vanilla, beat until combined, then 1 more minute to whip it further.

puddings, frozen things, etc.

blackout brownie waffle sundae

makes 3 waffles for 6 sundaes

For my son's 6th birthday, we marched his friends from the playground to a local ice cream parlor for a make-your-own-sundae extravaganza. The tables were set with a dreamland of sprinkles, hot fudge, butterscotch, whipped cream, cherries, chopped nuts, and more. Can you imagine the delicious chaos? Multiply that by twenty-six and imagine the sundaes getting more complicated by the minute. But not one child's. When asked which two ice cream flavors she wanted, she said, "Chocolate." "You can pick two, though." "Chocolate and chocolate." When offered caramel sauce and whipped cream, she wanted only hot fudge. Offered rainbow sprinkles, she chose chocolate. She was a girl after all of our hearts, with a single-minded determination for an experience unfettered by inferior, nonchocolate flavors.

We were definitely thinking of her when we decided to make an all-chocolate brownie sundae. But why waffles? It doesn't just look cool; it's about the fastest way to cook a brownie, and thus, a brownie sundae. Guys, I am just here to help.

hot fudge sauce

⅓ cup (80 ml) heavy cream

3 tablespoons (45 ml) light corn syrup, golden syrup, or honey

3 tablespoons (35 grams) packed dark-brown sugar

2 tablespoons (10 grams) cocoa powder

⅛ teaspoon fine sea salt

3 ounces (85 grams) bittersweet chocolate, chopped, or about ½ cup bittersweet chocolate chips

1 tablespoon (15 grams) unsalted butter

¼ teaspoon vanilla extract

brownie waffle

3 ounces (85 grams) unsweetened chocolate, roughly chopped

6 tablespoons (3 ounces or 85 grams) unsalted butter, plus more for the pan

1 cup plus 2 tablespoons (225 grams) granulated sugar

3 large eggs

1 teaspoon (5 ml) vanilla extract

½ teaspoon flaky sea salt, or ¼ teaspoon table salt

¾ cup (100 grams) all-purpose flour

½ cup plus 1 tablespoon (45 grams) cocoa powder

½ cup (85 grams) semisweet chocolate chips

assembly

1 pint (475 ml) chocolate ice cream

Whipped cream

Chocolate sprinkles

Maraschino cherries

make the sauce Combine the cream, syrup, brown sugar, cocoa, and salt in a small saucepan over medium heat and bring to a simmer. Cook, stirring, for 5 minutes. Add the chocolate, butter, and vanilla, and stir until smooth. Set aside.

make the waffles Melt the chocolate and butter together. Whisk in the sugar, then the eggs, vanilla, and salt. Stir in the flour, cocoa powder, and chocolate chips.

Heat your waffle maker to medium-low. Coat the waffle grates with nonstick cooking spray, or brush with melted butter. Cook the batter in three batches, opening the iron's lid for 1 minute before carefully, gently removing each waffle (in sections, if that's easier). Transfer to bowls or plates. Add ice cream, drape with hot fudge sauce, whipped cream, chocolate sprinkles, and a cherry.

lemon meringue pie smash

makes 8 servings

This was, in part, inspired by an Eton mess—a traditional English dessert in which macerated strawberries are mixed with whipped cream and crumbled meringue cookies (and if *that* isn't British enough, it's served at an annual cricket match between two 400-plus-year-old schools). But it is equally inspired by lemon meringue pie, something I love endlessly . . . except for the dampness that is too often part of the meringue topping. A mash-up of the two components, cooked separately, has solved this problem, and also makes the whole thing a little less fussy. No rolled doughs or crimped edges, no piping bags to make your meringue topping Pinterest-ready. It's messy and wonderful.

You could, by the way, use jarred lemon curd and store-bought meringues (the meringue slab here clocks in at 3 ounces); a sane person would definitely do this. But I have to insist that you whip your own cream, because it must be sugar-free to counterbalance the sweetness of the curd and the meringue. Together, the tart sauce, melty crumbled cookies, and rich cream harmonize. The sweetness is in check, and there's a cloudlike, dreamy quality to the whole dessert.

meringue slab

2 large egg whites

¼ teaspoon cream of tartar

½ cup (100 grams) granulated sugar

⅛ teaspoon fine sea salt

lemon curd

Zest and juice of 2 lemons

¾ cup (150 grams) granulated sugar

4 large egg yolks

3 tablespoons (45 grams) unsalted butter

cream

2 cups (475 ml) heavy or whipping cream

make your meringue slab Heat oven to 250 degrees. Line a large baking sheet with parchment paper. Beat the egg whites with an electric mixer until frothy, then add the cream of tartar and continue to beat until they hold soft peaks. Very gradually add the sugar, then the salt, beating the whole time, and continue whipping the whites until they hold thick, glossy peaks. Spread the meringue to about a ¼-to-½-inch thickness on the prepared sheet. Messily swirled is fine—this is just for crumbling. Bake for 75 to 90 minutes, until the meringue slab is dry and firm but not browned on top. Usually, meringue recipes have you turn off the oven and let the cookies finish drying in there, but in this case I don't find it mandatory. Let the slab cool completely.

meanwhile, make the lemon curd Combine the sugar and zest in a heatproof bowl that will fit over a saucepan (double-boiler style), and use your fingertips to rub them together to release the most amount of flavor from the peel. Add the remaining ingredients, and set the bowl over an inch of boiling water; the bowl should not touch the water. Cook, stirring, until the mixture begins to gel or thicken slightly (reaching 170 to 180 degrees); it shouldn't simmer. Remove from the heat, and strain through a fine-mesh sieve. Cover, and let it cool; it will thicken as it does. The lemon curd will keep refrigerated for up to 1 week.

whip the cream Using clean beaters or a big whisk, whip the cream until it holds soft peaks. Resist the urge to add sugar; you won't need it.

assemble Crumble a little of the meringue slab in an 8-ounce cup, dollop with whipped cream, and spoon a little curd over the top. Repeat, finishing with a few crumbles of meringue. Repeat with the remaining cups.

note If you think you'll miss the torched meringue flavor of the classic pie, you can briefly run your raw meringue slab under the broiler until it picks up a little color before continuing in the 250-degree oven for the full baking/drying time. The resulting cookie won't be pristinely white, but it will have that recognizable depth of flavor.

cheesecake semifreddo with gingersnaps and cranberries

makes 8 servings

I own an ice cream maker. It's . . . up in a closet, I think? Using it requires bringing it down (plus the forty-two things in front of it, because that's what happens when you live in a small New York City apartment), finding space in the freezer (possibly the only situation worse than the hall closet), and giving it 48 hours to get cold enough so it can reliably churn ice cream—ice cream that, even once churned, will need the better part of a day to finish setting up. Are there people who decide they'd like some ice cream but 3 days from now will be just fine? It seems to go against the nature of ice cream, and also of wanting things.

Instead, I obsessively collect recipes for frozen creamy things that don't require me to use the machine. Milkshakes and popsicles, granita, no-churn ice cream pies, ice cream sandwiches that are just as good with store-bought—and semifreddo, the Italian half-frozen dessert, too. With this last one, the joke's on me, however, because, even though semifreddo doesn't require churning, the custard portion is no less complicated. Still, I've done everything here to keep it manageable, and I promise that it's worth it. When you try it, you're going to be, like: Whoa, *this*. Forget the turkey, forget the pie, *this* is how a November/December should taste, equal parts cheesecake and semifreddo with a glorious light texture, faint gingersnap crunch, and tart cranberry syrup drizzled all over. You can make it long (weeks, even) before you serve it, so go ahead and get it out of the way today, and pat yourself on the back come the holidays.

semifreddo

1 cup (235 ml) heavy or whipping cream

¾ cup (150 grams) granulated sugar

6 large egg yolks

8 ounces (225 grams) cream cheese, softened

1 teaspoon (5 ml) vanilla extract

Pinch of salt

½ cup (2⅛ ounces or 60 grams) finely ground gingersnap cookie crumbs

to finish

12-ounce bag (3 cups or 340 grams) fresh or frozen cranberries, roughly chopped

¾ cup (150 grams) granulated sugar

1 cup (235 ml) water

prepare the pan Line the bottom and sides of a 9-by-5-inch (or equivalent 6-cup) metal loaf pan with foil, then plastic wrap, leaving enough excess to hang over the ends and sides. (Why both? Foil will make it easy to lift out—

thin plastic film is eager to tear—and the plastic will keep anything from leaking and gluing itself to the sides.)

make the semifreddo Beat the heavy cream with ¼ cup sugar until it holds medium peaks.

In a saucepan, bring 1 inch of water to a simmer. Whisk the yolks and ½ cup sugar together in a heatproof bowl that can fit over the saucepan of water (or in the top half of a double boiler), then set the bowl over the top. Whisking the whole time, cook until the mixture is pale, thick, and creamy and the temperature registers 160 degrees. (This takes all of 2 to 4 minutes for me.) Remove it from the heat, then whip with electric beaters at high speed until thick and pale, if it's not already there. Rest the bowl in ice water, and cool completely, stirring once or twice. Mine cools in no more than 5 to 10 minutes.

Beat the cream cheese with the vanilla and a pinch of salt until soft and light. Continue beating as you pour or spoon the cooled egg mixture into it, then beat until fluffy. Fold in the whipped cream.

assemble the semifreddo Pour a third of the cheesecake custard into the bottom of your prepared pan (this will be about 1⅓ cups). Set aside 1 tablespoon gingersnap crumbs for garnish. Sprinkle (I find it easiest to get an even layer by using my fingers) the custard with half of the remaining gingersnap crumbs. Repeat with another third

of the custard and the remaining crumbs, then finish with the last third of the custard. Smooth it flat, and transfer to the freezer; freeze until solid, at least 8 hours, but it's safest to give it a full 24. Once the top is solid, you can fold plastic wrap over it to protect the surface. This semifreddo loaf will keep for weeks.

make the cranberry syrup Combine the cranberries, sugar, and water in a medium saucepan, and bring to a simmer. Simmer, mashing the berries up a bit to get the most out of them, for 5 to 8 minutes. Strain the syrup. Let it cool in the fridge until needed. (You'll have double the 1⅓ cups that you need, but the remainder will keep so well and is so lovely on yogurt or ice cream and in drinks, you'll be glad you didn't split a cranberry bag to make just enough.) The syrup keeps in the fridge for 2 weeks.

to serve Place your serving dish in the freezer for a few minutes. Unfold your plastic wrap, and use the foil overhang to remove the semifreddo loaf gently from the pan. Invert it onto the chilled serving dish, and peel off and discard the foil and plastic. Cut the semifreddo into 1-inch slices, and serve with cranberry syrup and a pinch of crumbs.

note For a summery vibe, you could use graham or other cookies instead of gingersnaps, and a fresh berry sauce.

danish rice pudding with cherry black pepper sauce

makes 8 servings

For the last 20 years, I have willfully neglected the great Jewish tradition of Chinese and a movie on Christmas Eve in favor of spending it with my best friend's family. We catch up over cheese and champagne. We decorate the tree. We listen to John Denver and the Muppets. Her mother makes us an incredible meal of soup, salad, red cabbage, roast duck or pork, and potatoes, and then, when we cannot eat another bite of food, she brings out a gigantic bowl of rice pudding, more than we could or should consume, and we more or less finish it, because somewhere in there is a whole almond, and the person who gets it gets a prize. I'm pretty sure I haven't gotten that prize in a decade, but this year is my turn, I just know it. However, I'm not going to tell anyone until the end, because half the fun is tricking others into eating more than they will ever be rewarded for.

This—all of it, from the red cabbage to the whole almond (okay, but maybe not the Muppets)—is a Danish Christmas Eve tradition. The Danish way is to boil or bake rice for a very long time in milk, or milk and water, with a vanilla bean, and then fold in an abundance of lightly sweetened whipped cream and chopped almonds, and to finish it with a warm cherry sauce. The result is cool, barely sweet, and fluffy somehow—really, the opposite of American-style rice pudding in every way—contrasted with the warm, stunningly red sauce.

Making it in my own apartment feels completely strange. Where's the candlelight? Where's Fozzie? Have I even earned the right to make a recipe so intimately tied to a person, place, and time? But, for once, the easiest part is not changing it—well, everything but the sauce. I find the sparkly kick of black pepper to be wonderful in a cherry sauce, especially against the equally speckly vanilla bean pudding; I couldn't resist. With or without the interloping ingredient, I hope this becomes your holiday tradition, too.

pudding

1 cup (185 grams) short-grain white rice, such as Arborio

3 cups (710 ml) water

1½ cups (355 ml) milk

1 vanilla bean, split

Pinch of salt

1 cup (140 grams) chopped almonds, toasted (well chopped but not powdery)

1 whole skinned almond

cherry sauce

24 ounces sour cherries (about 5 cups or 680 grams), pitted (frozen are fine)

½ cup plus 2 tablespoons (125 grams total) granulated sugar

2 tablespoons (15 grams) cornstarch

½ cup plus 2 tablespoons (150 ml total) water

A few grinds of black pepper

to finish

2 cups (475 ml) heavy cream

2 tablespoons (25 grams) granulated sugar

cook the rice Bring the rice, water, milk, and vanilla bean to a simmer, then cook at a low simmer, stirring frequently, until the rice is very tender and the mixture is thick but loose, like a risotto, another 20 to 25 minutes. A spoon dragged across the bottom will clear a brief path in the rice. Remove the vanilla-bean pod and save it for another use, such as infusing vanilla sugar. Cool the mixture completely, and press a piece of plastic film against the surface so no skin is formed. Chill it in the fridge for several hours—ideally, overnight.

make the cherry sauce Place the cherries and sugar in a medium saucepan. Stir the cornstarch and 2 tablespoons of the water together until smooth, then pour this into the pan, along with the remaining ½ cup water and a few grinds of black pepper. Bring the mixture to a simmer, and, stirring frequently, cook for 2 to 3 minutes. Let rest for 5 minutes (the sauce should be served hot).

finish and serve Shortly before serving the pudding, whip the cream with the sugar to soft peaks. Fold the whipped cream, along with the chopped almonds and one whole almond, into the cold rice. It will be stiff at first but will eventually lighten and become fluffy. Serve in big scoops, and ladle with warmed cherry sauce.

note This recipe calls for sour cherries, which have an availability in New York of approximately 2½ minutes every June—even less consoling in December. Frozen sour cherries are ideal here, but if you cannot find them, frozen sweet cherries will do, and are pictured here. When using sweet cherries, I use 2 tablespoons less sugar in the sauce and stir in the juice from half a lemon at the end. I have tried, in testing, to use canned sour cherries, but found them to be beige and falling apart, not quite as nice here.

do ahead This pudding is best made over 2 days. On the first, cook the rice in milk and let it fully chill in the fridge. It will keep there for up to 3 days, if needed. Just before serving, whip up and fold in the cream and nuts.

peach melba popsicles

makes 10 popsicles

I have yet to find peach melba on a restaurant menu. It's too bad; I realize it sounds dreadful, like something an ancient aunt named Melba would eat or, worse, something someone snuck melba toast into (fair enough, as they're named after the same person), thinking we wouldn't notice, but as it's in fact a scoop of vanilla ice cream, a poached peach half, and a cascade of tart raspberry sauce, it's probably the most perfect August dessert ever. Escoffier created the dessert in 1892 to honor the opera singer Nellie Melba, who was performing at Covent Garden. On an ice sculpture of a swan, which had been featured in the opera, was a dish of peaches resting in a bowl of vanilla ice cream, all topped with spun sugar. A few years later, when his restaurant opened at the Ritz Carlton in London, Escoffier added raspberry purée to the dessert.

I'm sorry if you were hoping for ice swans, though; I hope ice popsicles will suffice. A fifty-fifty marbling of fresh peaches (although frozen will work fine), vanilla ice cream, and fresh raspberry sauce that together is like the highest calling of a Creamsicle, each bite a different intersection of sweet, sour, and creamy, no two tastes or popsicles exactly alike. Realistically, this will lead to needing more, so I trust you'll plan accordingly.

½ cup (120 ml) water

½ cup (100 grams) granulated sugar

1 cup (120 grams) fresh raspberries

2 cups (340 grams) peeled chopped peaches in small/medium chunks

⅛ teaspoon almond extract (optional)

1½ cups (305 grams) vanilla ice cream, frozen yogurt, or nondairy vanilla ice cream of your choice, slightly softened (think: soft-serve consistency)

Combine the water and sugar in a medium saucepan and bring to a simmer; stir until the sugar dissolves. Pour ¼ cup syrup (just eyeball it—it's about a third of the mixture) over the raspberries in a bowl. Add the peach chunks to the remaining syrup in the saucepan, bring back to a simmer, and cook for 1 to 2 minutes, until the peaches

soften. Let both the raspberries and peaches cool in the syrup. The raspberries will cool quickly, but you can hasten the peaches along by setting them in a larger bowl of ice water for 10 to 15 minutes. In a blender or food processor, purée the peaches and their syrup first, then scrape the mixture into a measuring cup with a spout and stir in the almond extract, if using. Purée the raspberries and place in a smaller spouted cup. (The raspberry color will muddle the peach purée much more than vice versa, so blend the peaches first.)

Pour a tiny splash of raspberry (you'll want to use only half of your total sauce in this step) into the bottom of each popsicle mold or small glass that you're using as a mold (I like champagne flutes, for this and really everything), followed by a larger splash of peach (again, using about half the purée), and dollop in a little softened ice cream. Repeat with the remaining raspberry, peach, and ice cream. Use a skewer to lightly marble the mixtures together—I get the best swirls by swiping the skewer right along the inside of each mold. Freeze the popsicles according to the manufacturer's instructions.

note You can use either fresh or frozen peaches and berries here. For the berries, use a little less than 1 cup as they're more collapsed from the freezer. For the peaches, if yours are a little overripe and soft, you can probably get away without cooking them and just purée them. The same goes for frozen peaches, which will no longer be firm once defrosted. The cooking is just to ensure a smoother purée. I learned about using simple syrup as a sweetener in popsicles from Fany Gerson's fantastic *Paletas* book; it freezes to a better texture than just sugar alone.

toasted marshmallow milkshake

makes 4 shakes

Many years ago, I met a friend for lunch at a long-since-closed burger joint called the Stand on East Twelfth Street, and we finished the meal with something the menu declared a toasted marshmallow milkshake. I don't remember a thing about the burger, but I do know that pretty much every conversation I had in the weeks that followed went like this: "The weather is so nice today!" "It would be perfect for a toasted marshmallow milkshake, don't you think?" "How is your son sleeping these days?" "Did I tell you about this toasted marshmallow milkshake I had? Let me tell you about this toasted marshmallow milkshake I had." "Can you believe the news?" "Toasted marshmallow milkshake, toasted marshmallow milkshake, toasted marshmallow milkshake . . ." You could argue it had *some* impact on me.

Years later, when I finally went to re-create it at home, I was shocked to learn that the restaurant had shared their recipe with a magazine, but get this: it didn't actually have any toasted marshmallows inside, only one on top, and in the glass beneath it was more or less just a vanilla shake. This was unacceptable. The flavor of toasted marshmallows—I like mine blackened and drooping off the stick, by the way—is everything. It's a burnt-sugar whiff of vanilla coating a stretchy white cloud. It's summer, and time spent outside, and crackly campfires, and I know this is getting really twee but I don't care, I just want to stuff everything awesome about toasted marshmallows into a frosty glass and slurp it through a straw. I hope you join me.

10 ounces (285 grams) large marshmallows

½ cup (120 ml) milk, preferably whole

Seeds scraped from ½ small vanilla bean, or 1 teaspoon (5 ml) vanilla extract

2 cups (400 grams) vanilla ice cream

2 tablespoons (30 grams) sour cream, plain yogurt, or crème fraîche

¼ cup (60 ml) heavy cream, beaten to soft peaks with 1 teaspoon powdered sugar, for garnish (optional)

Place your glasses in the freezer. Heat your broiler. Line a baking sheet with foil, and coat it lightly with nonstick spray. Set aside the number of marshmallows you'll want for garnishes (estimate 1 or 2 per shake), and spread the rest on the tray. Broil—keeping a close watch, because the marshmallows will take on color very quickly—1 to 2 minutes, until they're the color you like. Don't be afraid of a little char; it really enhances the shake. Cool the tray in the freezer for 5 minutes, until the marshmallows are no longer warm, then transfer the broiled marshmallows to your blender. Blend with the milk until they are as puréed as you can get them, then pause to toast the garnish marshmallows individually over a gas flame, or under your broiler, for a moment. This ensures that they're warm when they hit the glass. Add the vanilla bean or extract, ice cream, and sour cream to the marshmallow mix in the blender, and blend until thick and smooth. Pour into the chilled glasses, and finish with a dollop of whipped cream, if using, and a warm marshmallow. Slurp through a straw; repeat very soon.

cannoli zeppole

makes 24 zeppole

I am obsessed with carnivals and boardwalks. I haven't met a balloon race, Ali Baba, bumper car, Ferris wheel, haunted house, carousel, mini-zipper, Gravitron, or Hurricane I didn't like. Give me all the strung lights, popcorn in red-and-white boxes, and musical reels that haven't changed in 50 years. I delight in the vague creepiness of clowns; we regularly go to boardwalk amusement parks in the summer—you know, "for the kids."

What I am not allowed to do, however, is to go near the stands that make zeppole, because fried dough is my undoing. Even being within a city block of it, I will catch a trace of the aroma in the air and suddenly redirect all of my energies into getting to the root of it, and then getting that root in my belly, which is why it was definitely not one of my better ideas to recently look into exactly how difficult they were to make. It turns out: not at all. And so, instead of making it easier on myself (not making them), I made it worse, teaming fried dough up with my other favorite Italian-American bakery dessert, cannoli. I mean, the good kind, the kind that's in a hand-formed shell that's been deep-fried to a crackly crisp and is not filled until you order it, so the outer crunch isn't compromised. A proper cannoli has orange and lemon peel and a whiff of Marsala, chopped pistachios, and always, always, always the miniature chocolate chips. Mashing these two beloved things into cannoli-flavored fritters is at once dangerous and brilliant—dangerous because I somehow have made doughnuts even harder to resist, but brilliant because I get two desserts in one.

1 cup (250 grams) ricotta

2 large eggs

2 teaspoons (10 grams) granulated sugar

2 teaspoons (10 ml) sweet Marsala or another white wine

½ teaspoon each finely grated lemon and orange zest

¼ teaspoon ground cinnamon

Pinch of allspice

1 cup (130 grams) all-purpose flour

2 teaspoons baking powder

¼ teaspoon kosher salt

¼ cup (30 grams) finely chopped pistachios

½ cup (85 grams) miniature chocolate chips

Neutral oil or shortening, for deep-frying

½ cup (60 grams) powdered sugar, to finish

Mix all the ingredients except the oil and powdered sugar in a medium bowl.

Heat 2 inches of oil to 350 degrees in a heavy frying pan or pot.

Drop tablespoons of dough into the oil, and fry them until they are golden brown; zeppole are magic in that they turn themselves over. Drain on paper towels. Finish with powdered sugar.

apps, snacks, and party food

kale-dusted pecorino popcorn

makes 8 cups

The first time I made kale chips, I thought I had done something wrong, or at least was being punished for some unobserved slight. What else could explain how terrible, bitter flatness was being cruelly passed off as a chip? Chips were something I previously knew in puffy foil packages, salty, fried, and delicious; you dipped them in sour-cream-and-onion sauce; you bought them covered in chocolate at candy shops. These were . . . green, and tasted it, too. So I did the only sensible thing and ground the chips into a powder, renamed it "kale dust" so it would sound as magical as possible, and sprinkled it over freshly popped popcorn.

It was kind of amazing how something so unpleasant magically transformed itself once it became a garnish. It was even better when I starting using more olive oil, sea salt, black pepper, and a good helping of Pecorino Romano. Pecorino is one of my favorite cheeses. I like to joke that it's dainty Parmigiano-Reggiano's loud Roman cousin—saltier, funkier, and a little goes a much longer way.

Given that it's green and has the word "kale" in the title, this popcorn has proved to be shockingly popular among the preschooler set (to whom I'd bring it for class snacks when it was our turn) as well as adults.

kale dust

A bundle of lacinato kale (aka dinosaur or Tuscan) (usually 9 to 10 ounces or 255 to 285 grams; see notes)

1 tablespoon (15 ml) olive oil

Sea salt

to finish

4 to 5 tablespoons (60 to 75 ml) olive oil

⅓ cup (70 grams) popcorn kernels

⅔ cup (95 grams) finely grated Pecorino Romano

Fine sea salt and freshly ground black pepper, to taste

make the kale dust Heat the oven to 300 degrees. Rinse and dry the kale; no worries if you don't get every last droplet of water off. Remove and discard the tough stems.

Lightly brush two large baking sheets with olive oil—the thinnest coat is just fine. Arrange the leaves in one layer on the prepared baking sheet(s), sprinkle lightly with salt, and bake for 12 to 14 minutes, until the leaves are crisp. Let cool completely. In a food processor, with a mortar and pestle, or even with a muddler in a bowl, grind the kale chips down into a coarse powder.

make the popcorn Place 3 tablespoons olive oil and 2 or 3 kernels of popcorn in a 3-quart or larger pot. Turn the heat to medium-high, and cover with a lid. When you hear these first kernels pop, add the remaining kernels and replace the lid. Using pot holders, shimmy the pot around to keep the kernels moving as they pop. When several seconds pass between pops, remove from the heat.

to assemble Transfer to a bowl, and immediately toss with the remaining 1 to 2 tablespoons olive oil, kale dust,

Pecorino, salt, and a few grinds of black pepper. Toss until evenly coated. Taste, and adjust the seasonings if needed.

notes

Seek out the Pecorino with the black rind, if you can; it's got my favorite flavor.

You could start with store-bought kale chips to save time.

Though kale chips can be made from either major variety of kale—curly or flat—I get a much better yield from the flat variety. If you're using curly kale instead, bake the chips for 20 minutes and begin with a 1-pound (455-gram) bunch to achieve $\frac{2}{3}$ cups dust.

herb and garlic baked camembert

makes 4 servings

The first time I hosted Thanksgiving, I wildly underestimated the amount of time it would take the turkey to cook. By some miracle, or perhaps foresight, I remembered that I had bought the ingredients for a melted fontina dip—a little chopping and a few minutes under the broiler later, a mess of cubed cheese, minced herbs, garlic, and olive oil was bubbling and glorious in a skillet, and when I put it out on the table, it was like a pride of lions came out of nowhere and eviscerated their prey with chunks of crusty baguette. Within 5 minutes, there was barely a scrape left and I had learned a few important things:

1. Appetizers are a good thing, a very good thing, especially when people have been drinking wine for nearly 2 hours on empty stomachs. They free you from stressing over dinner taking longer than expected.
2. Cheese baked until gooey with herbs and garlic is the most unbelievable party snack there could ever be, especially if you (also) do not delight in buying and setting out eight types of cheese and crackers with those little cheese knives from your wedding registry that you pull out once a year. (Okay, maybe I'm projecting.) Think: queso. Think: fondue. *Melted cheese will always win.* Drop it like a mic before hungry people and walk away (before they take your arm with it).
3. Melted cheese doesn't need to be an investment. The original recipe I used called for an expensive cheese, but because I cannot make a regular thing of spending $30 on cheese (my mom is going to yell at me when she reads this), I looked for a more reasonable alternative, and I found it in the 1990s, under a scoop of apricot jam, encased in crescent dough.

Baked Brie and Camembert, rescued from the ordinary, are even better with an herby garlicky mess slathered over them before hitting the oven. Camembert is especially party-sized, available at all price ranges (and the low-end stuff is just splendid here), and most wheels come in little wooden baskets you can warm the cheese in directly. It stays gooier longer than firmer cheeses and never looks split, and I've found you can even rewarm it later and it stays smooth. Just one more thing: eating this without drinking a glass of red wine would be like having a warm chocolate chip cookie without milk; I know you won't let that happen to you.

One 8-to-9-ounce (225-to-255-gram) wheel Camembert

1 tablespoon (15 ml) olive oil

1 teaspoon minced fresh thyme leaves

1 teaspoon minced fresh rosemary leaves

¼ teaspoon kosher salt

¼ teaspoon ground black pepper

1 large garlic clove, sliced very thin

Crackers, preferably long enough to dip with, for serving

heat the oven To 350 degrees.

assemble Most Camembert comes in a little wooden crate. If yours does, remove the crate lid and any packaging or wrappers around the cheese, and place it back inside the basket. Yes, it is safe to bake it right in there for the short time that this recipe calls for. If you're nervous about leakage, you can wrap the Camembert in foil or line the basket with parchment paper as a layer of protection. Place the cheese in the wooden crate on a baking tray.

With a thin sharp knife, make gridlike cuts in the cheese, 3 or 4 in each direction, about 1 inch apart and going about 1 inch deep into the cheese but without cutting through the bottom rind. Use your knife tip to "open" each cut and your fingers to press a little sliver of garlic into each cut. Combine the olive oil with the thyme, rosemary, salt, and pepper in a small dish. Spread thickly on top of the cheese.

bake For 15 to 20 minutes, until the cheese is loose inside the rind. Serve immediately with crackers.

chopped liver on rye, roumanian steakhouse style

makes 2 cups chopped liver

On Chrystie Street below Houston and above Delancey is an in-shambles-looking restaurant front that takes you four steps down (always easier going down than up a few hours and vodkas later) to a place with low, dingy ceilings, yellowed business cards for wallpaper, an even murkier yellow substance in syrup dispensers on every table, and a Jewish cabaret singer, heckling everyone from his keyboard in the back. Before you go, there are a few things you should know: (1) There will be a hora and everyone will participate—yes, even you; (2) Vodka is served by the bottle in blocks of ice; this rarely ends well; (3) That's not syrup in the syrup dispensers; and (4) Sammy's Roumanian Steakhouse may not be the place to go for the eponymous steak, or chicken, or latkes, and, my God, definitely not rugelach, but it makes the best chopped liver there is. It is impossible to argue otherwise.

While elsewhere on the Lower East Side restaurants are serving truffled and foie-grased tufts of nouveau chopped liver on artisanal crostini, Sammy's serves it the way it always has. A waiter comes to the table with a giant bowl of chopped liver, grated radishes, a heap of very dark caramelized onions, and a smattering of *gribenes* (salted, crispy-fried chicken skin), picks up the syrup dispenser, and pours its contents—schmaltz, in case you were too scared to ask—from up high all over it and stirs it together with a fork before dropping it without ceremony on the table with a basket of bread and walking away. It's everything I always wanted chopped liver to be—crunchy, salty, a little sweet from the onion and refreshing from the radish (don't question it; it just works)—but never is, and so I started making it at home. For better or worse, I do not keep a dispenser of schmaltz in my kitchen, but if there ever was an argument to rethink that decision, this recipe is it.

Vegetable oil

4 medium yellow onions, peeled, halved, and sliced thin

Salt and freshly ground black pepper

A splash of Madeira (optional)

½ pound (225 grams) chicken skins, roughly chopped into ½-to-1-inch pieces

1 pound (455 grams) fresh or frozen and defrosted chicken livers

1⅓ cups (6⅔ ounces or 190 grams) coarsely grated daikon radish

caramelize your onions Heat a large frying pan over medium heat. Add 1 to 2 tablespoons vegetable oil; once it is hot, add the onions, tossing them with the oil and seasoning them lightly with salt. Reduce the heat to low and place a lid over the pan. Cook, stirring occasionally, for 10 to 15 minutes, until the onions are limp. Remove the lid and bump the heat up to about medium again and cook the onions, stirring, until they are deeply browned and totally caramelized, about another 20 minutes. Don't skimp on this step; their flavor is what sets the liver apart. At the restaurant, they're dark brown.

Pour a splash of Madeira in the pan, if using, and use it to scrape up any stuck bits. Transfer the onions to a bowl, then cool in the fridge until needed.

make the gribenes Rinse the chicken skins, but don't bother blotting them dry. Place the chicken skins in the now-empty frying pan over low heat and season with salt. Cook, stirring frequently. They will start picking up color and releasing their fat, and are done when they're tan and crispy, about 15 minutes. Scrape the chicken fat and skins into a fine-mesh sieve set over a small bowl. Drain the skins; save the chicken fat. You should have about ½ cup crispy skin and ¼ cup chicken fat.

cook the livers Heat the frying pan to medium-high and add 2 tablespoons vegetable oil to the pan. Add the livers, seasoning them well with salt and pepper, and sauté them, turning them once, until golden brown on the outside with the insides still slightly pink, 4 to 5 minutes.

assemble and finish Remove the livers and let cool slightly, then transfer to a food processor and blend until finely chopped but not as smooth as a paste. Alternatively, you can use a potato masher to do the same in the bottom of a large bowl.

Transfer the mashed livers to a large bowl if they're not already in one. Add all but a pinch (reserved for garnish) of the caramelized onions and crispy skins, plus the grated radish, salt and pepper to taste, and all the reserved chicken fat. Stir with a fork to combine. Taste the seasoning and add more if needed. Sprinkle with the remaining onions and skins. Smear generously on rye bread.

mom's bread bowl with spinach *liptauer* and pickled red onions

makes 1 big bread bowl

My mother's go-to dish for cocktail hours and entertaining in the eighties, like that of many other hostesses of the era, was a loaf of bread, scooped out like a bowl and filled with a spinach-and-sour-cream dip that had been seasoned with a packet of onion soup mix but also included thinly sliced scallions and chopped water chestnuts. The bread was always pumpernickel and the edges of it were cut into fingers that could be torn off and used to scoop the dip in the center.

I thought it was brilliant and perfect, but I still make it my way because at some point I experienced the wonder of *liptauer*, an Austro-Hungarian spicy cheese spread. Made from quark, cottage, or farmer's cheese, or even cream cheese, and seasoned with everything from paprika to mustard powder, grated onion, fresh herbs, minced capers, and small sweet pickles (and there are versions with garlic, caraway, Worcestershire, and anchovies, too), *liptauer* spread on dark bread is a perfect food. Here, I use pickled red onion instead of fresh onion for both the crunch that was Mom's water chestnuts and a garnish; it plays off the cheese and spinach deliciously.

onions

¼ cup (60 ml) red wine vinegar

¼ cup (60 ml) cold water

1½ teaspoons kosher salt

1½ teaspoons (5 ml) granulated sugar

1 small red onion, peeled and sliced into very thin rings

dip

½ pound (225 grams) baby spinach, washed (no need to dry it)

1 cup sour cream (240 grams) or plain, thick yogurt (ideally Greek-style)

1 cup (225 grams) farmer's cheese, cottage cheese, quark, or cream cheese, softened

1 teaspoon sweet paprika

1 teaspoon dry mustard

1 teaspoon kosher salt

¼ teaspoon freshly ground black pepper

3 tablespoons (30 grams) finely chopped cornichons (about 6)

3 tablespoons (35 grams) minced pickled red onions

assembly

1 medium-sized firm loaf of pumpernickel, rye, or another bread of your choice

Additional cornichons

Combine the vinegar, water, salt, and sugar in a small bowl and stir. Add the onion and toss to coat with the mixture. Cover and refrigerate for at least 30 minutes and up to 2 weeks.

In a large skillet, heat the spinach with just the water clinging to the leaves over medium-high and cook until it is wilted. Transfer to a colander and let cool until you can pick it up, then wring it out, handfuls at a time. Chop it well and set aside.

If using cottage or farmer's cheese, you might prefer to press it through a fine-mesh sieve first for the smoothest texture. In all cases, combine the sour cream or yogurt and cheese in a large bowl. Add the paprika, mustard, salt, pepper, and cornichons, and stir to combine. Drain about half the pickled red onions, chop small, and stir into the mixture. Add spinach and stir to distribute. Taste and adjust the flavors and seasonings to your preference.

Hollow out your loaf of bread. Use a bread knife or kitchen shears to cut the sides of the bowl into 1-inch-wide fingers, still attached at the bottom. Slice or cut around from the top of the bread into extra fingers. Spoon the dip into the bowl and garnish with a few rings of pickled onion. Serve with extra bread fingers, the remaining pickled red onions, and additional cornichons.

Keep leftover bread and filling wrapped in fridge for up to 3 days.

crushed olives with almonds, celery, and parmesan

makes 2 cups, serving 4 to 6

The recipe for having friends over—or at least my friends, tonight or any night—is wildly simple: some wine, something spritzy for those who don't drink wine, some cheese, some crackers or a baguette, and a few dishes of stuff like olives, small pickles, and nuts; hopefully, all three. My favorite thing about this is that you can do a mad dash through about any grocery store at 5:30 p.m. and have this happen within 15 minutes of getting home, including time to, you know, taste test the wine to make sure it's good enough for anyone else. Why mention all this? It's probably not news, after all, that wine plus cheese plus crackers plus a quick group text for drop-ins is all that a blah evening needs to be a much better one—but the thing is, I forget, too.

This is my plus-one, the thing I put out if I have even 5 minutes more to spare, or mix up and put in a little jar if I'm going somewhere else. It requires no cooking, just a little chopping and stirring, and you can get everything you need in that same grocery run. The crunch is everything; fresh celery, roasted almonds, and Parmesan cheese rubble, plus garlic and a little oil and vinegar, transform an ordinary bowl of olives into something worth anticipating that vanishes quickly.

2 cups (270 grams) large green olives, pitted and drained

1 cup (140 grams) diced celery (from 2 to 3 medium ribs)

½ cup (65 grams) roasted almonds, roughly chopped

2 ounces (55 grams) Parmesan, crumbled with a fork or knife point into ½ cup rubble

1 large garlic clove, very thinly sliced

2 tablespoons (30 ml) olive oil

1 tablespoon (15 ml) white wine vinegar, plus more to taste

Kosher salt and red pepper flakes, to taste

Leaves from celery ribs, roughly chopped, for garnish

Toss all the ingredients except the celery leaves together in a medium bowl. Taste and adjust the seasonings to your preference. Garnish with the chopped celery leaves. Refrigerate until needed, and for up to 5 days.

note If serving as part of a cheese spread, keep the pieces chunky and put out toothpicks. If it's a first course, you can chop everything smaller and let people eat it with forks. People will tell you they don't like celery (someone always does), but I find that if you ignore them and make this anyway, there are never leftovers.

garden gin and tonic with cucumber, lime, and mint

makes I drink

About cocktails, I'm a Luddite. The thought of a bartender adding liquid smoke or rosemary syrup to my beloved Manhattan or offering some hot new take on a rum sour makes me want to sputter, "But . . . it wasn't broken!" So I'm a total bore about gin and tonics as well. I like unfancy gin and nonbespoke tonic; the "wildest" I've ever had was at a nondescript bar in London where they pour you a full glass of gin and hand you a bottle of tonic and let you work out how you're going to mix the two over a bag of crisps you've opened sideways because that's what everyone else was doing when you looked around and you wanted to fit in.

So when, several years ago, I walked into the Breslin, a Britishish restaurant in Manhattan, to discover they had a gin and tonic menu with variations on the classic, I had already said "absolutely not" before remembering I had very little to lose, and instead discovered the best thing that I think has ever happened to a great tradition: cucumber. Yes, the vegetable. They called it the Garden Gin and Tonic and it used cucumber bitters, too. This is the rare deviation on a classic so good, I only wanted them made this way going forward. Because I can't leave delicious alone, I began adding mint and the traditional squeeze of lime that pulls all gin and tonics together and I lightly muddled everything because that's easy and messy, and the results are crisp, refreshing, and spectacularly summery—fitting when it's warm out and happily transporting when it's anything but.

2 thin slices cucumber

2 large mint leaves

About ¼ cup (45 grams) ice

¼ cup (60 ml) gin

½ cup (120 ml) tonic water

1 big lime wedge

Stack one slice of cucumber, one mint leaf, and then the second of each in the bottom of an 8-to-9-ounce glass. Muddle lightly. Add the ice, then the gin, then top off with the tonic water. Squeeze the lime wedge and drop it in. No garnishes needed, but an extra slice of cucumber or the tip of a sprig of mint is never unwelcome.

notes

Some people like their gin and tonics 1:1; others like them more like 1:3, heavier on the tonic. I'm in the middle—I like a good 1:2. With gin and tonics especially, adjust to your taste. The amount above makes 1 solid drink.

Tonic water sold in the United States is quite sweet. Should you be buying a less sweet or more classic tonic water, you might add a pinch of sugar to the cucumber-mint muddle, if you like.

pomegranate and orange peel fizz

makes 4

n the almost 6 years between the times I waddled around the city in the name of procreation—I know, I make it sound so glowy and glamorous—to my delight, a key thing changed: more bars and restaurants began making really excellent mocktails. People who choose not to drink, whether due to beliefs, lifestyle, diet, or due date, are no longer expected to sip a club soda and twist of lime they could have bought at the local bodega for pennies to take part in what I consider one of the holiest social rituals—hanging out with friends at happy hour after a really long week.

One of the best mocktails I envisioned during my first pregnancy was a Negroni without any of the three alcohols that normally compose it. And I realized that the magic was in the bitterness; there are a lot of drinks for those who crave the sweet, tart, or fizzy, but what about those of us who miss the bracing bitterness of Aperol or the way a dash of bitters laces a glass?

This is my far simpler attempt to embrace the cocktail I missed most in teetotaling times. Here, pomegranate juice provides the deep, garnet tartness that makes a cocktail sing. A simple syrup, simmered long enough with orange peels so that it is as much bitter as it is sweet, provides the rest—well, that and the fizz (I use seltzer, but cava or prosecco is a seamless natural swap for those who drink), plus a muddled fresh orange slice and crunchy arils of fresh pomegranate. It looks fashionable, feels festive, and will leave you with absolutely no headache in the morning.

---

1 orange, any variety

1 cup (235 ml) water

1 cup (200 grams) granulated sugar

A few small ice cubes per glass

1 cup (235 ml) pomegranate juice

1 cup (235 ml) seltzer or club soda

¼ cup (45 grams) fresh pomegranate arils

Use a knife to cut the skin and all white pith off the orange in large peels. Place the peels in a small saucepan with the water and sugar and bring to a simmer. Simmer gently for 15 minutes, then let cool with the orange peels inside for maximum flavor infusion. Strain before using.

Cut the peeled orange into 8 slices and cut four of the slices in half, forming half-moons. Place one full and one half slice in the bottom of each glass and muddle them lightly. Add a couple small ice cubes to each 8-ounce glass, followed by 1½ tablespoons of the orange peel syrup and ¼ cup each of the pomegranate juice and seltzer, and stir to combine. Sip and add more syrup, juice, or seltzer to taste. Garnish each glass with one of the halved orange slices (you should have one left for each) followed by the pomegranate arils. The fresh orange slices float and should hold up some of the pomegranate prettily. Cheers!

note You'll have more syrup than needed for this recipe, but, once strained, it keeps for a month in the fridge.

acknowledgments

"No one who cooks cooks alone."
—LAURIE COLWIN

To everyone who has come to the Smitten Kitchen to read, to cook, and to share over the last 11 years: Thank you for inspiring me every day to become a better cook and writer. You are the very best part about this gig.

A huge humbled thank-you to everyone at Knopf, especially Paul Bogaards, Chris Gillespie, Laura Wanamaker, Kathy Hourigan, Kathleen Fridella, Cassandra Pappas, Lisa Montebello, Carol Carson, and Janet Hansen. Before my first book, Alison Fargis warned me that the best way to proceed with a publisher was "Just don't be a Difficult Author." She tried, okay? I appreciate the care and quality you put into getting these books out into the world.

To Lexy Bloom, for otherworldly patience and kindness putting together this book and for believing in it even when I often did not. Tom Pold, thank you for working tirelessly behind the scenes to keep things running smoothly.

To Alison Fargis, for going above and beyond what any book agent has done in the history of book agency. I feel lucky to have walked into your office 8 years ago, even if it was just to tell you that you were out of your mind if you thought I would ever in a million years write a cookbook.

To Sara Eagle, for being the better half of my professional brain: organized, responsive, and full of bright ideas.

To Leda Scheintaub, for your careful, detailed, and inexhaustible recipe testing and editing.

To Patricia Austin, for lending your deep baking knowledge to whisk these baking recipes into shape.

To Anna Painter, for coaxing me off the crumb cake ledge and for years of testing and cheer.

To Jessie Sheehan, for getting those cakes ready for a party.

To Rebekah Peppler, for the eleventh-hour styling rescue.

To Angela Moore, for being my copilot on all things fishy.

To Gail Dosik, for changing my cookie game forever.

To Julie Touber, for helping my strawberry tart loosen up.

To Magnus Lundström, for making the most beautiful cutting boards.

To Rachel Roddy, for introducing us to Rome and helping to unlock the mystery of *foccacia ripiena*.

To Daniel Shumski, for guidance waffling everything.

To Venetia Iliopoulos at Fresco, for the best croissants, Americanos, and spiral pies.

To Inger Ladegaard, for nearly two decades of Danish Christmas inspiration and hospitality.

To both my families: Thank you for your endless support, babysitting, and recipe tasting; and for ducking flying objects when you've had the audacity to ask when this book would be done.

To my bear and my bunny: Thanks for being the two finest little people we've ever met and for bursting through the door cheering on chicken noodle soup days.

To Alex Perelman, my favorite person, my support system, and the best dad out there: This would be no fun without you.

measurements

metrics

Eager to make this book as useful as possible to a wide range of readers, I have included metric weights in recipes, just as I did in *The Smitten Kitchen Cookbook*. Because most digital scales these days switch easily between ounces and grams, I listed most ingredients only in grams. I did try to include ounces on items that most people in the United States buy by weight, such as meat and cheese, and items that are packaged by their weight. If your scale reads only in ounces,

Google will happily do the math for you: simply type, e.g., "15 grams in ounces" into the search bar, which will return the result ".52 ounces," or half an ounce. I have also included the spoon/cup-to-weight and volume equivalents below.

I also excluded very tiny weights, usually items that are a tablespoon, a teaspoon, or less, so small that including them bordered on quibbling.

Still new to scales? Please let me convert you.

how to use a kitchen scale
(and ditch your measuring cups forever)

Count me among those who rejoice whenever a recipe is presented in weights. Why? Because nothing is more accurate. A cup of flour, packed different ways, can clock in anywhere from 115 to 200 grams. You could end up with almost double the flour the recipe's writer intended in your cake! But a 130-gram cup will always be a 130-gram cup. Plus, I am all about using fewer dishes and nothing minimizes clutter in a kitchen like a scale. Measuring 2¾ cups flour into a bowl requires a 1-cup measure, a ½-cup measure, and a ¼-cup measure, plus a bowl—that's 4 dishes. On a scale, you *only*

need that bowl and to fill it until the number hits 360 grams. Then you can add your next ingredient, and the next, and voilà! You've nearly made a one-bowl recipe!

But enough of the sales pitch. So, you bought a kitchen scale. Now what?

Place your empty bowl on the scale and "tare" or "zero out" its weight. (On scales without "tare" button, the "on/clear" button usually does the same job.) Add your first ingredient, slowly, until the scale reaches the weight you need. Zero it out again. Add the next ingredient. Zero it out again. If the recipe calls for you to whisk, whip, or blow gentle kisses across the surface of your ingredients, go do that, too, but when it calls for the next ingredient, re–zero out the weight of the bowl so that you can continue.

You'll have this method down in no time. You'll wonder why you didn't try it sooner. And now, you can use all the extra space in your drawer that was once devoted to a tangle of measuring cups and spoons to stash more chocolate.

useful conversions

fahrenheit/celsius/gas mark equivalents

275°F = 140°C = gas mark 1
300°F = 150°C = gas mark 2
325°F = 165°C = gas mark 3
350°F = 180°C = gas mark 4
375°F = 190°C = gas mark 5
400°F = 200°C = gas mark 6
425°F = 220°C = gas mark 7
450°F = 230°C = gas mark 9
475°F = 240°C = gas mark 10

length equivalents

¼ inch = .5 cm
½ inch = 1 cm
1 inch = 2.5 cm
6 inches = 15 cm
1 foot (12 inches) = 30 cm

volume equivalents

½ teaspoon = $\frac{1}{12}$ fluid ounce
1 teaspoon = ⅙ fluid ounce
2 teaspoons = ⅓ fluid ounce
1 tablespoon = 3 teaspoons = ½ fluid ounce
2 tablespoons = 1 fluid ounce

3 tablespoons = 1½ fluid ounces
¼ cup = 4 tablespoons = 2 fluid ounces
⅓ cup = 2⅔ fluid ounces
½ cup = 4 fluid ounces
⅔ cup = 5⅓ fluid ounces
¾ cup = 6 fluid ounces
1 cup = 8 fluid ounces
1 pint = 2 cups = 16 fluid ounces
1 quart = 4 cups = 32 fluid ounces
2 quarts = 8 cups = 64 fluid ounces
1 gallon = 4 quarts = 128 fluid ounces

weight equivalents

½ ounce = 15 grams (rounded/approximate/practical equivalent; exact is 14)
1 ounce = 30 grams (exact = 28)
2 ounces = 55 grams (exact = 56)
4 ounces = ¼ pound = 115 grams (exact = 113)
5⅓ ounces = ⅓ pound = 150 grams (exact = 151)
8 ounces = ½ pound = 225 grams (exact = 227)
12 ounces = ¾ pound = 340 grams (exact)
16 ounces = 1 pound = 455 grams (exact = 454)
24 ounces = 1½ pounds = 680 grams (exact)
32 ounces = 2 pounds = 905 grams (exact = 907)

a guide for special menus

Keeping in mind dietary preferences and restrictions, I've created a guide (also reflected in the index of the book) that will, I hope, make it easier for you to select options or create menus that cater to vegetarian, vegan, gluten-free, and dairy-free diets.

vegetarian

Note that the rennet used in cheese making is often animal based. For recipes containing cheese, look for labels that indicate an animal-free rennet (vegetable rennet or microbial rennet) is used to ensure that the cheese is completely vegetarian. For recipes that call for stock, choose the vegetable stock option. Also note that because all of the baked goods, desserts, and drinks in the book are vegetarian, they are not listed below.

- Artichoke and Parmesan Galette
- Broccoli, Cheddar, and Wild Rice Fritters
- Broccoli Melts
- Brussels and Three Cheese Pasta Bake
- *Cacio e Pepe* Potatoes Anna
- Caramelized Cabbage Risotto
- Carrot Salad with Tahini, Crisped Chickpeas, and Salted Pistachios

- Cauliflower Wedge
- Crispy Tofu and Broccoli with Sesame-Peanut Pesto
- Crushed Olives with Almonds, Celery, and Parmesan
- Cucumber Yogurt Gazpacho with Mint, Almonds, and Grapes
- Dry-Rub Sweet Potato Steaks with Green Bean Slaw
- Fall-Toush Salad with Delicata Squash and Brussels Sprouts
- Fennel, Pear, Celery, and Hazelnut Salad
- Flipped Crispy Egg Taco with Singed Greens
- Fried Green Plantains with Avocado Black Bean Salsa
- Grilled Yogurt Flatbreads
- Halloumi Roast with Eggplant, Zucchini and Tomatoes

- Herb and Garlic Baked Camembert
- Kale Caesar with Broken Eggs and Crushed Croutons
- Kale-Dusted Pecorino Popcorn
- Leek, Feta, and Greens Spiral Pie
- Mango Apple Ceviche with Sunflower Seeds
- Mini–Matzo Ball Soup with Horseradish and Herbs
- Mom's Bread Bowl with Spinach *Liptauer* and Pickled Red Onions
- Mujadara-Stuffed Cabbage with Minted Tomato Sauce
- One-Pan Farro with Tomatoes
- Parmesan Dutch Baby with Creamed Mushrooms
- Pea Tortellini in Parmesan Broth
- Polenta-Baked Eggs with Corn, Tomato, and Fontina
- Potatoes and Asparagus *Gribiche*
- Red Lentil Soup, Dal Style

- Roasted Tomato Picnic Sandwich
- Roasted Tomato Soup with Broiled Cheddar
- Romesco, Chickpea, and Smashed Egg Bowl
- Smashed Cucumber Salad with Salted Peanuts and Wasabi Peas
- Spaghetti *Pangrattato* with Crispy Eggs
- Spiced Carrot and Pepper Soup with a Swirl of Couscous
- Spinach, Mushroom, and Goat Cheese Slab Frittata (skip the sausage option)
- Spring Fried Barley with a Sesame Sizzled Egg
- Sushi Takeout Cobb
- Tomato and Gigante Bean Bake / Pizza Beans
- Wild Mushroom Shepherd's Pie
- Winter Slaw with Farro
- Winter Squash Flatbread with Hummus and Za'atar
- Zucchini-Stuffed Zucchini with Sorta Salsa Verde

vegan

For recipes that call for stock, choose the vegetable stock option to keep the recipe vegan. For recipes with an option for butter or oil, use the oil. And bypass any optional dairy garnishes such as yogurt or cheese.

- Carrot Salad with Tahini, Crisped Chickpeas, and Salted Pistachios
- Crispy Tofu and Broccoli with Sesame-Peanut Pesto (skip the honey)
- Double Coconut Meltaways
- Fall-Toush Salad with Delicata Squash and Brussels Sprouts
- Fried Green Plantains with Avocado Black Bean Salsa
- Garden Gin and Tonic with Cucumber, Lime, and Mint

- Magical Two-Ingredient Oat Brittle
- Mango Apple Ceviche with Sunflower Seeds
- Mujadara-Stuffed Cabbage with Minted Tomato Sauce
- Olive Oil Shortbread with Rosemary and Chocolate Chunks (use dairy-free chocolate)
- One-Pan Farro with Tomatoes
- Pomegranate and Orange Peel Fizz
- Red Lentil Soup, Dal Style
- Smashed Cucumber Salad with Salted Peanuts and Wasabi Peas
- Spiced Carrot and Pepper Soup with a Swirl of Couscous
- Sushi Takeout Cobb

gluten-free

Where strict gluten sensitivity is a concern, labels—in particular for corn tortillas—should be checked for stray gluten-containing ingredients, and choose products, in particular oats, polenta, cornmeal, and other grains, that are packaged in gluten-free facilities. Use gluten-free tamari rather than soy sauce.

- Alex's Bloody Mary Shrimp Cocktail
- Bacony Baked Pintos with the Works
- Baked Oatmeal with Caramelized Pears and Vanilla Cream
- Beefsteak Skirt Steak Salad with Blue Cheese and Parsley Basil Vinaigrette
- Brick Hens with Charred Lemon
- Broccoli, Cheddar, and Wild Rice Fritters
- *Cacio e Pepe* Potatoes Anna
- Caramelized Cabbage Risotto
- Carrot Salad with Tahini, Crisped Chickpeas, and Salted Pistachios
- Cauliflower Wedge
- Charred Corn Succotash with Lime and Crispy Shallots
- Cheesecake Semifreddo with Gingersnaps and Cranberries (use gluten-free gingersnaps)
- Chicken and Rice, Street Cart Style (use gluten-free pitas)
- Crispy Short Rib Carnitas with Sunset Slaw
- Crispy Tofu and Broccoli with Sesame-Peanut Pesto
- Crushed Olives with Almonds, Celery, and Parmesan
- Cucumber Yogurt Gazpacho with Mint, Almonds, and Grapes
- Danish Rice Pudding with Cherry Black Pepper Sauce
- Dry-Rub Sweet Potato Steaks with Green Bean Slaw

- Fennel, Pear, Celery, and Hazelnut Salad
- Flipped Crispy Egg Taco with Singed Greens
- Fried Green Plantains with Avocado Black Bean Salsa
- Garden Gin and Tonic with Cucumber, Lime, and Mint
- Grilled Squid with Chickpeas, Chiles, and Lemon
- Halloumi Roast with Eggplant, Zucchini, and Tomatoes
- Herb and Garlic Baked Camembert (serve with gluten-free crackers)
- Kale Caesar with Broken Eggs and Crushed Croutons (use gluten-free panko; omit croutons)
- Kale-Dusted Pecorino Popcorn
- Lemon Meringue Pie Smash
- Loaded Breakfast Potato Skins
- Magical Two-Ingredient Oat Brittle
- Mango Apple Ceviche with Sunflower Seeds
- Miso Maple Ribs with Roasted Scallions
- Mujadara-Stuffed Cabbage with Minted Tomato Sauce
- Peach Melba Popsicles
- Polenta-Baked Eggs with Corn, Tomato, and Fontina
- Pomegranate and Orange Peel Fizz
- Pork Tenderloin *Agrodolce* with Squash Rings
- Potatoes and Asparagus *Gribiche*
- Red Lentil Soup, Dal Style
- Romesco, Chickpea, and Smashed Egg Bowl
- Smashed Cucumber Salad with Salted Peanuts and Wasabi Peas
- Smoky Sheet Pan Chicken with Cauliflower
- Spinach, Mushroom, and Goat Cheese Slab Frittata
- Spring Fried Barley with a Sesame Sizzled Egg
- Strawberry Cloud Cookies

- Sushi Takeout Cobb
- Toasted Marshmallow Milkshake
- Tomato and Gigante Bean Bake / Pizza Beans
- Wild Mushroom Shepherd's Pie
- Zucchini-Stuffed Zucchini with Sorta Salsa Verde (use gluten-free panko)

dairy-free

For recipes with an option for butter or oil, use the oil to keep the recipe dairy-free. And bypass any optional dairy garnishes such as yogurt or cheese.

- Alex's Bloody Mary Shrimp Cocktail
- Bacony Baked Pintos with the Works (use dairy-free sour cream for serving, or omit altogether)
- Brick Hens with Charred Lemon
- Carrot Salad with Tahini, Crisped Chickpeas, and Salted Pistachios
- Charred Corn Succotash with Lime and Crispy Shallots
- Chopped Liver on Rye, Roumanian Steakhouse Style
- Crispy Short Rib Carnitas with Sunset Slaw
- Crispy Tofu and Broccoli with Sesame-Peanut Pesto
- Double Coconut Meltaways
- Dry-Rub Sweet Potato Steaks with Green Bean Slaw
- Fall-Toush Salad with Delicata Squash and Brussels Sprouts
- Fried Green Plantains with Avocado Black Bean Salsa
- Garden Gin and Tonic with Cucumber, Lime, and Mint
- Grandma-Style Chicken Noodle Soup
- Granola Biscotti
- Grilled Squid with Chickpeas, Chiles, and Lemon
- Magical Two-Ingredient Oat Brittle
- Mango Apple Ceviche with Sunflower Seeds
- Manhattan-Style Clams with Fregola
- Mini–Matzo Ball Soup with Horseradish and Herbs
- Miso Maple Ribs with Roasted Scallions
- Mujadara-Stuffed Cabbage with Minted Tomato Sauce
- Olive Oil Shortbread with Rosemary and Chocolate Chunks (use dairy-free chocolate)
- One-Pan Farro with Tomatoes
- Peach Melba Popsicles (use dairy-free ice cream)
- Pomegranate and Orange Peel Fizz
- Pork Tenderloin *Agrodolce* with Squash Rings
- Potatoes and Asparagus *Gribiche*
- Quick Sausage, Kale, and Crouton Sauté
- Red Lentil Soup, Dal Style
- Sizzling Beef Bulgogi Tacos
- Smashed Cucumber Salad with Salted Peanuts and Wasabi Peas
- Smoky Sheet Pan Chicken with Cauliflower
- Spiced Carrot and Pepper Soup with a Swirl of Couscous
- Spring Fried Barley with a Sesame Sizzled Egg
- Strawberry Cloud Cookies
- Sushi Takeout Cobb

Index

Page references in *italics* refer to illustrations.

A NOTE ABOUT THE AUTHOR

Deb Perelman is a self-taught home cook, photographer, and the creator of smittenkitchen.com. She is the author of the *New York Times* best-selling *The Smitten Kitchen Cookbook*, which won the IACP Julia Child Award. Deb lives in New York City with her husband, son, and daughter.

A NOTE ON THE TYPE

This book was set in Minion, a typeface produced by the Adobe Corporation specifically for the Macintosh personal computer and released in 1990. Designed by Robert Slimbach, Minion combines the classic characteristics of old-style faces with the full complement of weights required for modern typesetting.

Printed and bound by C&C Offset Printing Co., LTD, China

Designed and composed by Cassandra J. Pappas